MORE PRAISE FOR *PATRIOT NUMBER ONE*

"Lauren Hilgers's *Patriot Number One* tells a great story spanning China and America, shedding light on the most complex and tangled relationship between any two nations in the world. It's a great yarn."

—JOHN POMFRET, author of *Chinese Lessons* and
The Beautiful Country and the Middle Kingdom

"*Patriot Number One* is an intricate and engaging dual portrait of the struggles of New York Chinese working-class immigrants and the struggles of China's village democracy. Its carefully rendered scenes offer a rare depth to worlds we know mostly from headlines."

—JENNIFER 8. LEE, author of *The Fortune Cookie Chronicles:
Adventures in the World of Chinese Food*

"The humanity, sly humor, and drama of *Patriot Number One* make it a delight to read. Its intertwined China-and-America narrative is revealing about both countries. This joins the list of books that easily convey larger messages through a vivid focus on the particular."

—JAMES FALLOWS, author of *Postcards from Tomorrow Square:
Reports from China* and *Our Towns*

"*Patriot Number One* brilliantly captures the bittersweet combination of joy, sorrow, and transformation of Chinese immigrants in New York City. Lauren Hilgers's vibrant, compassionate writing transports readers to the gritty streets and vertiginous world of the recently arrived, enabling you to see America with a set of new eyes."

—ROB SCHMITZ, author of *Street of Eternal Happiness*;
Shanghai correspondent, NPR

"*Patriot Number One* is a page-turning tale of the sub-world of exiled Chinese dissidents in American society. While Chinese immigration dates back generations, Lauren Hilgers has tapped into the more recent wave of Chinese political exiles and asylum seekers—and she astutely tracks their various struggles adjusting to life in America. A fascinating read."

—DAVID SHAMBAUGH, author of *China Goes Global*; professor of political science, George Washington University

" In *Patriot Number One*, Lauren Hilgers expertly weaves history and current events into a compelling human narrative, writing with clarity and compassion about how the outsized dreams of immigrants can collide with an indifferent world. True patriotism, this book shows us, means demanding better of the place that you love."

—LAUREN MARKHAM, author of *The Far Away Brothers: Two Young Migrants and the Making of an American Life*

"Lauren Hilgers captures with poignancy and humor the courage of immigrants who reach for the American dream. As we follow the tale of Zhuang and his wife, Little Yan, we stumble along with them, suffering the indignities of those new to this culture and language, buoyed by their successes. The result is a touching and insightful portrait of modern Chinese immigrants and their community."

—JEAN KWOK, author of *Girl in Translation*

PATRIOT

NUMBER

ONE

AMERICAN DREAMS IN CHINATOWN

Lauren Hilgers

CROWN
NEW YORK

Copyright © 2018 by Lauren Hilgers

All rights reserved.
Published in the United States by Crown, an imprint of the Crown
Publishing Group, a division of Penguin Random House LLC,
New York.
crownpublishing.com

CROWN is a registered trademark and the Crown colophon is a trademark
of Penguin Random House LLC.

Library of Congress Cataloging-in-Publication Data
is available upon request.

ISBN 978-0-451-49613-3
Ebook ISBN 978-0-451-49615-7

Printed in the United States of America

Jacket design by Michael Morris
Jacket photograph by Juni Xu

10 9 8 7 6 5 4 3 2 1

First Edition

FOR KAIZHI, AND FOR JUNE

CONTENTS

1 Escape
   逃逸 / *Táoyì*   1

2 A Fisherman's Son
   渔夫的儿子 / *Yúfū de Érzi*   15

3 Wukan! Wukan! Revolution
   革命 / *Gémìng*   27

4 In Queens
   皇后区 / *Huánghòu Qū*   39

5 Work
   工作 / *Gōngzuò*   55

6 The Chairman
   主席 / *Zhǔxí*   67

7 Sanctuary
   避难所 / *Bìnànsuǒ*   83

8 Wukan! Wukan! A Death
   死亡 / *Sǐwáng*   99

9 Little Yan
   小燕 / *Xiǎo Yàn*   109

10 Brewing Tea
    泡茶 / *Pào Chá*   123

11 Fortress Besieged
    围城 / *Wéichéng*   139

12 Paper Sons
    契约儿子/ *Qìyuē Érzi*   155

13 Wukan! Wukan! Land and Committee
    土地和村委会 / *Tǔdi hé Cūnwěihuì*   167

14 The Moon Represents My Heart
    月亮代表我的心 / *Yuèliang Dàibiǎo Wǒ de Xīn*   179

15 Personal Shopping
    代购 / *Dàigōu*   193

16 Strangers
    陌生人 / *Mòshēngrén*   205

17 Services
    服务 / *Fúwù*   215

18 Wukan! Wukan! Rule of Law
    法治 / *Fǎzhì*   227

19 A Man of Wukan
    乌坎人 / *Wūkǎn Rén*   237

20 Dissent
    异议 / *Yìyì*   251

21 Politics
    政治 / *Zhèngzhì*   265

22 Labors
    劳动 / *Láodong*   277

23 Blocking Traffic
    拦车 / *Lánchē*   289

24 Simplicity
    单纯 / *Dānchún*   301

    AUTHOR'S NOTE   311
    ACKNOWLEDGMENTS   315
    NOTES   317

PATRIOT

NUMBER

ONE

1

Escape

逃逸 / *Táoyì*

MARCH 2013–FEBRUARY 2014

Zhuang Liehong had made three plans to get from his village in China to New York. In the first, the American embassy would simply send someone to pick him up. He envisioned a midnight escape—cars waiting in the shadows along the uneven, trash-filled fields on the outskirts of his village. He felt sure, when he considered the plan, that the Americans would be sympathetic to his situation. He was a lover of democracy trapped in a corrupt corner of Guangdong Province. If the plan were to work, it would have to be secret. His friends would wake the next morning to find him vanished. By the time the news spread, he would be on a plane, heading toward a new life.

In a second plan, Zhuang would flee by sea. He had learned that Guam, a mere two thousand miles from the Guangdong coastline, was U.S. territory. This plan made it closer to execution: he went to work on a friend's fishing boat in Wukan Bay in preparation—ten grueling hours on a wooden plank boat, fully exposed to the sun—and purchased slightly too much fuel each time, stockpiling it slowly, so no one would notice. He planned to buy two motors. "Just in case one died," he said. "I would use one some of the time and then switch them. Sometimes I would use them both, and *vrrrmm*!" He would wait until the two months of the year when the intervening stretch of ocean was at its calmest, the swells low and rolling, the water undisturbed by typhoons. Then he would take a tiny boat out into the expanse of the South China Sea. He estimated the trip would take about ten days. He could make it, if he had to.

Zhuang was a man of Wukan Village, a proud former village leader on the ragged outskirts of Guangdong Province's manufacturing boom. He was on the verge of thirty, stocky and compact, meticulous about his appearance but always slightly out of style. His crooked teeth gave away a childhood spent in poverty, but he was not self-conscious about them. He grinned while greeting people on the street, pouring tea in his tea shop, or singing at the local KTV. He smiled relentlessly in the face of danger or embarrassment. He suffered from the occasional lapse in reading social cues and fought it with volume, warmth, and a strong handshake.

During the summer of 2013, paranoia overtook Zhuang's home village, and he recognized the feeling of trouble on the horizon. The shadowy forces of the county-level government—people he had rebelled against a few years before—were returning to Wukan. His friends were sure that their phones had been tapped by local security forces, the lackeys of corrupt officials. A propaganda official had taken up residence in a local school. Zhuang took the extra precaution of hiding his cell phone in the back of his tea shop whenever he discussed politics. He had heard rumors that government spies could turn them on remotely and listen in.

There was a time when Zhuang had run headlong into political turmoil. He had led protests, helped spark at least one riot, and argued with police interrogators over cigarettes. He had seen his friends kidnapped by thugs and his village invaded, and he had mourned a friend who died in police custody. But now Zhuang had a wife and a son. Now he understood the consequences of protest and revolution. He did not want to end up in jail, fearing for his life, worrying about his family. So he made plans and counterplans. He schemed while sitting in his tea shop, a storefront business he had opened along the smaller of the two main arteries that ran through his village. He pulled up the storefront barrier and sat behind sliding glass doors, watching the rain hit the metal awnings that shaded the shops, and the sun return to bake the scoured concrete of the lane. Zhuang first opened the shop in late 2012, when it was nice out and the political pressure more remote. He left the glass doors open to the street and blasted Michael Jackson. He brewed pot after pot of tea, serving it to his friends, who threw around cigarettes before they sat down on the pleather-encased stools Zhuang had placed around a monstrous wooden desk.

Later, the more worried Zhuang grew, the more likely it was you'd find the store shuttered. Eventually, as the pressure increased, he gave up the business entirely and planned in his tiny apartment, still serving tea to passing friends, watching his son struggle to maintain a wobbly sit, and doing his best to put his schemes into action.

Zhuang would subsequently tell people that, as he thought it over in his shop, he considered many possible destinations. An increasing number of Chinese emigrants were choosing Australia as a new home. Germany, he had heard, was welcoming. But the interest was passing. The moment he decided to leave Wukan Village, he thought of the United States. It had an allure no other country could match. It was a country of justice and freedom, a place with values that paralleled his own. He had to whisper when he said it: *America*. He had heard its asylum policies were favorable, and he understood it to be a wealthy country that took care of its citizens. Work would be easy to find there. People would be friendly. Some might even know his name. He imagined a warm welcome from Western democracy advocates. He thought of returning to Wukan years later, a success. He envisioned himself on a boat passing Liberty Island, a little windblown and visibly, palpably free.

At the tail end of his plan, the point at which it trailed off into a haze of hard work, success, and prosperity, was Flushing, Queens. Zhuang had carried out his scheming largely online, and had been wise enough to realize that New York City was too large a place to approach uninformed. He had skimmed through online discussion boards and squinted his one nearsighted eye at photographs. Manhattan's Chinatown, he decided, would be too dense and urban for his village sensibilities, and in the center of the city, real estate would most likely be expensive. Flushing, on the other hand, had become the destination of choice for most working-class immigrants from Mainland China. He looked up photos and saw a clutter of signs in Mandarin. He saw restaurants, driving schools, supermarkets, and even a sign for the Democratic Party of China. He made up his mind that this, at least temporarily, would be his destination in the United States.

Flushing, as far as Zhuang understood it, was a new, more modern kind of Chinatown. It was dominated by the working class, the result of an influx of new immigrants from new parts of China—inland and northern provinces that had little history of exploration or emigration overseas. Flushing wasn't controlled by the family-based patronage systems that had once ruled Manhattan's Chinatown or by the human smugglers who had brought in tens of thousands of Fujianese in the 1990s. It was a neighborhood where people would speak Zhuang's language and the food would suit his palate. There would be opportunities for work and a community of activists who would respect him. He would make friends, explore the neighborhood, and plan his next steps from there.

Zhuang had no family in the United States. He spoke no English and had never graduated from middle school. But he did not worry that he might get lost in a crowd of new arrivals or have to struggle to find work. After all, he had the advantage of being at least a little famous. Journalists had been coming to his village since 2011, when he had helped catalyze a particularly explosive protest. He had given interviews and appeared on Chinese-language television. He would wait until he got to the United States to contact the journalists he knew and make a statement, but he imagined it would create quite an impression—a man of Wukan in New York City.

• • •

Zhuang's third plan, the one that would finally bring him to New York, was the simplest and least flamboyant: he would acquire two tourist visas to the United States, one for himself and the other for his wife, Little Yan. This plan had none of the daring of a maritime or midnight escape. Its difficulties were largely bureaucratic. Zhuang had to hope that the local office would ignore his history of troublemaking and issue him a passport, and that the nearest U.S. consulate would grant them the visas. Then he and Little Yan would have to find a place to keep their infant son, Kaizhi, safe. And then the pair would join a tour group. Their exit from China would be led by a distracted young woman hoisting a tiny stuffed bear on a pole, bobbing through the crowds in one of Shenzhen's ferry ports.

If Zhuang had taken a boat, he would have traveled alone—it would have been too dangerous for Little Yan to come with him. Once he decided to go by air, however, he felt they should travel as a couple. He presented the plan to his wife one night, sitting on the long wooden bench that passed for a sofa in most Wukan homes. Baby Kaizhi was asleep on their metal-framed bed. He had just started to crawl, military style, around their one-room apartment during the day, bent on exploring the small concrete courtyard. Kaizhi regarded the outside world with great seriousness. He grabbed leaves and looked at Little Yan before shoving them into his mouth. He rarely cried. He slept well. Little Yan could watch him all day long and not feel bored. She did not want to leave China.

Little Yan had known Zhuang for three years, and for three years she had stood in flattering relief to her husband. She was quiet and petite; pretty, but with a slight underbite that made her shy about smiling. She had grown up in a village in Guangxi Province, one even smaller and less prosperous than Wukan. She allowed Zhuang an air of worldliness. He could drive the conversation while she happily cooked for his friends and took care of their son. She didn't make too many demands or spend too much money. And she appreciated his dogged sense of right and wrong. He was honest, which was more than Little Yan could say for a lot of the men she had met in Guangdong Province.

When Zhuang described his plan, Little Yan had concerns that came in quick succession, neatly pricking holes in his confidence.

He had been prepared for some questions—he had thought carefully about what to do with their son—but she was persistent. She asked why she and Kaizhi couldn't follow him to the United States after he got settled. She wondered how hard it would be to get by in an English-speaking country with an English vocabulary that was almost nonexistent. She had studied the language in high school but could barely remember a word. She wanted him to delay so she could take classes.

Little Yan had come to understand that the more stung Zhuang felt, the quicker and louder he was with his defenses. "You don't understand at all!" he told her. He did not want the local government to suspect the couple were planning to run, he said. He worried that any delay could put him in further danger. And she was dense if she didn't think he was in danger. He felt sure that, the moment he gave them an excuse, local officials would send goons to arrest him. And his fiery nature would eventually give them an excuse.

Zhuang was more careful when he talked about Kaizhi. It was natural, he thought, that Little Yan would worry about their son—she would always be connected to him. But the affection between two grown people might not survive across an ocean. Kaizhi could stay with Little Yan's parents, who would take good care of their grandson, he told her, but no one could help the two of them keep up their relationship when they were separated. It could take him years to get a green card. They would find a Chinese neighborhood, he would look for work on a fishing boat, and she could study English. Kaizhi would come as soon as they could bring him over.

"*Suan le ba*," she said, mid-discussion. It doesn't matter.

It was a terrible choice—between her husband and her son—but she did not blame Zhuang for forcing it. He made his points, and she accepted them. If he could make the escape happen, Little Yan would go with him.

Escape to America had to be undertaken in steps, each with the potential to derail the entire undertaking. Zhuang was so nervous about applying for a passport that he tested the waters by first applying for a permit to visit Hong Kong. It came in a little blue booklet that said *Travel Permit* on the front. He then took a ferry from Shenzhen into Kowloon and wandered the streets for a few nervous days. He met with a handful of journalists he knew from his days as a protest leader and told them about his plan. He asked them to help him keep a low profile—Zhuang had gotten the travel documents, he guessed, because local officials were too busy to monitor him, and he didn't want to give them a reason to start paying attention. He talked loudly on the phone about his vacation plans, in case someone was listening in.

When he went back to his village, he applied for two passports. He stood in line for over an hour, and when he was face to face with the agent, the man barely looked at his name. He purchased two suitcases in his-and-hers pink and black and hid them, just in case. He researched the weather in New York, and Little Yan invested in leggings that were nearly an inch thick with padding. They bought impossibly puffy coats, the volume-to-warmth ratio as high as might be expected in a region where winter bottoms out around fifty degrees Fahrenheit. In with his clothes, Zhuang stuck a little clay teapot, some small cups, and a plastic bag full of tea leaves. Other necessities would be easy to come by in New York. There would be time for everything once they arrived.

• • •

I did not set out to befriend Zhuang Liehong. When we first met, I was visiting his village to research a magazine story about the Wukan Village protests, the mini-revolution that Zhuang had helped lead. I was on my way to the village council office, a salmon pink affair on the eastern side of the village, when I passed his tea shop. The doors were wide open, and music was pouring out. It was otherwise a hot, sleepy day, and I paused at the noise. Zhuang's head popped around the expanse of his wooden desk, a cigarette hanging loosely from his lips, and he waved me inside. In no time, my cell phone was hidden in back, and I was sitting on a pleather stool, sipping tea out of a thimble-size cup and listening to Zhuang chatter in rapid Mandarin, giving his account of the previous two years. "I always knew I wasn't suited for government," he told me right away, adopting a more serious air while he selected a video to play on his computer and blast over his speakers. He haphazardly settled on a video in French that appeared to be about Marie Curie.

"Have you ever watched the Chinese period dramas on TV?" he asked me, half-shouting over the sound of a French man speaking in a semimonotone. Zhuang was referring to a genre of Chinese television that imagined China's imperial past as full of poisoners, wise old men, and young martial arts masters, usually just coming into their own. In that narrative, he explained, he was like the young heroes. "I am more a swordsman!" he shouted. "I've never had the patience to be a village head." As a member of the village council, Zhuang had been in charge of village security and trash disposal.

Zhuang had made friends with reporters from Hong Kong and Germany. He had done interviews with the *Sydney Morning Herald*, the *South China Morning Post*, Reuters, Radio Free Asia, Al Jazeera, Bloomberg, *Le Monde*, and others. He kept the phone numbers of students who visited the village and sat down with him in his tea shop. And he was persistent in his hospitality. I visited the village a handful of times over the next year and always, at one point or another, ended up with Zhuang. He invited me to eat fresh shrimp in his one-room apartment, the adjacent concrete courtyard half covered in debris from the construction that was constantly going on in the village. I held his baby and chatted with Little Yan as she cooked in their tiny kitchen—a structure added to the outside of the building as an afterthought. I drank endless small cups of tea. And then I moved from Shanghai, where I had been living for six years, to New York. We had kept in touch only sporadically. But then Zhuang's plans solidified. He had many journalist friends to choose from in Hong Kong. He knew filmmakers in Beijing and foreign correspondents in Shanghai. But as he got closer to his date of departure, he realized that I was the only person he knew in the United States.

I was living in Brooklyn when two photos arrived over a messaging app that Zhuang used. They had been sent with no explanation. One photo showed Zhuang and Little Yan standing by a beach. Little Yan was scowling into the wind, the face she makes to hide her underbite. She was wearing a fake Chanel sweater with fake pearl buttons, and Zhuang was standing beside her, grinning widely in one of his best button-down shirts. In the second photo, Zhuang was posed, indoors, next to a red Harley-Davidson, still wearing the button-down shirt, still grinning. They could have been in a mall anywhere in the world, but he looked thrilled to be there.

I might have dismissed the photos as a mistake, but the next day Zhuang followed up with a phone call. It came from a strange number, and his voice crackled and echoed over the connection. He could have been calling from another world. "We are in Hawaii! We might be seeing you in New York soon!" He laughed. "Someone is letting me borrow their phone! I will contact you later!" He suggested we use Skype for our next call, then hung up. I was too slow to pick up on it at the time, but Zhuang was giving me advance notice, indirect and polite, that he was on his way to my doorstep.

Zhuang had, in fact, told me about his plans when I saw him in Wukan, but I had not taken him seriously. He had popped out of his tea shop and asked me to meet him in secret, later, at his friend's house to discuss the first of his escape plans. Our phones were hidden, and we sat, conspiratorially, in the corner of a room packed with metal bunk beds. We whispered while Zhuang's friend splayed out beside us, playing games on her phone. Zhuang balanced a stack of papers on his knees. "I have all the evidence in order," he told me. "I just need someone to help me contact the U.S. consulate."

I shook my head. It was unrealistic. At the time, I thought I was letting him down gently. But I was making the same mistake that the corrupt village government had made two years earlier, just before the Wukan protests erupted: I was telling myself that Zhuang was all talk.

To get to the United States, Zhuang had decided a group tour would provide a good cover and help with a visa. Most agencies required their customers to leave a large deposit, thus guaranteeing their return to China, but he had found a place that offered to waive the requirement. He borrowed a friend's motorcycle and drove three hours to the outskirts of the city, where a girl in street clothes met him outside a storefront plastered with travel posters. He perused travel brochures with exaggerated interest. He made a show out of considering which trip would suit him, then held out the brochure he decided he liked. "For a honeymoon!" he said, grinning. The trip he selected would take them through Hawaii and California, ending in Las Vegas. The woman took down his information and a small payment. A few weeks later an agent met him at the U.S. consulate and walked him through his visa interview. Zhuang had been prepared to act excited about his vacation, but it wasn't necessary. The visa was approved in what seemed like no time at all.

In the few weeks before Zhuang and Little Yan left, he deposited his wife and son in Guangxi Province with Little Yan's parents and went back to the village to quietly sell a modest plot of land he had purchased a few years earlier. Land values in Wukan had been skyrocketing, and he was paid nearly thirty thousand dollars. The money would be enough to cover the cost of the tour and leave a reasonable amount for the months they would spend in the United States before he could find a job. He bought multiple new cell phones and SIM cards. When he took the bus to Shenzhen, he told his uncle to drop his suitcases off at the station, concealed in large plastic sacks, and spoke loudly on the phone about helping out a friend with some packages. He did everything he could to maintain plausible deniability.

Zhuang and Little Yan decided to make the most of the tour they had purchased, keeping up the charade until the last minute. If the pair deviated from the brochure's itinerary, Zhuang felt sure it would alert someone back home and possibly derail their plans. They followed the tour guide out of Shenzhen to the Hong Kong International Airport. They entered the United States, ironically, at a stop in Guam, then continued on to Hawaii. The tour operator ensured that every restaurant they visited offered Chinese food. Every stop involved at least one shopping trip, so when Zhuang took his first photos in the United States, some were set against the backdrop of a mall.

Zhuang and Little Yan were traveling with two wealthy factory bosses and their wives, a pair of teachers, and a couple planning on visiting their son in the United States. He and Little Yan were the poorest couple on the trip, but they tried to keep up. They shuttled through Honolulu, San Francisco, Los Angeles, San Diego, and Las Vegas so quickly that they would wake up and have to remind themselves which city they were in. They withdrew piles of cash at every opportunity. Zhuang suspected the teachers and the couple visiting their son of motives similar to his own.

As Zhuang and Little Yan's tour group made its way to the West Coast, I received a few more phone calls and messages from Zhuang, all initially telegraphic: "We're in San Francisco!" "We're in Los Angeles!" As they traveled from Los Angeles to San Diego, his messages became more pointed.

"Can you help us find a place to stay in New York?" he asked in a Skype message. "You are the only person we know in the city."

By the time Zhuang's intent became clear, I had laid no groundwork, gained no helpful knowledge. I had spent six years in China and was doing my best, nearly two years into my life back in New York, not to cling to my experience as an expatriate. The only Chinese people I knew in Brooklyn ran the cavernous local laundry. Every day a handful of immigrant women wheeled around baskets full of clothes, folding them perfectly while standing at a long table surrounded by machines. An overflowing laundry bag would be returned so neatly packed that it was barely half the size. After a week of messages from Zhuang, I went to the laundry and asked the folding women for advice.

"Are they coming with papers?" a woman from Fujian Province, with a ponytail that reached halfway down her back, asked. "Do they have family?" She offered to call her sister about a place to stay, then flagged me down a few days later with word of an apartment. It would cost five hundred dollars a month and had a shared bathroom and kitchen. "It's a good deal," she assured me. I tried to contact Zhuang over Skype, but the offer came out sounding miserly. So I wrote back and gave him my own address. He sent back an outsize yellow emoji—a giant thumbs-up.

Little Yan spent the trip watching the other tourists. She had a feeling of being swept along, moving from place to place without effort, with no control over where she ended up. She stuffed all the dollars they withdrew into her pink pleather purse, preparing for Las Vegas, where they planned to jump ship. Once there, they spent a day touring and then caught a taxi to the Las Vegas airport. They had been practicing the words they would need for the occasion. Little Yan's pronunciation was better, but when the time came, it was Zhuang who gave the driver directions, over-pronouncing his consonants and adding a stutter to the center of the word—"Air-hah-por-tah." They exited the taxi, smiling and pointing to determine how much money they owed, then walked in and squinted at the unreadable signs. Zhuang walked up to the closest airline desk and pronounced the second piece of vocabulary they had practiced in preparation for the day: "New York."

It took them what seemed like hours to communicate their destination. The people behind the desk spoke, at first, in complete sentences. Then single words. One of them ran off to find someone able to speak Mandarin. Finally they handed a phone over the counter, with someone who could translate on the other line. All the money Little Yan and Zhuang had stashed into her purse would not be enough for two tickets, so the attendant pointed out a nearby ATM.

That night Zhuang told the tour guide that he and Little Yan would be staying in the United States for some extra holiday travel. The guide made them sign a form explaining that the cost of their return ticket would not be refunded and asked when they planned to return to China. Zhuang made something up. The next afternoon they joined the tour bus to the airport and said goodbye to everyone in the entry hall. Then they set off on their own, wandering the building and holding up their tickets for strangers to read, following pointing fingers until they found their gate.

· · ·

Zhuang Liehong and Little Yan showed up at my apartment in Brooklyn in the middle of a snowstorm. Their flight had been delayed, and it was well past ten p.m. when a yellow cab crunched over the salt that had been spread on the road and stopped under a streetlight. I could see Zhuang from the window, stepping out of the car with false confidence, his huge coat pulled over a button-down shirt. He waved dollar bills at the cabbie, saying thank you over and over. He surveyed the sidewalk, and the snowdrifts piled up between parked cars, with his hands on his hips, his eyes scanning left and right nervously, a grin fixed on his face. Zhuang gets more blustery the more out of place he feels.

My husband and I hurried to the door and helped them haul their suitcases over the snowbanks at the edge of the sidewalk. Zhuang shook my hand vigorously and introduced himself to my husband, who had lived in Shanghai with me and was busy acting like their arrival was the most natural thing in the world. Zhuang rolled his suitcases into our spare room and disappeared into our bathroom to fix his flattened hair. Little Yan picked at the pasta I had made for dinner and apologized, explaining that they just weren't used to Western food. She sat carefully on the sofa, keeping herself as compact as her enormous puffy jacket allowed, until they went into the bedroom to sleep.

The next morning Zhuang occupied the bathroom for forty-five minutes, turning on and off various faucets and emerging, finally, with his hair carefully spiked and his pant legs rolled up. Little Yan had joined me on the couch and had been quietly flipping through some Chinese-language newspapers I had purchased. We watched Zhuang back across the living room, toting a bag of toiletries that he had taken from a hotel during their travels. Little Yan smiled. "Before I got married, I assumed women were the ones who spent all their time in the bathroom," she said. "Then I met Liehong."

Zhuang looked around the apartment quietly, avoiding the bagels and lox I had naïvely put out for breakfast. "Why do you have so many knives?" he asked, peering into the small kitchen. "We've never needed more than one knife." Little Yan wondered about the absence of a washing machine. When I explained that we used a laundromat, she wondered how much clothing Americans must own, to go a week or two between washings. In Wukan she had done laundry almost every day, cleaning the sweat off the handful of outfits they owned. Zhuang went outside to smoke a cigarette on the sidewalk, in jeans and tennis shoes and without his puffy coat. He tested the piles of snow with his foot. It was twenty-three degrees, and he had never seen snow before. "It's not cold!" he said upon coming back inside. "I really didn't think it was too cold. I was expecting much worse!"

2

A Fisherman's Son

渔夫的儿子 / *Yúfū de Érzi*

1983-2009

Before Zhuang saw snow, before he boarded the boat to the Statue of Liberty, before he took pictures of himself next to the Wall Street bull, he had been a part-time crab fisherman in Wukan, a dusty village outpost along the coast of southern China. He had been born there in 1983, sometime in September or October—the office responsible for issuing identification in his hometown regularly entered dates incorrectly, out of either laziness or the hope that people would return to correct the mistake, offering bribes tucked into red envelopes. His mother had given birth at home, in a two-room house with a tile roof and dirt floors that the family was renting. It was dark and earthy inside, stained with smoke from the stove where Zhuang's mother prepared meals. They put the new baby in the bedroom with them and their middle son. Zhuang's eldest brother and his older sister slept in the main room. Outside, two pigs rooted in an entry courtyard, watched over by a yellow dog that came and went.

Zhuang arrived in the village on the threshold of China's economic opening. Wukan was close enough to the booming manufacturing center in Shenzhen that you could smell the coal-charged changes in the air. It was far enough away, however, that people in the village felt sidelined. Zhuang was destined, by virtue of the time and place of his birth, to be a migrant. He just did not expect to travel so far.

Zhuang was the third son of a fisherman with a quick temper. Zhuang Songkun drank and gambled and yelled at his wife when things went wrong. His skin was leathery and tan from pulling up crabs in the sun, his brow heavy and his mouth wide, stretched across the bottom half of his face in a set grimace. In a poor village, the family was poorer than most.

Zhuang Songkun, like most fishermen in Wukan, ran a side business smuggling goods in from Hong Kong. Unlike most fishermen, Songkun also had a reputation as a bad business partner and a dishonest man. Even among family—hundreds of people in Wukan shared the last name Zhuang—Songkun was a man to avoid.

Zhuang's mother, on the other hand, barely registers as a presence in his memory. She worried about the pigs getting loose and her sons coming home by nightfall. She did everything—cleaning the family's clothes, cooking meals, descaling fish—slowly, as though moving underwater. She quietly endured her husband's moods and swings of fortune. Thinking back, Zhuang has trouble ascribing much of an inner life to his mother. He suspects she was at least a little bit stupid. Whether it was fair or not, from the moment he was born, Zhuang ranked above her in the family hierarchy. She was made to work and suffer. There wasn't much use in talking about it.

When Zhuang thinks about his home village, he prefers to remember it as it was in his childhood. Wukan had been truly rural, filled with orchards, gardens, and ramshackle fisheries. It was cooler then—shaded by groves of trees that would eventually give way to new construction. Children played and swam not far from their houses during the day while their parents farmed or went fishing. When it rained, unpaved alleys filled with puddles of unpredictable depth, and the croaking of bullfrogs echoed off the surrounding houses, a racket that could go on most of the night. At the center of the village, a nest of old houses were connected by narrow streets and punctuated by little rocky courtyards. Wukan had one main square and one good-size temple—a place where traveling troupes would stage Chinese operas or project black and white films on outdoor screens. A handful of other small temples were hidden among the houses, many of them barely more than heavy iron tubs set out for burning incense. Summers were hot and humid, and winters mild.

Zhuang, unlike his mother, was born excitable. He had a talent for mischief and ran unsupervised through the village while it was light outside and sometimes again well after dark. He trapped bullfrogs and climbed trees. He enlisted friends to help steal sweet potatoes from other people's gardens and cook them in barrels. (A stolen sweet potato, they observed, tasted much better than any other kind.) In other boys, a talent for pranks and petty theft might have evolved into something criminal. But Zhuang had an acute sense of right and wrong, a sense of injustice that welled up inside him and made him speak up. He felt it when other boys taunted his second brother, who had a dragging limp and a foggy, good-natured mind, the result, his mother said, of a childhood illness. Zhuang would never be entirely sure what had happened—it was another thing that no one saw much use in talking about—but he spent his childhood outyelling bullies. Zhuang was small, but he could be loud.

Zhuang's sharpest memories are of the family's nameless yellow dog—a scruffy, gangly mutt. He would call it home by leaning out the front door and shouting over and over, "Dogdogdogdog!" He had purchased the yellow dog from a neighbor for a few yuan and, along with his eldest brother, had taken the puppy to the local dump. It was customary, in Wukan, to wipe a puppy's butt with a handful of garbage. The ritual was intended to leave the dog with a lifelong preference for cleanliness and an aversion to leaving home in favor of the trash heap. The animal grew up to be unusually loyal and smart. The only times it went back to the trash heap was when the pigs found their way out of the front courtyard. Fear of losing the pigs weighed heavily on Zhuang's mother, and sensing her distress, the dog would track the pigs to where they were eating rubbish and lead them back, dragging one by its ear while the other came trotting after.

Zhuang was only six when he left his dog behind in the village, but he remembers the day with clarity. His father loaded him onto a scooter, squeezed in with their belongings and his middle brother. He remembers setting out down the main road through the village, humid air in his face, and turning around to see his yellow dog loping after them. Zhuang's father was moving the family to a port town a few hours away, a place where he could find better work. The dog kept up with the scooter through the slower village streets, but as soon as they turned onto a larger road, it fell behind. It chased them past the boundaries of the village. It ran hard, tongue hanging out, until it finally gave up and sat down by the side of the road. Zhuang watched the dog disappear behind them. His father had asked a family friend to look after it, but the dog ended up getting shuffled from home to home. A few years later the dog returned to one of the village dumps and ate rat poison.

• • •

By the time Zhuang was born, Deng Xiaoping had launched the Shenzhen Special Economic Zone. He offered cheap land and favorable tax treatment to foreign investors willing to put money into the new zone—at the time still just a cluster of villages on the edge of Hong Kong. And he offered the rest of China a chance to apply for temporary residency. He was giving people the freedom to move. It was 1989 when Zhuang's father left Wukan. Compared to a lot of the other villagers, Zhuang Songkun had gotten the message rather late.

The move was Zhuang's earliest introduction to transience. China's strict residency rules left him unable to attend school in the port town where his father had moved. So he was shuffled closer to home, moving from family member to family friend. He stayed with relatives in surrounding villages for months at a time, then moved back with his parents, then back to Wukan. He was just seven and already part of what people in China were calling "the floating population." He had been raised to never quite belong anywhere besides his home village, yet he was never there for long.

After Zhuang's first year of school ended uncomfortably, with him unhappy in the care of an uncle, his parents sent him to his mother's home village, a place called Shangchen. Zhuang remembers stripping to his underwear on the banks of the little river that ran through his grandparents' village. He would wade into the shallow water with his grandfather, their backs tan and bare, the water going up to his waist at its deepest, the older man bending down to sweep his net back and forth. They would fill buckets with little fish and lug them back together, Zhuang scurrying after the old man, working hard to carry a load with his spindly arms. His grandmother would cook the fish up for dinner, and they would share it with neighbors. Zhuang would run out and buy his grandfather cigarettes. One pack, he still remembers, cost seven and a half yuan—a luxury no one would have considered a decade earlier.

Even with his grandmother and grandfather watching after him, Zhuang worried about money. In the summer, he earned pocket money gathering cicadas, climbing trees that were dangerously close to the pools of night soil that farmers kept for fertilizer. He could sell the bugs to people who ground them up and ate them. Near the end of his time in Shangchen, he fell out of a tree and nearly drowned in one of the waiting pools of shit. When he arrived back home, stinking and breathless, his grandmother was furious.

Zhuang loved his grandparents' village, but he loved Wukan more. He loved the open-air dentist's office along the central road and the noodle shops that served bowls half filled with fresh seafood. He loved the stubborn, bickering villagers who filled the streets in the afternoon, squatting on their haunches or sitting on plastic stools while they gambled, the clang of dice hitting the rim of metal bowls.

People of ambition, however, did not stay in Wukan. By the time Zhuang was old enough to understand, he knew he would have to become his own person. He did not want to share his father's reputation. He did not want to be limited to a life of pulling up crabs in the bay. He wanted to be respected.

. . .

For Wukan, like most of the rest of China, opportunity required travel. China's economic miracle was engineered to be lopsided. The cities that Deng Xiaoping opened to foreign investment boomed while others fell behind. City residents benefited from better schools, better healthcare, and higher incomes. Reforms allowed them to sell their government-issued housing, buy apartments in new high-rises, and start a booming real estate sector. And while all this was happening, rural China stayed poor. On average, a Chinese farmer in the late 1990s died nearly six years earlier than his urban counterpart. Rural children were and are far less likely to go to college. And Zhuang was part of this rural underclass.

Getting from Wukan to Shenzhen required obtaining a special travel permit, and nearly without exception, every able-bodied boy in the village got it by the time he was sixteen. As a general rule, the earlier someone left the village for Shenzhen, the more successful they were. The earliest migrants had applied for jobs in factories before anyone else got there. They became managers and supervisors. They sent money back to the village and built impressive homes, all variations on the same floor plan. A Wukan man with money would build a three-story concrete and tile home with a large front courtyard. He would shut himself off from the rest of the village with a large concrete wall and a gleaming, polished steel door.

It did not take long, however, for Shenzhen to fill up with migrants from all across China. Wukan villagers found themselves in competition with people from places that were poorer and more remote. The available pool of factory workers grew so large that people from the village, for the most part, did not bother. Instead, they set up side businesses in Shenzhen. They opened corner stores and stalls in local fish markets, feeding the tide of workers from other villages and provinces. As time went on and the streets grew saturated with similar shops, more and more villagers looked to their neighbors for connections and guidance. The most common venture for a Wukan villager in the big city became the storefront clothing shop.

Zhuang grew up barely aware of the United States. America loomed somewhere past the shipping crates at the port where his father found work. Instead, he thought about Shenzhen and Guangdong.

By the time he was sixteen, most of Zhuang's friends had left for the city. He imagined the skyscrapers and highways and the money to be made. He had moved around so much that he had not yet finished middle school and could not imagine a world in which more education would benefit him or his family. No one in Wukan made it much past high school, and if Zhuang fell further behind, he would be embarrassingly old for the classroom. He would have to keep paying school fees. He worried that he had been a drain on everyone for too long—a burden on every cousin, friend, and family member who had taken him in.

In Wukan Zhuang's options were severely limited. His family had no land and no boat to take out in the bay. The only way for him to make money was to go to work on someone else's boat. The only respectable thing for him to do was to follow all the young people who had already left the village to look for ways to make money.

• • •

Zhuang's move to Shenzhen did not go as smoothly as planned. Every Wukan villager there relied on his village network to find a job, but Zhuang's network had collapsed before he even left. The trouble began when his eldest brother moved to Shenzhen and got a job at a clothing shop owned by another Wukan villager. He struggled to balance his work with a developing heroin habit. At one point he complained to his father, Zhuang Songkun, that his boss was mistreating him. He was not paying him the agreed amount, not giving him the respect he was due. It was, in fact, disrespectful to the whole family, he said—a terrible loss of face.

Zhuang Songkun, his temper smoldering, made the trip to Shenzhen. On the afternoon he showed up at the little storefront, he screamed at the shopowner in their local dialect. He flung his arms, pointing wildly. When the shopkeeper didn't agree with his complaints, Zhuang Songkun tried to pull down the metal grate in front of the store. The pair struggled, yanking the grate up and down, shoving each other in the street. By the time Zhuang Songkun stalked off, his family's reputation for troublemaking had solidified.

Zhuang wanted to escape his father. He wanted to be a new man. But his father cast a long shadow.

Back in Wukan, Zhuang bought new clothes and packed a few essentials. He spoke his goodbyes with such gravity that you would have thought he never expected to see his friends again. He longed to be an adult and return home unrecognizable. He caught a midsize bus at an unmarked spot on the side of the road, a place where people swarmed on with woven plastic bags. Sometimes it seemed as though the buses didn't so much stop as get caught in some sticky gravitational force, the driver impatiently letting the wheels roll forward toward the city.

Zhuang wanted to move to Shenzhen officially—not for a night of gambling in the low-slung fringes of the city center. He had applied for a permit to live there temporarily and appealed to an uncle with a small clothing shop. Zhuang imagined he would help out in the shop for a couple of months or, if that wasn't possible, look for work with another relative. He had grown sensitive to soliciting help from his extended family, but he hoped that in a month or two he would become a seasoned entrepreneur, ready to strike out on his own. After he made it, he planned to be so generous, it would embarrass anyone who had ever begrudged him a bowl of rice.

With his uncle on the bus to supervise, Zhuang stayed glued to the bus window as the farmland gave way abruptly. Dusty white and tan high-rises clustered around elevated highways, each covered in a grid of windows and tiny balconies. Mirrored glass towers varied the skyline. Zhuang thought Shenzhen was beautiful.

When he got off the bus, Zhuang beamed at his uncle. He was

already in the habit of trying to shift reality with the force of his own optimism. He grinned his lopsided grin when they reached his hosts' apartment, a handful of cramped tile rooms atop the family-run shop, and received a lukewarm reception. He was stuffed into a room with one of their three children and offered no invitation to join the family meal. Zhuang smiled at his hosts when they equivocated about his job prospects. He acted confident as long as he could—to the point that his optimism started to slip into the territory of delusion.

Out in the world, people from Wukan were generally willing to trust only other people from Wukan. If they were feeling expansive, they might include people from the surrounding county in their circle of friends. People outside these boundaries, it was understood, were predatory. It was easy to be cheated by someone whose customs you did not know. Zhuang learned this lesson when he was still a child and his father recruited him to travel to the outskirts of Shenzhen during Spring Festival. Every year Zhuang helped run a night of gambling, quietly monitoring some fixed dice at a table of people playing Fish Prawn Crab. He operated a little machine that shuffled the dice, rigged with magnets so that he could change the outcome. No one ever suspected the kid hovering over the gambling tables was helping cheat them out of their money.

No one wanted to give another son of Zhuang Songkun a job. He slunk from relative to relative offering to help out at fish markets or to work as a security guard. Few of his relatives told him no directly. Instead they hemmed and hawed and skirted the issue. One man, with a business selling fish, told Zhuang he would contact him first when there was space for a new hire. A few days later Zhuang learned the man had hired another cousin from Wukan. Zhuang went home after a few weeks. He joined his father on a fishing boat and spent his nights in a shed behind his family's rented house.

The next few years of Zhuang's life passed in a fog of work and humiliation. When the job with his father became too tense, he would get back on the bus to Shenzhen. It was a matter of which hell he preferred. In the city, he made a slim profit hawking train tickets at the station, catching a few hours' sleep in a local park before the police kicked him awake. When he grew too dirty to stand it, he would stop by an aunt's apartment and shower, ashamed of how bad he smelled. He sometimes fell asleep there, his head down on a little desk she kept in the apartment. His aunt was the only person in his extended family who helped him in his worst moments.

Zhuang had seen the worst of his village, but he still loved it. He longed to win the respect of the family members who had rejected him—the people who had resented looking after him as a child, who refused him work as a teenager, and who had bullied his middle brother. He vowed not to be like them. His heart was big. He would be accepting of everyone, no matter their circumstances. He was determined to love his fellow villagers, but he would remain wary of the people around him. He held his moral sensibility—his determination to stand up to injustice—around him like armor.

In Wukan, in order to escape from his father, Zhuang took a more dangerous job, on a boat that took him out into the choppy open ocean. He did it alone. He spent long, hot days setting crab traps and singing at the top of his lungs. He lay on the floor of the boat, looking up at the sky. When he was out on the bay, he thought, at least he didn't have to deal with the demands of his family and the judgment of other villagers. It was a kind of freedom.

Zhuang's teenage years were his worst. He would say, looking back on them, that spending months sleeping in a park gave him perspective. He would never be as tired or as dirty as he was then. Life would never be as humiliating. But he was young then. He had no reputation. He had nothing to lose.

By the time Zhuang reached his twenties, some of his school friends were coming into their own, and he no longer needed to rely on his father's generation for work. He worked for a few months as a security guard at a factory, living in a tent. And then finally he found an opportunity in a nearby city called Shunde. A friend had started a small business selling cigarettes and booze to local shops. He invited Zhuang to buy his own scooter and help make deliveries. Within a year, Zhuang was running his own delivery business, making enough money to send some home and rent his own apartment. He made friends. He found a girlfriend and hosted people for tea. In Shunde, he began to turn his life around. And then, unexpectedly and without a great deal of forethought, Zhuang Liehong started a revolution.

3

Wukan! Wukan! Revolution

革命 / *Gémìng*

On the night that Zhuang became Patriot Number One, the skies over Wukan Village were unusually clear. It was April 4, 2009, the night before Tomb Sweeping Festival, and the village houses were packed with family members come home to pay respect to their ancestors, the streets quiet following an evening of homecomings and big family meals. Zhuang had arrived from Shunde with a stack of papers so tall that, if placed on the ground, it nearly reached his knees. He had made thousands of copies of a letter entitled "Open Letter to the People of Wukan: We Are Not the Slaves of a Conquered Village." "It doesn't matter what generation you are in, or what place, you cannot avoid corrupt officials!" he had written. "Over ten thousand *mu* of collective land has gone missing!" He signed off with a pseudonym: Patriot Number One.

Zhuang had arrived with only the bare outline of a plan. He borrowed an electric scooter from a friend and waited until three in the morning to slink out of his father's ramshackle house. He wedged the papers between his legs and began a slow circuit of the village. He grabbed fistfuls of his open letter and let the breeze take them out of his hand. At first he went quietly and cautiously, keeping the headlight turned off, but as he wound his way through the village, he grew bolder. He tossed stacks of papers at doorways. He scattered the letter outside the village temple and around the police station. He buzzed through the alleys and drove through village squares. He had written, in the letter, about the sweet, freeing breath of Wukan air, and he felt it on his scooter. He raced out onto a larger road, past a string of fancy new sea-food restaurants. He whipped around the contours of a single, out-of-place traffic roundabout. And then he hit a rock.

He had been moving too fast in the pitch black and hadn't spotted it in the road. The bike spun out from under him, clatter-ing onto the pavement. He lay low for a moment, waiting to see if the noise had woken anyone up, then limped back to the scooter. He was unharmed, but the scooter would need some repairs. He wheeled it home quietly, chastened, and parked it outside his fa-ther's house. At the bottom of his letter, he had included an anon-ymous number for an online chat group. He sat down on his bed as the sky was lightening, wondering what would happen when the village woke up.

• • •

Long before Zhuang set off on his three a.m. ride, land had become the preoccupation of every villager and local official in Wukan. It was valuable now, situated close to both Shenzhen and the coast-line. According to China's constitution, however, village land was collective. Farmers could sell land use rights to other farmers, but only for agricultural purposes and only with the approval of a village council. If, on the other hand, a developer was looking to buy land—to build a factory, hotel, or apartment tower—the only way to do it was to have the government requisition and sell the land itself. According to China's constitution, the government can requisition rural land as long as it does so in the public interest. What constitutes the public interest is left up to interpretation.

People in Wukan had noticed for years that village land was disappearing. Their farmland was situated on the edge of a city called Lufeng, a dusty metropolis of 1.7 million people, filled with the rubble of discarded construction materials. Lufeng was ex-

panding quickly, its streets growing in the direction of the coastline, threatening to swallow the little fishing hamlet whole. By
the time I made my first visit to Wukan, in 2012, the city had
constructed an avenue of new government buildings not far from
the village. The new street was adorned with white streetlights,
and one of the new buildings had a dome-shaped roof, painted
gold and glowing in the sun, visible even from a distance.

Lufeng City is the county seat of an area that includes more
than 280 villages. Its mayor, Qiu Jinxiong, is responsible for a district that is famously unruly. (In 2015, during a raid on a village
not far from Wukan, three tons of methamphetamines were con-
fiscated, the wares of a village-level party leader.) In addition to
keeping his 280 villages in line, Qiu was tasked with funding and
overseeing a sprawling county bureaucracy. There were planning
commissions, tax commissions, bureaus for fish, grain, weather,
and salt; there were county-run schools, hospitals, and factories.
Counties, in China, are expected to oversee 20 to 25 different government departments. In reality, most have between 40 and 50.

Above Qiu, at the prefecture level, was a man named Zhen
Yanxiong, who held responsibility for the economic development
of all the villages, towns, and cities under his purview. In China,
leaders like Qiu and Zhen were responsible for fulfilling mandates
passed down by the central government in Beijing—to build cultural centers, improve hospitals, develop infrastructure, and expand GDP—that are frequently underfunded. Local governments
receive, according to World Bank estimates, about 40 percent of
the nation's tax revenue but are responsible for twice that amount
of government spending. The gap has to be made up somehow.

In the 1990s local governments in China often tried to balance
their budgets by levying illegal taxes on villages and towns. When
authorities cracked down on this practice, local officials turned to
land sales. Corrupt local officials could requisition collective land,
collude with developers, help balance the budget, and line their
own pockets all at the same time.

The village chief of Wukan, Xue Chang, had been selling off
blocks of Wukan's land since the 1990s. He had registered the

Wukan Port Industrial Development Company, listing himself and his deputy village council chief as the corporate representatives. Xue went about selling land to developers and pocketing the money: his buyers put up a garment-dyeing factory. Some land was parceled off for a pig farm. The village chief went so far as to lease out some of the bay for a seahorse-breeding operation. Soon a pink hotel complex sprang up along the more picturesque part of Wukan's bay. Most villagers accepted the new developments with a fatalistic shrug. They were focused on the money they might make outside the village. No one farmed anymore.

The Wukan villagers were not the only ones in China to watch their land disappear at the hands of the local government. In a survey of seventeen hundred village households conducted three years after Zhuang first papered Wukan with pamphlets, 43 percent of the people interviewed had seen their agricultural land taken by the government and sold to developers.

Like the other villagers, Zhuang himself had shrugged until sometime in 2008, when he logged on to the work computer of his first steady girlfriend. He was waiting for her shift to end, and without thinking much about it, he typed in the two characters for his village: 乌, meaning "dark," and 坎, a character that, in Daoist philosophy, represents water. He was shocked at first that anything came up at all. And then he got angry.

The first entry that caught his eye was a website advertising Wukan real estate. It called the village beautiful and industry-friendly. In 2007, the website stated, every one of Wukan's ten thousand villagers had received 6,688 yuan, nearly a thousand U.S. dollars, from collective industry and agriculture. It was a perfect place to do business. A model village. Except that the advertisement was false. No one Zhuang knew had ever received a penny from the land that had been developed. It was illegal, he realized, what the village chief was doing. And if it was illegal, Zhuang thought, there might be something he could do about it.

Zhuang opened an anonymous instant messaging account on QQ, a popular service that offered a platform for chatting online, joining discussion groups, and playing games. It allowed Zhuang to use his cell phone to send messages and access his account. He was taking it one step at a time, he told himself. First he would find out if anyone would support him. Then he would think about step two.

· · ·

Zhuang picked the name Patriot Number One after he decided to pen the open letter to the people of Wukan. He praised the ancestors who had cleared the land for Wukan Village during the Song Dynasty, then pointed out how corruption during the Qing Dynasty in the 1800s had made the country weak. Chinese soldiers had fought against Japanese invaders during World War II. "So many heroes were sacrificed in waging guerilla warfare," he wrote. "It was only because of these patriots that we were able to achieve victory." Why had they done it? "To defend thousands of years of culture and history, a thousand years of toil by their ancestors." The message was clear: protecting Wukan from corruption was a patriotic endeavor. Those who joined Zhuang in his cause would be defending the hard work of Wukan's ancestors, preserving the village for future generations.

If it weren't for QQ, Zhuang might simply have called himself "Patriot." The "Number One" was a feature tied to social media: if people joined him online, there might be Patriots Number Two, Three, and so on. It was marketable, he thought. And it was accurate.

The morning after Zhuang papered the village with his open letter, people requested to join Zhuang's QQ group faster than he could add them. Cell phone service was bad in the village, but Zhuang tried his best to keep up. He would add a slew of people, moving through the text messages one by one, and then his phone would stall. After his phone caught up, he would go back to adding people. For the first time in his life, he wasn't scheming on his own. Hundreds of people joined his QQ group.

The people who joined were all, like Zhuang, in their twenties or younger. They used the Internet and had QQ accounts. Most of them were migrants who worked and lived outside the village and used QQ to keep in touch. Zhuang joined the group, too, pretending he didn't know Patriot Number One.

At first Zhuang was thrilled by the idea of a little open rebellion. He went back to Shunde and kept up a steady stream of messages with his new allies. People in the group talked about their struggles to find housing in their home village. They complained about the factories. On Wukan's last big piece of open land, a sign had recently gone up—it looked like another factory was going to be built. Zhuang purchased a computer to keep up with his QQ habit and went about making friends online. He grew close to a twenty-five-year-old villager named Hong Ruichao, who had been one of the first to join the group. Later, when they finally met in Guangzhou, they would make an odd pair: Hong, tall and dashing, with a heavy, serious brow and a regal nose, and Zhuang, voluble with his crooked teeth, outsize grin, and small, energetic frame.

Another villager, Zhang Jianxing, who was all of seventeen at the time, sought out Patriot Number One online and offered to help with running errands, gathering evidence, and promoting their cause. Jianxing was young and awkward, with hair that spiked across his forehead and a smattering of acne across his cheeks. Eventually, however, he would grow into his role as a protester, mastering every new app and online service, spreading the word farther than Zhuang had imagined possible.

• • •

Zhuang and Hong Ruichao met on the street in Guangzhou, outside the headquarters of the Guangdong Provincial Government Propaganda Bureau. After a month of chatting online, the group had settled on a name, Wukan's Hot Blooded Patriotic Youth League, and a course of action. A handful of the members—not quite twenty people—had decided to petition the provincial government in Guangzhou. It was, they agreed, the proper thing to do. Petitioning was a holdover from Imperial China, intended to give local people a way to bypass corrupt officials. Zhuang and his friends drafted a letter of complaint and planned to deliver it to the proper office in Guangzhou. If all went well, the provincial government, or maybe even the party secretary himself, would come to Wukan and investigate. Wukan's local officials might not obey the law, but the Hot Blooded Youth were determined to do things by the book.

Zhuang and his friends were not seasoned activists or dissidents. Most of the people in the chat group were afraid to reveal their real names. Among the few exceptions were Zhuang, who announced himself without revealing his connection to Patriot Number One, and Hong Ruichao. A few days before the group met in Guangzhou, he made a point of using his name: "I am Hong Ruichao, and I am going to attend this action!"

As soon as the Hot Blooded Youth decided to petition, however, they realized the QQ group was not secure. The party secretary from the village called Zhuang Liehong and urged him not to go to Guangzhou. A deputy party secretary from the village showed up at the home of Hong Ruichao's father and asked the older man to corral his son. Later, when Hong told Zhuang the story, he recounted his father's answer: "My son is already grown, he makes his own decisions! I can't tell him what to do!"

The plan hatched by the Hot Blooded Youth was to meet on Sunday, June 21, and protest outside the provincial government's propaganda bureau; they would submit the petition the next day. For the first day of protest, the group planned to meet at eleven a.m. outside the block of offices. Zhuang rented a car and penned another open letter, this one to the Guangdong Provincial Government, about corruption in Wukan. He blew it up and pasted it onto a wooden board. On Sunday he showed up with a car full of supporters—mostly strangers whom Zhuang had coordinated with over QQ.

Waiting for them, they encountered a group of Wukan Village officials, accompanied by a village security team, who had made the trip to Guangzhou to stop them. By Zhuang's count, there were more than twenty. The village party secretary approached him. "Don't do this," he told Zhuang. "There's a teahouse around the corner. Why don't we go there and chat?"

"Can we do it on another day?" Zhuang replied. "Today I'm busy." He set up his blown-up open letter, leaning it against a fence. Village security officers gathered around him, arguing with him, telling him to leave, raising their voices. Zhuang argued back. "I am Zhuang Liehong!" he yelled at them. "I'm not afraid of you!" He held them off for two hours by himself, wondering if all the other members had forsaken him—the people he had arrived with were scared and had fallen back.

And then, hours behind schedule, Hong Ruichao pushed his way toward Zhuang. "Where have you been?!" Zhuang demanded. "I've been here by myself!"

"Lao Xiang!" Hong Ruichao responded, using a familiar greeting for a fellow villager. "I meant to be here earlier, but there was terrible traffic!"

With Hong by his side, Zhuang felt emboldened. The pair pointed to the supporters who were hanging back and encouraged them to step up. To Zhuang, the day felt like an enormous victory.

That night seven protesters stayed over in order to submit their petition on Monday. They had rented a room with only three beds, and when they arrived, Hong Ruichao threw himself across all three of them. "They're mine!" he said, and his friends tried to drag him off, euphoric. The village chief, Xue Chang, called Zhuang's cell phone, and Zhuang put him on speaker. "We'll stop protesting when you give us back our land!" he yelled into the phone as his new friends shouted their support in the background.

• • •

On that first trip to Guangzhou, Zhuang felt as if he had found his purpose. The protesters looked to him for guidance and valued his opinion. Young villagers looked to him for instruction, volunteering to help him gather evidence of land grabs. The day after he met Hong Ruichao, someone photographed Zhuang and the group of petitioners walking on a street in Guangzhou, smoking cigarettes and looking tough. Zhuang looks thrilled to be there. His clothes aren't quite as hip as the others'—his baggy white button-down shirt is no match for their leather jackets and faded jeans. His hair sticks up unevenly, and he has a hint of a smile on his face while everyone else looks thoughtful and serious. Zhuang couldn't help himself. He kept grinning.

Looking back, Zhuang would not say he had been naïve. He knew that challenging the local government could have consequences, but the Hot Blooded Youth made him a better man. He learned how to use a computer, how to write for an audience, and how to inspire others to action. He felt himself taking hold of his fate, rising above his circumstances.

From that time on, they went to Guangzhou every few months, always on the twenty-first, to try again to submit a petition. Every attempt to reach the petition office resulted in another shouting match with the local Wukan officials who showed up to stop them. Zhuang, still preoccupied with respectability, worked hard to balance his naturally fiery nature—his talent for shouting down local officials in the street—with research. His instinct was to do things by the book, to assemble evidence and build his case. Zhuang made a habit of going to Internet cafés, trying to understand how much land had been appropriated. Young Jianxing wandered around Wukan taking photographs of walled-off pieces of village land—farmland that lay fallow for no apparent reason—and forwarding them to Zhuang on QQ. They all went about their daily business at the shops, boats, and fish stalls where they worked, then chatted on QQ at night. Now when Zhuang returned to Wukan, people on the street knew him. They had heard about his petitioning. People grinned back and shook his hand. They called him brother.

Zhuang used his budding computer skills, along with his new zeal for documenting conditions in his village, to create promotional material for the Hot Blooded Youth. He downloaded video software and made short films in which photos of Wukan swirled and faded in and out. For music, he recorded a karaoke version of Michael Jackson's "Earth Song." He rewrote the lyrics and sang about local corruption:

My home village Wukan, you've lost the sunrise
My beautiful home, you've been polluted

After four hundred years of hard times
Of selfless dedication
In clouds of sentiment
We were assaulted with no warning!

• • •

The petitioning began in 2009 and continued for two years. It became less glamorous and more routine. The early cloak-and-dagger methods of Patriot Number One seemed almost laughable by the summer of 2011. Protesting was not such a big thing, it seemed. So Zhuang and his friends decided to try a new strategy, something a little more daring. They decided to organize a protest in the streets of Wukan Village.

The Hot Blooded Youth worried that their age undermined their message. None of the older villagers would listen to a bunch of twenty-year-olds. It didn't help that most of the members were shy when it came to public speaking. Zhuang was confident in an argument, but he developed a stutter every time he had to speak in front of a crowd. So Hong Ruichao invited an impish, deeply tanned villager named Yang Semao to help them organize. Yang was in his late forties, a former fisherman and a successful entrepreneur. He was a strong swimmer and had the energy to match Zhuang himself. He was one of the rare villagers who could be found jogging on the streets around the village—sweating in the humidity and dust as the occasional car roared past him. "I grew up by the sea, so my mind is as broad as the sea," Yang told his young companions.

Zhuang did not, at first, like Yang Semao. The older man was too sure of himself, too controlling, too ready to tell Zhuang what to do. The petitioning had, up to this point, been an adventure. Zhuang had been a respected leader, alongside Hong Ruichao. Then Yang arrived with his own ideas, his own lofty rhetoric about democracy, and inserted himself at the top of the protest hierarchy. The movement had grown. It didn't belong only to Zhuang and his friends anymore. It was difficult to sit back and let someone else take the lead.

Yang, however, was more focused than Zhuang. He quit his job and sold off his stake in his company to help organize the young petitioners. He was concerned about the land grabs, but focused mainly on democracy. He thought the problems that Wukan faced could be solved only by a local election. He pushed the group of young protesters to expand their message. And he pushed their plans for protest forward. Yang didn't put much stock in petitioning. Democracy required people on the street.

For the first Wukan protest, the group kept their expectations modest. They were edging toward a line they could not precisely locate, moving from creating a nuisance to organizing real and dangerous dissent. They planned to gather a few hundred people in the village and march to the golden-domed government offices in Lufeng. They would show the local government that they were not giving up, then return home. Zhuang posted flyers anonymously in the days before the protest was scheduled. Yang bought a ream of paper that everyone could sign to express their support for the petitioners. The protest was a departure, Zhuang knew, but an exciting one. And then, on September 21, 2011, three thousand people showed up.

The organizers watched as the crowd filed into the square in front of the village temple. They improvised. People shouted through bullhorns and told the crowd where they were marching. They poured down past the temple onto the main road, talkative and disorderly, slogans about land coming and going, picking up in one spot and then dying down, only to be taken up somewhere farther down the line.

The flow of marchers broke against the government gates, and an official told them to go talk to their village head if they were unhappy. "I don't know anything about it!" the man said.

So the crowd marched back and found the deputy village chief already in an argument with Yang Semao. "Give back our land!" they shouted.

The official pretended not to know what they were talking about. He got flustered and red in the face. "We didn't sell the land! If you want to go smash the Hetai Industrial Park, I don't care. Go smash it!"

Three thousand villagers took a collective breath and then followed the instructions of their village councilman. They ran back down the road and jumped onto their scooters and motorcycles. They smashed the temporary housing for the construction workers. They smashed the construction equipment. They went to a pig farm and a restaurant owned by a rich villager and smashed those. They overturned cars. Police drove in from Lufeng, and villagers overturned their cars. Some of the rioters were detained and held inside a police station located in the middle of the village, as a crowd grew outside. Some of the original Hot Blooded Youth members fled the village, afraid they would be punished.

Zhuang Liehong had known it was out of control from the moment thousands of people showed up in the square. He was elated and overwhelmed. He yelled directions at the rioters, telling everyone he met that they could smash things, but they couldn't steal. One villager grabbed a wine bottle out of a cabinet and, grinning at Zhuang, chugged most of it, then smashed the bottle on the floor.

4

In Queens

皇后区 / *Huánghòu Qū*

Flushing, Queens, lies at the end of the number 7 train, under the shadow of a giant metal globe that someone, in 1964, named the Unisphere. It was mounted atop a rehabilitated ash heap, a trash pile so notorious that it was the likely inspiration for the "Valley of Ashes" described in *The Great Gatsby,* lying along the road from West Egg to New York City. The Unisphere was the crowning structure of the 1964 World's Fair. Lights were placed to indicate capital cities, and circles of steel around it represented orbiting satellites, an intended tribute to "man's achievement on a shrinking globe, in an expanding universe."

Three hundred years before the World's Fair, Flushing was a small Dutch settlement nestled on the forested banks of the East River. It became, in 1657, a haven for the Quakers who had been banned by the last acting director-general of New Amsterdam, Peter Stuyvesant. (He banished them, initially, to Rhode Island, but the Quakers circled back.) From their new home, the group released the first declaration of religious freedom penned in the United States. In what came to be known as the Flushing Remonstrance, the Quakers condemned "hatred, war, and bondage." The laws of love, peace, and liberty extended to everyone, they wrote, including "Jews, Turks and Egyptians, as they are considered sonnes of Adam."

Flushing, in the centuries that followed the Quaker agitation, had been reinvented as a horticultural center full of orchards and nurseries, then was transformed once again by the enormous ash heap on the edge of the neighborhood. The ash heap, in turn, was transformed to make way for the 1939 World's Fair, and then, in 1946, the park served as the temporary headquarters of the newly formed United Nations.

Neither the ash nor the nurseries lent themselves, particularly, to the formation of a Chinese community. The UN, on the other hand, did. Taiwanese diplomats made their homes in the neighborhood. And over time, that handful of anchor families attracted other immigrants from Taiwan—people who were more likely to speak English than they were Cantonese and who, as a consequence, felt unwelcome in Manhattan's Chinatown. For the most part, these early immigrants were educated. They had money or the means to make it. They invested in real estate and opened restaurants. When immigrants came from other parts of China—places where they spoke Mandarin rather than Cantonese or Fujianese—Queens beckoned. By 2014 the U.S. Census Bureau estimated there were more than two hundred thousand Chinese people living in the borough.

From where I lived in Brooklyn, it took over an hour on trains and buses to get to Flushing. Zhuang and Little Yan would have to switch trains twice or start out on a bus. They would have to decipher a maze of signs that could confuse even English-speaking newcomers. Zhuang grinned at me in the morning, apologetically. "We are such an annoyance," he said, tiptoeing toward our bathroom. "But if you show us once, we can do it by ourselves next time!"

Zhuang had not arrived in the United States preoccupied with making money. He did not obsess over exchange rates and changing dollars to yuan. He had the luxury of arriving free of debt, having never met a human trafficker. These were advantages over other working-class Chinese immigrants, many of whom had paid tens of thousands of dollars to get a visa. On the other hand,

Zhuang knew nothing about the United States. He knew no one who had done what he was attempting to do. New immigrants tend to follow roads traveled by family members or friends who came before them. Zhuang was busy forging his own way.

One of the most useful suggestions offered by the women at the Chinese-run laundry around the corner from my house was that I go buy a Mandarin-language newspaper. The manager threw out a few names while eating her lunch, her eyes darting back and forth from the Qing Dynasty drama she was watching on her phone. "You could try the *Singtao Daily,*" she said. "Or the *World Journal.*"

So a few days before Zhuang's arrival, I made a visit to one of the pharmacies on Mott Street in Manhattan. The neighborhood was in the full flush of its Lunar New Year celebrations, and the streets were covered in glitter. "You can't set off actual fireworks in New York," the shopkeeper said woefully. "In China, every street is full of explosions!"

I held on to the papers for a few days and brought them out to Zhuang and Little Yan on their first morning. When they avoided the bagels I had brought for breakfast, I served them tea instead, and Little Yan crouched over her cup and flipped through the sections of the two papers. She moved past articles welcoming the Year of the Horse; skipped over photos of Taiwanese-American business leaders gathered, clapping, in a middle school auditorium; and thumbed through to the classifieds in the back. There were ads for all three of the most popular Chinese neighborhoods: Sunset Park, Manhattan, and Queens. There were listings for jobs, vocational schools, real estate agents, and lawyers specializing in immigration. In the real estate section for Flushing, she moved slowly, borrowing a pen so she could carefully underline some of the listings.

The advertisements in the two newspapers offered a quick survey of life in the neighborhood. There were hostels, called family hotels, where beds ran from ten dollars a night to about thirty. The hostels were stuffed into apartment buildings, some separating rooms with curtains, the cheaper ones stacking bunks toward the ceiling. There were men-only hostels and ones that charged slightly extra for shared rooms that boasted the luxury of an attached bathroom. The private rooms—rented by the month rather than by the night—were in shared apartments or houses. Here shared bathrooms and kitchens were almost a given, and rents went up closer to the heart of the neighborhood.

Zhuang looked over his wife's shoulder at the listings. "Six hundred dollars?" he said, pointing at a listing she had circled. "And look, it has a shared bathroom." A married couple, Zhuang thought, should always have their own bathroom. It was part of being a respectable adult. "Especially," he said, "for six hundred U.S. dollars every month."

Zhuang had arrived in New York with a figure in his head. He hoped to pay about four hundred dollars a month and save some of the money he had brought with him. After the plane tickets, the hotels, and the meals, he had a little under twenty thousand dollars left from his Wukan land sale. But he wasn't sure he could get a job. They would need to buy things to set up their new home. They would have to eat and live. He wanted to make his small fortune last.

With just the tourist visas he and Little Yan were carrying in their passports, Zhuang imagined the path to becoming an official resident would take some time. Meanwhile he had a list of things he wanted to accomplish. He saw no point in sitting around and looking at the newspaper, avoiding the cold. "We will go to Flushing," he said, "and we will walk around until we find a real estate office. I want to open a bank account and then find a cell phone . . . then an apartment . . . then a green card." He was sorry they couldn't find their way themselves, but he was afraid he wouldn't be able to read the subway signs. He would learn English soon, he promised.

By the time we left the house that morning, Zhuang and Little Yan were starving. They had barely eaten dinner and had shunned the bagels. We wandered out into the icy midmorning, Zhuang and Little Yan wearing tennis shoes, making their way carefully on the ice. We turned off a side street onto Nostrand Avenue, and I jokingly pointed out a Japanese restaurant called Sakura Tokyo that, I had recently discovered, was run by a Chinese family. Virtually no Chinese immigrants lived in my neighborhood, but the more I paid attention, the more Chinese businesses I discovered near our home. There was the laundry, two takeout restaurants, a 99-cent store, and a fish market. Chinese bosses drove vans in every morning from Flushing and Sunset Park, depositing their employees or working themselves, in the kitchen or behind the cash register.

Zhuang paused under the paper lanterns hanging outside Sakura Tokyo. He laughed half-heartedly and exchanged looks with his wife.

Little Yan turned. "Aren't you hungry?" she asked, aiming the question at me, the only one of the three of us who had eaten breakfast. "You should at least have a little something."

They pulled open the door to the restaurant, passing a window plastered with sushi dishes. The menu was loosely Japanese, and photos of noodles, rice bowls, and sashimi platters decorated the walls. Three tables were squeezed into the front room; a young woman and an older man in a white paper hat staffed a little counter toward the back. Cooks clanged pans in a back kitchen, occasionally visible through the Japanese curtain that covered the doorway. A deliveryman separated boxes of food into plastic bags on a foldout table along the back wall.

Zhuang looked at the photos on the wall, walked straight up to the young woman at the counter, and grinned. "Good morning!" he said. It couldn't be common for two Chinese people to wander in on this particular street in Brooklyn. "What do you have that suits the Chinese palate?" he asked. "I don't want anything too warming." His throat had been hurting, and he was pretty sure he needed to adjust his diet to accommodate the cold weather and the sudden lack of tea. The woman behind the counter suggested noodles. Zhuang and Little Yan each ordered a bowl and settled into one of the tables in the tiny dining space. Zhuang ate his noodles and refilled a tiny plastic cup of barley tea over and over. "Your tea is excellent!" he complimented the waitress. ("They were very happy when I said that," he said, once we finished up and left the restaurant.) He and Little Yan were very happy with the noodles. For the rest of the week, they would eat all their meals—breakfast, lunch, and dinner—at Sakura Tokyo.

The second stop, on the walk to the subway, was the laundromat. Little Yan was interested in seeing the inside of one—she couldn't imagine what they looked like. We walked in to meet the small army of laundry-folders. "These are your friends?" the manager asked me. She told them about the room her sister had to rent. The woman was from Fujian, a coastal province in China that had experienced an exodus in the 1990s: entire villages emptied out as people spent fortunes to find their way to the United States. The apartment the manager was offering was in Sunset Park, an immigrant neighborhood dominated by Fujianese. It had a shared bathroom and kitchen and was renting for five hundred dollars.

"We are going to Flushing today," Zhuang said, worried that the woman was trying to cheat them. "I think we want to live in Flushing."

The woman nodded and took them around the laundromat, explaining how to work the machines.

Little Yan peered curiously at the women folding clothes. She asked about work. "Here you make about a thousand dollars a month," the woman told them. "If you don't have papers and you don't speak English, that's about what you make." Little Yan followed up with a question about how the machines worked, but Zhuang narrowed his eyes. "Well, we don't need to look for jobs now," he said. "We should probably be on our way." The laundry ladies were not family, he explained—they were not from Wukan. It could be dangerous to take them at their word. Zhuang did not want to be a gullible villager in the big city.

• • •

New York City has the largest Chinese population of any city in the United States. Immigrants from China make up the second-largest (after immigrants from the Dominican Republic) and fastest-growing immigrant group. The city has no single

Chinatown. If you take the term in its most expansive sense—
designating an enclave of Chinese immigrants—there are several. In each neighborhood the working class built upon the ones
that came before it. Manhattan's Chinatown came first, settled
by immigrants from southern China. Nearly a century later, after
immigration restrictions had been imposed and then loosened,
people from Fujian came en masse, thousands of people travers-
ing the globe on airplanes and rickety boats to sneak over borders
and onto New York's beaches and docks.

When, in the 1990s, the influx of Fujianese found Manhattan too crowded, they moved along the N train into the Brooklyn
neighborhood called Sunset Park. They kept their ties to Manhattan through dollar vans and easy train access, traveling back to
the old neighborhood to look for jobs and visit lawyers.

Zhuang had learned Cantonese when he moved to Shenzhen,
and Little Yan had learned it in school. They could have, had
Zhuang chosen to, fit in on the streets of Manhattan's Chinatown,
where the dialect of Hong Kong and southern China still dominates. His local dialect is not far from the language spoken by the
Fujianese—he could have made a home for himself in Brooklyn
alongside the immigrants from around Fuzhou. But Zhuang had
heard about Flushing: the neighborhood in Queens had developed a reputation as the best landing spot for the truly rootless.

That morning the three of us wandered onto the platform at
the Nostrand Avenue A/C subway stop, and Zhuang cleaned his
teeth with a toothpick. Little Yan and I found two seats together,
and Zhuang settled down across from us. The arrangement didn't
last long. Whenever Zhuang got a seat, five minutes later he would
offer it to someone else. He stood up for an elderly man and then
a woman weighed down with shopping bags. Somewhere under
the East River, he jumped up when a woman wrapped in three
coats and toting a baby wandered down the length of the subway
car, asking for money. He gestured gallantly toward the empty
seat as she pushed her cardboard sign toward him. They looked at
each other, both confused, and the woman scurried off the train
at the next stop. Zhuang crossed the subway car, bewildered.

Little Yan discreetly pointed out all the different hair colors in evidence on the train. She had never, she admitted, met a black person before. There was an African community in Guangzhou, she explained, but she had never spent much time there. When Little Yan thought about it, she hadn't met that many white people, either. "How would I talk to them anyway?" she said, shrugging. She paused for a moment, then returned to the topic of clean clothes.

If you take the term *Chinatown* in its strictest sense rather than its most inclusive, Flushing is no Chinatown at all. The word occupies a particular place in U.S. history and has an attending folklore. America's Chinatowns were built on the opening and closing of doors, the mix of opportunity and xenophobia that greeted Chinese immigrants to the United States. In the popular imagination of many Americans, their neighborhoods were mythologized as impoverished and densely packed, cut off from the rest of the United States, places with a history of smoky alleyways, criminal networks, and opium dens. (A 1903 guide to eating chop suey in the *New York Times* went so far as to interview a policeman about the safety of eating at Chinese-run restaurants.) Today's Chinatowns are at once immigrant enclaves and tourist destinations, with entrances marked by shiny red pagoda-topped arches.

Flushing, however, offers little to the curious tourist. Its restaurants and groceries cater to a largely Chinese clientele. Its streets are expansive compared to the compact ones in Manhattan; its storefronts and apartment buildings quickly give way to rows of brick houses. Its Chinese population has grown during the years of smartphones and widely available Internet. Chinese-language websites aimed at the immigrant community advertise job openings and offer local news. People can join interest groups on WeChat, a phone application that started as a messaging service and expanded. (In China, WeChat users can pay bills, find doctors, and search the Internet.) And yet Flushing's immigrant economy—its underground banks, dollar buses, and packed housing—is a variation on a theme established a century ago. Zhuang Liehong was entering a community still shaped by a history of isolation and self-sufficiency. Flushing was both new and old, and Zhuang, fleeing the political forces at work in his village and expecting to make a success of an alien life in a new place, was the same.

. . .

Flushing's Main Street cuts a curving north–south path, running from the last narrow drops of Flushing Bay. It moves past Flushing Meadows and the Queens Botanical Garden before continuing into other neighborhoods, finally joining the Van Wyck Expressway. A few blocks from the street's origin point, the number 7 train comes to a stop at the corner of Roosevelt Avenue, dropping off commuters heading home from Manhattan in the center of the Chinese district. The daily pedestrian traffic here is second only to that of Times Square.

The day we traveled to Flushing for the first time, Main Street was a mess of slush and mud. Puddles had gathered at street corners, some still enough to trick people into judging them patches of ice before they plunged a foot in. Despite the booby traps, the sidewalks were dense with people moving at different paces, weaving in and out, sometimes slipping, dodging into gaps that could scarcely be considered human-size. Strollers encased in plastic bubbles spun past elderly people handing out flyers. Parking attendants struggled against the flow, wearing orange vests and warm hats pulled down over their ears. They spread their arms and held out their palms, in fat gloves, to pause the flow of people just long enough to let cars in and out of an underground lot.

As soon as we got off the subway, Zhuang dove into the crowd, winding among people with his face tilted up toward the shop signs. He took in the clutter of advertisements for driving schools, hair salons, lawyers, Internet cafés, and restaurants but found none announcing a real estate agency. His ears turned red in the frigid sunlight. (When I suggested he buy a hat, he worried that it would mess up his hair.) We walked past a shop selling hot soymilk and steamed buns, then threaded under some scaffolding.

Just as we came out into the sun, Zhuang stopped walking and looked thrilled. "Aha!" he shouted. "I have walked these streets many times before!!"

Little Yan raised her eyebrows. "He's joking," she said, unsure of herself. "He's never been here before."

"No!" Zhuang said. "I have strolled these streets before . . . on Google!" He erupted in giggles. "I'll take you on a short tour!" He wheeled around and started walking back the way we came. Flushing's Main Street is shadowed by the tracks of the Long Island Rail Road, and the sidewalk traffic is broken up, somewhat, by the clean lines of the Flushing branch of the Queens Library. Just past the library, a man sat shivering inside a kiosk, surrounded by pictures of bloody faces and calm-looking people sitting cross-legged. The kiosk, a sign proclaimed, was run by the Center for Quitting the Communist Party.

As we walked, the smoke from a Chinese barbecue cart followed us, sticking to everyone's winter clothing. Zhuang turned left. "See, there is the teahouse!" he said, pointing out a store selling loose tea leaves on one side and bubble tea on the other. "Down here we will find the offices of the China Democracy Party." We turned onto another side street, and there they were, but he walked past them, having decided, for now, not to go in. "I have to be careful about getting caught up in someone else's political agenda," he explained. Another turn, and he saw a park that he had walked through on Google. "Yes, I remember this little park!"

Zhuang and Little Yan walked back to Main Street and eased into the strolling pace on the sidewalk, reading all the signs they could without coming to a complete halt. Zhuang finally stopped in front of a storefront selling Chinese medicine. Dried mushrooms and herbs sat out in boxes, but he wanted something specific for his sore throat. He threaded his way into the white-tiled shop. He sought out a man in a white apron, explained his symptoms, and walked out with a small box of pills. We headed south, having yet to find a real estate office.

Then we saw a sign hanging above an open doorway that said 888 REAL ESTATE.

Zhuang led the way, full of confidence, climbing the dimly lit, narrow stairs until he reached the locked glass door of an empty-looking office. He located a doorbell and pressed it, drawing out a man in a gray suit. The man unlocked the door and opened it halfway. "Hello?" he said.

"We're looking to rent an apartment," Zhuang told him.

The man nodded and let us in. He took us past some cubicles into a conference room and left us there to find our seats.

A well-dressed Chinese woman in bright red lipstick and a bouffant hairdo walked in smiling, handed out business cards, and shook everyone's hand. "Now, you're looking for an apartment," she started.

"Yes!" said Zhuang, grinning. "We would like something in this neighborhood, not too far from the center."

"Great! I've got something you can rent for fifteen hundred," she fired back, opening a file and shuffling through some papers.

Zhuang gave me a glance from across the table, allowing the briefest flicker of alarm. The woman had him at a disadvantage. He turned back to her, his grin waning a bit. "We're looking for something cheaper," he said.

The woman tut-tutted, and her hands came to rest atop her folder, no longer shuffling. "I've got a basement for eight hundred."

He looked over at me again, pained. He had put effort into acting confident and at home on Flushing's freezing streets, but now he was losing his footing. "I was thinking of finding something below six hundred dollars," he said carefully, raising the estimate he had given that morning by 50 percent. "Do you have anything at around that price?"

The woman slammed her folder shut. "No way! You want something that cheap, you have to get away from Chinese people. If you want a cheap apartment, go somewhere in Queens with only white people. Chinese people drive up prices. We don't offer anything that cheap!" She stood up and ended the meeting, smiling through her lipstick and pushing us back past the cubicles and out the door. "If you want anything more expensive, come back and see me!" The door clicked and locked behind us.

On the stairs, Zhuang lost his grin. The woman hadn't been very friendly, he complained. Was it because she had seen he was with a foreigner and assumed he had money?

Little Yan laughed. "You can't call her a foreigner!" she said. "Aren't *we* the foreigners now?"

Zhuang stepped back out onto the sidewalk and stuffed his hands into his pockets. His mood had changed, and he didn't feel like taking us on a tour anymore. He walked past another grocery store and came to a stop outside a kiosk selling SIM cards. An older man had stuffed himself into the tiny kiosk, his winter coat wide enough to brush the wall behind him. Zhuang channeled all his residual embarrassment into a barrage of officious-sounding questions. Twenty-five-dollar SIM cards were available with un-limited international calling, but Zhuang would have to change his phone number every month. For slightly more money, he could keep the same number. He deliberated, hemming and hawing.

Little Yan looked through a table of gloves and tights set out on the sidewalk. "I don't think I need a card," she said. "We're always together anyway."

Zhuang settled on the twenty-five-dollar card, slipped it into his pocket, and asked the man the best way to find an apartment. "Go look in the newspaper," the man said.

That day's issue of the *World Journal* had the same list of cheap rooms, shared bedrooms, and family hostels. Some requested women or men only. Most had shared bathrooms and kitchens. Zhuang carried the paper under his arm into a little dim sum shop filled with a sparse after-lunch crowd of elderly men, most of them sitting alone, drinking tea, and staring at newspapers.

Zhuang ordered more steamed dumplings than he could pos-sibly eat and looked over the classifieds with Little Yan. They circled some of the ads in pen, starring any that did not mention a shared bathroom. The list they came away with was not long. With a new U.S. SIM card in his phone, Zhuang called the adver-tisers in quick succession, asking about rents and bathrooms and when he could look at the room. Half the advertisements he had circled had shared bathrooms after all. Most of the others were already rented. One was really just a bed in a shared room.

Finally Zhuang reached a landlord who seemed agreeable. The room had its own bathroom and a shared kitchen, the landlord explained. But if Zhuang wanted to rent it, he needed to come over as soon as possible. Zhuang said he would come right away. He scribbled the details onto a torn slip of paper and hung up beaming. The room sounded promising. He was whittling down his to-do list. The day was improving.

We took two buses—first the wrong bus and then the right one—to get to the address he had written down. The sidewalks had been shoveled only partially, the lane between snowbanks only wide enough for us to walk single file. Zhuang led the way toward a white clapboard house that was slightly dingy, packed tightly into a block of similarly dingy clapboard and brick houses—the Flushing approximation of suburbia. It boasted two stories perched above a garage that sank below street level. The driveway, slick with snow and ice, sloped down from the street at a steep angle, flattening out just before it met the permanently closed garage doors.

Zhuang climbed gingerly up the slippery porch steps and peered into the front window. Inside, a skinny Chinese kid with spiked hair and plastic slippers was painting the walls in the vacated room. Zhuang rapped on the window and, when the kid, no older than twenty, opened the door, offered a firm, vigorous handshake. The kid waved us in. The last tenant, he explained, had gone back to China for Spring Festival. "I don't know if he'll come back," he said. "If he does, he'll rent another room somewhere."

The room for rent was little more than a hundred square feet, with a door that opened into a narrow hallway and a small kitchen. It was empty and paint-speckled but had its own bathroom and a big window that kept it from feeling musty. The windows offered a view out over the front porch toward the street, catching the top of the driveway. The garage, the young landlord explained, was used as an office. The inside door leading there was kept permanently locked.

The little house had been split into two by the family's patriarch, an immigrant from Fujian who had saved money for years to buy it. He had placed his two sons in charge of managing it. The upstairs was for the family—a spare five hundred or so square feet. The two downstairs rooms, each big enough for a mattress and a small desk, were for rent. The young man in the plastic slippers, along with his brother, placed advertisements, managed tenants, and made the occasional gesture toward keeping things clean.

The room being painted was far more expensive than Zhuang had hoped—seven hundred dollars a month—but he decided that a private bathroom was worth the extra expense. He looked around with a carefully impassive expression on his face. He ventured into the bathroom and asked if the faucets worked. "You can try them if you like," the kid said.

In the kitchen, Zhuang opened all the cabinets and tested the sink. The only communal space in the little downstairs, it curled around the locked door leading to the garage. A card table stood in the corner, dusty and unused. Zhuang scuffed his feet on a little welcome mat set outside the second bedroom door. "It's a girl," the kid offered. "She's quiet."

Zhuang peered into the refrigerator, which had been separated into sections, each of the crispers divided into two. He pointed at a little toaster oven and swept his finger over to the stove. "Can we use these?" The kid nodded.

The room came close to meeting Zhuang's standards, but there was no furniture. He had not been expecting this. In China, most rentals come with a bed at the very least. "It's very clean," said Little Yan, nodding at the walls. Zhuang grunted in agreement, then beckoned her over to a corner. "It's expensive," he stage-whispered, "and we would have to buy our own furniture."

"I could take you to a furniture place," said the kid. "It's not too far."

"Is it cheap?" asked Zhuang.

"I don't know . . . depends on what you consider cheap."

"Do you think you could help us pay for the furniture?" Zhuang countered. "We just got here yesterday, and seven hundred dollars is already very expensive." He waited a beat and then changed tactics. "Where are you from?" he asked.

"Fujian," said the kid.

"We are from right near there!" said Zhuang. "We are all one big family! Shake my hand!"

The kid shook his hand and looked sideways. "We can't help pay for furniture," he said.

After a day of feeling unsure of himself, and with a small audience now observing him, Zhuang was in the mood to be decisive. "We'll take it!" he announced to the room.

The kid looked unsurprised. "Okay," he said, with no celebration. "You'll have to put down some money now." And they wouldn't be able to move in for another week while he finished painting. Zhuang agreed to a two-hundred-dollar payment, and the kid told Zhuang he could come by and pick up the keys at the end of the week. He could move in whatever furniture he had after that.

The young landlord scurried down to the garage and came back with a pen and a piece of college-ruled paper. He wrote out a receipt, reserving the room and noting the payment. Little Yan pulled a wallet out of her purse and handed it to Zhuang. He counted out the amount in twenty-dollar bills.

He left the house grinning, having ended his first day triumphant. He felt he had been exacting and held to his standards. He wasn't going to get hoodwinked by the United States. He wasn't going take everything new at face value or act impressed by everything he saw.

We headed back to Brooklyn and, on the way, stopped in a corner store. "I want to check the price of instant noodles," Zhuang told me. He ran into the store and scrutinized every variation of instant noodle in the shop, asking what meat was in which container. "Can you ask him the price?" Zhuang said to me, pointing to the Yemeni man who runs the store. "Can you ask him if he has any beef jerky?"

I did, and the Yemeni man pointed to a display near the register. Zhuang peered at his options. "Can you ask him if he has any beef jerky that's a bit thinner?"

Over the next few weeks, as Zhuang settled in to New York, he began to contact the journalists and academics he knew from his days as a protest leader. He announced his arrival and his intention to apply for asylum. Reuters dispatched a photographer to document him standing in the snow, frowning at the sidewalk. In an interview with Radio Free Asia, Zhuang predicted that a crackdown would follow a coming village election in Wukan. "There were many signs that I would be the target of political persecution if I didn't leave," he said. And during the Wukan protests in 2011, according to an interview with the *South China Morning Post* in Hong Kong, Zhuang had learned an important lesson: "The biggest fortune in life is not health but freedom."

5

Work

工作 / *Gōngzuò*

A month after they moved to Flushing, Little Yan asked Zhuang to wake up early and walk her to a nearby street corner. She had gotten a job at a nail salon over the phone and was expected to start that morning. Her new employer was planning to pick her up by the side of the road. Little Yan had never painted a nail in her life. She had no idea where she was going and only a vague idea where she was. She had never learned to read a map. When the boss asked her where she lived, Little Yan had answered, "Flushing, Queens. I'm not sure what street."

When Zhuang and Little Yan settled into their single-room apartment, with a single hard mattress, a single set of sheets, and a little pasteboard desk where Zhuang set up his computer, he had admonished her not to worry about money. They weren't like other immigrants, he told her. They weren't desperate. They still had money left over from Zhuang's land sale, and they had Zhuang's network.

He was still busy calling the various journalists and academics he had met in Wukan, updating them on his whereabouts and mining them for introductions to friends in New York. Zhuang's process was habitual. In Shenzhen, people from Wukan relied on a network of family and friends to help them settle. In New York,

Zhuang was attempting to build a support network from scratch, and he was sure an opportunity would come up sooner or later. It might take some time, but there were more important things in life than finding a job.

Little Yan had, for the first few weeks, listened to her husband's advice. She did her best to put aside her practical concerns about building a new life. Instead, she and Zhuang did everything together. They learned how to take the bus that ran in a straight line down Flushing's Main Street. They purchased a few items of furniture and went to the grocery store to buy noodles. They carried their clothes through the snow to the laundromat and looked up English-language classes online. At night they called Little Yan's parents and asked for updates on their son.

As the days passed, Little Yan's worries grew to fill her idle time. She tried to study English but spent most of her time watching Chinese television online. Zhuang left their door open, hoping to meet their neighbors, but no one came. They had made no new friends. Quietly, Little Yan decided to keep her own counsel and find a job. The problem was how to go about it in the United States.

She found her solution in a barbershop. Zhuang would browse job advertisements on local Chinese websites, but Little Yan didn't trust the impersonality of the Internet. She wanted to talk to a real person about getting a job. So one day when he took her with him to get a haircut, she asked the barber what she should do. She had no experience, she told him, limited English, and no work permit. The barber had no trouble answering. He told her to find work in a nail salon. "Go get a newspaper and look at some of the ads," he said. So she picked up the same Mandarin-language newspapers they had used to find the apartment and circled the nail salon ads. Some listed openings in Brooklyn, some in Manhattan, others in Long Island. There were nail salons in New Jersey and upstate New York. There were vans that would run workers to Connecticut and rural Maryland. Little Yan called numbers for salons in New York City, but beyond that, she didn't ask where they were. The locations were all the same to her.

The job that Little Yan got was at a shop in Long Island City, in a bad part of town, where no one tipped. She got the job, she later understood, because no one else wanted to work in that area and because summer was coming, peak season for nail salons. When she couldn't produce her address over the phone, the boss didn't hesitate and asked, "Is there a grocery near your house?" People commonly navigated according to the Chinese groceries. Little Yan said yes and named one on a corner a few blocks away. The boss instructed her to go stand in front of that store the next morning. She would pick her up and take her to work.

The night before, Little Yan had been worrying that she would be kidnapped and sold into slavery—get into the boss's car and never come back. Before she met Zhuang, when she was living as a migrant worker in Guangzhou, she had heard horror stories about women who had not been cautious. Little Yan hadn't been in New York long enough to hear cautionary tales, but she didn't need to. Migrant workers from rural areas were vulnerable in Guangzhou, cut off from their families; New York was much farther away, and Little Yan didn't speak English. If she found herself stranded in another part of the city, she would have no idea how to get home or even ask for directions. But she was determined to work. She asked Zhuang to walk her to the corner so he could memorize the license plate of the car that picked her up.

On the morning of her first day, Little Yan and Zhuang worked their way around snowdrifts and passed a handful of women lingering on street corners waiting for other vans. They arrived at the grocery store a little too early and stood quietly, Zhuang smoking a cigarette with a pinched efficiency brought on by the lingering cold. And then a van pulled up, a door opened from the inside, and the woman driving asked Little Yan's name. "Get in," she said. Little Yan did, and the van sped off.

• • •

Little Yan had expected New York to be luxurious. She had seen movies. She had watched episodes of *Friends* and absorbed the fabulous large apartment and big windows. New York had to be the wealthiest city in the world, she thought. And then on her first day in the city, she had taken the subway to Flushing. The neighborhood had looked worn out, as if it needed a break from the daily traffic. Little Yan had lived in big cities before and on their outskirts. Flushing did not measure up to them—it was like a third-tier city in China. The bridge carrying the Long Island Expressway over Main Street was dripping and old. The storefronts were dirty and packed together. Little Yan had prepared herself for hardship, but she had imagined a metropolis that was ordered and clean, even in its poorest neighborhoods. She had not considered that she would be packed in with thousands of other Chinese immigrants, walking streets that were cluttered and chaotic. She talked to no one. She saw rats on the subway and out in the open, and no one else blinked.

For nearly a hundred years, the Chinese immigrants who had come to the United States were men. In 1890, Chinese men living in the United States had outnumbered women more than twenty to one. They were not necessarily bachelors—in some cases, a village family arranged for a young man to be married just days before he left town—but they were alone. They worked long hours in laundries and restaurants. They pooled their money to start new businesses. The Chinese Exclusion Act of 1882 had prevented immigrants from bringing over their families, so the imbalance only grew with time. Men packed boardinghouses and gambling dens. They lived according to their village connections, filling up buildings with distant cousins. Their limited family lives helped darken the reputation of Chinatown; lonely men were more likely to smoke opium or frequent prostitutes.

Little Yan's Chinatown in Flushing was different. In the 1960s, a change in immigration policies eliminated a quota system based on nationality and focused on reuniting families. Thereafter women made their way from China to the United States in ever greater numbers. In the 1970s, wealthy Chinese investors opened sewing factories, and in the 1980s and '90s sweatshop clothing manufacturing was tucked into warehouses in Brooklyn and Queens. Bosses would not consider women for labor-intensive jobs like construction or stocking groceries, but they could work in nail salons or push carts at dim sum restaurants. Wealthy Chinese families needed nannies and housekeepers.

Many of the jobs available to women paid even less than what their husbands and sons were making. But when a woman spoke a little bit of English, her options expanded. Women were popular at the checkout counter in groceries or as salesladies in shops. Restaurants would hire women to answer phones and take orders or as waitresses—jobs that paid slightly more than the kitchen or delivery roles available to men. In Manhattan, some hostels still offered cheap beds to men only, but in Flushing the newspaper classifieds offered beds for women and families. Women had to pay a little more, fifteen dollars a night rather than twelve, but they could live as peripatetic a life as men.

• • •

The nail salon where Little Yan worked was a tiny operation—a narrow, dark shop with light coming in only through the front windows. In the winter the boss kept a skeleton staff of mostly part-time employees. There were two women in their fifties and a student who came in on the weekends. Each of them wore a little nametag that the owner would recycle as her employees came and went. If the women in the shop ever learned Little Yan's real name, they forgot it quickly. She had long ago picked the English name Angel for herself, but as a nail technician, she became Lisa.

Nail salons in New York occupy a low rung of the immigrant employment system. Most offer low wages and long hours, but many are willing to hire even the newest immigrants, paying wages under the table, no questions asked. Little Yan's boss did not worry that she had no papers. She took a hundred-dollar training fee and promised to give it back as soon as Little Yan worked in the shop for three months. It would take that much time, her boss reasoned, for her to pay back the expense of training her. It would also ensure that Little Yan stayed there for most of the summer, keeping the store running at peak efficiency during the busiest time of year.

Little Yan's boss didn't do much in the way of training. Instead, Little Yan learned by watching the older manicurists, practicing when business was slow. They told her what order to go in, how to cut cuticles with reasonable confidence, and how to keep the varnish neat. She learned the English words for upgraded services—gel polishes, hand massages, and moisturizing treatments. She was to keep her tools in a little sterilizer beside her desk. She didn't understand the allure of a manicure; no one she had known in China liked to paint their nails. It was, she decided, a quirk of American beauty. "They don't have to work with their hands," she said. The streets might have been chaotic, but New Yorkers liked their toes and fingers buffed and neat.

For the most part, Little Yan's co-workers did not open up to her. They talked impersonally about jobs and money but avoided divulging the details of their lives, wary of one another. After a few weeks, however, details started to trickle out, and Little Yan started to build a social map of immigrant life. It was not uncommon, she learned, for students to work at nail salon jobs part time as a stepping-stone to something better. Nail salons paid poorly because they accepted undocumented workers and everyone had to rely on tips. (A statewide investigation of nail salons undertaken by New York's Department of Labor in 2015 found that 85 percent of salons maintained inadequate payroll records.) Zhuang had been right about their advantages—he and Little Yan might live in a shared apartment, but many nail salon workers lived in shared rooms, stacked in bunk beds or separated from one another by hanging sheets.

The dangers of working in a nail salon were largely economic: long hours for poverty wages. But other industries in Flushing could be more hazardous for women. Massage parlors in particular had a reputation for paying well, but not all were straightforward in their services. Next to the nail salon job ads in the classified sections, it was possible to find ads that were explicit in their intent to hire "beautiful women" only; some offered suspiciously high daily wages. Other ads were deceptive. In previous years, multiple police raids on brothels masquerading as massage parlors in Flushing, Manhattan, and as far afield as Boston en-

snared women who claimed they had gotten into a van in Flushing on their way to a job as a masseuse, only to find out they were
expected to provide sexual services. There were stories of bosses
who held hostage the passports of women who traveled to jobs in
other cities and found themselves stranded.

On the other hand, for women who arrived in Flushing alone
and in debt, working as a prostitute could be a practical choice.
It paid far more than any other immigrant job and functioned
nearly the same as a nail salon: bosses picked up women in the
morning and delivered them home at night. In a 2012 book, the
sociologist Ko-Lin Chin explained that most of the brothel owners he met were not underground crime lords but former prostitutes or just regular immigrants who had rented a room, relying
on classified ads and word-of-mouth to build their business. Some
establishments served exclusively Chinese clients, others a mix.
Nail salon jobs were a safer choice for women, but they offered a
hardscrabble existence. They were for women who needed flexible
hours or who shared rooms, keeping their monthly expenses to a
minimum.

• • •

As time went on, Little Yan learned more about her co-workers.
The two older women had both divorced after coming to New
York. "Everyone in Flushing has a story like this," her boss told
her. Divorce was common among immigrants in Flushing. The
younger of the two admitted that she was looking for a boyfriend.
The other announced she was off the market, complaining that
many of the available men in their fifties were still married to the
women they had left behind in China.

When Little Yan came home and told Zhuang about her work-
mates, he started to worry. He still didn't like the idea of Little
Yan working in the first place, and he didn't want her gossip-
ing with divorcées. At his worst, he would get angry with her on
nights after she came home from a long day of bathing in nail
salon fumes. He had known that working would give her a bad
attitude, he said. "You don't understand anything!" he would tell

her. "People here are greedy and money-obsessed!" Little Yan was too easily influenced. "I tell you not to worry, and you don't listen to me!"

Little Yan was quieter in an argument but deadlier. She complained that Zhuang wanted her to stay home and sweep the floors—which would be fine with her if he would get a job. She would sweep all the floors her husband wanted as long as he was earning good money. But if he didn't, she was going to work. They had to send money to her family in Guangxi to help them take care of their baby. And Zhuang's family, with one brother crippled and the other a drug addict, had started demanding money as soon as they arrived. "You are not an expert on money," she told her husband.

While Little Yan worked, Zhuang searched listlessly for jobs online and worried about their asylum application, but mostly he obsessed over his past. He could not tear himself away from Wukan Village. Every day he followed the news coming out of the village and complained bitterly to Little Yan about the mismanagement there. He compiled stacks of the petitions he had filed in Guangdong. He took screenshots of his media interviews and wrote page after page of his story. Someday, he thought, he would turn his story into a book. He could find a publisher in Taiwan if someone helped him clean up his manuscript. He wrote as he was—a man with a middle school education, preoccupied with specific details and exact dates. He identified the quantifiable pieces of his past: dates, acres of land, number of protesters. People in Flushing might dismiss him as an uneducated fisherman, but the numbers were unassailable.

Otherwise he filled his time with trivial things. He took their laundry to the local laundromat. He smoked cigarettes with their neighbor's boyfriend, a young immigrant from Fujian who had finally, after weeks, introduced himself. When an argument turned too bitter, he would go into their shared kitchen and open a beer.

Zhuang was determined to come up with something that he could tell his friends in Wukan about without embarrassment. He felt he had a reputation to uphold; he would not lose face by failing to thrive in the United States. If a job on a boat didn't materi-

alize, he had a million other ideas. He kept his door open, hoping
to meet a neighbor who could offer advice. Their current neighbor's boyfriend told him about Chinese employment agencies that
connected immigrants to employers in New York, Florida, Chicago, and beyond. Offices in Flushing offered jobs, but mainly to
women hoping to work as nannies. In Manhattan, streets were
filled with agencies catering to the tens of thousands of Chinese
restaurants scattered across the United States.

Zhuang didn't want to leave New York, but in New York jobs
were harder to come by. He spent a week training at a travel
agency before he realized his entire salary would be on commission. Restaurants nearby were reluctant to hire someone like
Zhuang, in his thirties, with no English and no experience. And
the potential loss of face there was great: while he could imagine
working in a kitchen, he did not want to be a busboy taking home
a salary barely enough to pay rent. He walked Little Yan to her
street corner every morning and picked her up every night, and
he tried to think of a solution.

Flushing was full of face-losing situations. People on the street
looked down on Zhuang and his wife, both villagers and recent
arrivals. When they went to a sit-down restaurant, early on, and
didn't know to pay a tip, the boss openly scolded them. Every
transaction, every purchase they made, made it clear to Little
Yan and Zhuang that they were bumpkins. The real estate office,
that first day, had been just the tip of the iceberg. Every outing
revealed some new bit of ignorance—they stuttered while checking out at the grocery store, or they jumped off the bus too early
out of fear they would miss their stop. The veteran immigrants
would sigh, tired of the complications that the steady influx of
newcomers presented.

It hurt Zhuang more than Little Yan. The more he tried to
assert himself in his new city, the more he opened himself up
to disdain. After a heavy snow, he borrowed a shovel from the
neighboring house and cleared the sidewalk. He left a note for
his landlord suggesting that they buy a snow shovel that everyone
could use and take turns. The Chinese kid looked at him like he
was insane. Zhuang grinned but could see the condescension in

his landlord's face. He had struggled before. He had tasted humiliation. But he had no stomach for it anymore.

In retrospect, Zhuang would claim he came to New York with no expectations. He had known it would be hard, but the list of his disappointments was long: the crowded streets, the smell of garbage in summer, the cluttered sidewalks, and the dim, packed housing that cost so much more than anyone in China could imagine. His spending limits were constantly being pushed upward as he paid more than expected for groceries, rent, and bus fare. He took to eating at McDonald's for the cheap sandwiches. This, he supposed, was what American food tasted like. In the hours he spent indoors, he would scroll through advertisements on websites like 51nyc.com (a play on the similarity between the Mandarin words for "five" and "one" with "I want"). There were no openings to work on Chinese-run boats. He could work long hours on a fishing boat, but he would have to move to Boston. And even then he would have to wait until he got papers. Zhuang decided not to waste time worrying about money. Something would come along.

• • •

Every morning Little Yan walked to the street corner where the van would stop, passing other unmarked corners where other groups of women clustered—eddies in the stream of people in the sidewalk. People stood silently with their faces buried in their phones or their hands stuffed into their pockets. They would nod a quick hello and go back to staring at the ground. And then a van would pull up—black and white, mostly—and a nail salon boss would swing open a side door. Corners emptied out by late morning. Pedestrians were just pedestrians again.

About a year after Little Yan got that nail salon job, the *New York Times* would run an exposé on the working conditions and low pay at nail salons across the city, and the subsequent crackdown would scatter workers as salons suffered fines and shutdowns. Although she didn't know it, Little Yan had been lucky to find her job in Long Island City. The woman running the shop was honest—she returned the hundred-dollar deposit Little Yan had given her, a refund that the *New York Times* investigation found was not the norm. Little Yan worked six days a week, resting on Mondays, and her boss gave her a bonus every Friday, a little boost to her fifty-dollar-a-day base pay. She had learned, however, that a nail salon worker's income depended on tips, and so she wanted to find a shop in a better neighborhood. She also hoped for one with better ventilation. She was especially sensitive to the fumes, she decided, since other people worked all their lives in nail salons and never got a headache.

So after her three months were up, she quit and went back to stay in the little apartment with Zhuang. It would take her months to find another job.

6

The Chairman

主席 / *Zhŭxí*

During the unusually cold winter that welcomed Little Yan and Zhuang to New York, a man named Tang Yuanjun was spending the coldest days in his Flushing office, improving his hot-plate cooking, gluing together a small library of posters, and struggling to make peace with the sense of futility that had ebbed and flowed throughout his time in exile. Tang was the chairman of one of Flushing's Chinese Democracy Parties, the stable center of a swirl of longtime dissidents and newly arrived immigrants—the paranoid, the outspoken, the nervous, and the resigned. Tang listened to them all with the same series of nods and murmurs, settling people's fears and letting their expectations lower slowly, as painlessly as possible. "There is a saying that applies to life in the United States," Tang said. "In the first year you speak brave, bold words. In the second, nonsense. By the third, you have nothing to say at all."

Tang's office is located just half a block off Main Street, in a six-story glass and steel building grungy with neglect. He rents a space on the second floor, above a cheap restaurant and an express mail center. He leaves his door slightly ajar whenever he is in and keeps a carafe of tea on a foldout table. Activists and members come and go, drinking tea, talking politics, and trading gossip. After lunch, it is not uncommon to find an old dissident or two asleep at the table, wedged into a folding chair. Between working long hours, keeping in touch with family in China, and living in close quarters with other immigrants, it can be difficult, for an immigrant in Flushing, to find the time to sleep.

Tang is in his late fifties, with gray hair that sweeps across a wide forehead. He has grown distinguished during his time as chairman. In winter, he wears a long black coat that makes him look like a visiting dignitary. He uses his heavy-lidded eyes to great effect, lowering and raising them as he listens to the new people who file in and out of his headquarters. He dresses neatly, in slacks and a button-down shirt, and still wears a cell phone in a carrier strapped to his belt, in the style of China's small-town power brokers: a magnetic clasp lets him snap the phone in and out with every call. He has heard enough stories of persecution and nodded his head to enough half-baked plans for revolution (to make the China Democracy Party relevant! to contact the press! to pressure the government!) for a few lifetimes.

In the bathroom of his office, Tang stores a mattress that he sleeps on occasionally. When incredulous visitors wonder why he doesn't live in the office full time to save money, he explains that it is against the rules. "It's an office building," he says repeatedly. Nonetheless, in an armoire near the door, he keeps cooking supplies and bottles of Lao Ganma spices. In the bathroom, he stashes a hot plate that makes its appearance on a folding chair just before a meal. No one formally taught him how to cook, but he developed considerable skill on his own, perfecting the dishes he knew from China in the isolation of the neighborhood. People sometimes stop by just to pick up little jars of whatever Tang is serving.

• • •

In 1998 in China, the founders of the China Democracy Party signed their founding document and applied for legal status. "All political power can come only from the public," their declaration read. "The government is the servant of the public and not the one that controls it." By the end of the year, seven of the party's founders were in prison and their supporters, people like Tang, were being kept under close surveillance. The China Democracy Party, according to a report from Human Rights Watch, had been "nipped in the bud."

When Tang first opened his New York office, however, he found that China Democracy Parties had proliferated in Flushing. There were eleven located in the neighborhood—all of them separately allying themselves with the original. Now he estimates the number to be closer to eight; he has lost track. Democracy Parties are tucked into basements or above restaurants, or they share space with employment agencies. Party headquarters open their offices once a week for a matter of hours; Tang's office stays open late into the night.

Upon his arrival, Tang had been shocked that there were so many offices for the China Democracy Party. It was as if the first, the one he had belonged to before he left China, the one that the Chinese government had banned, had traveled to Queens and exploded.

Then someone had asked Tang if he owned the idea of democracy. "Is it yours, or does it belong to everyone?" He conceded the point. There was no reason to insist that the first party was the only one or even the best one. So he rented an office and started holding weekly meetings. Every Tuesday he talked about China's history and read the biographies of activists still in jail to a crowd of people sitting in folding chairs. On the final Tuesday of every month, he led his group to the corner of 42nd Street and Twelfth Avenue, across from the Chinese consulate. Tang's party planted itself there, to serve as a reminder that dissent still existed.

In 2014 Tang's protests faced frigid winter weather. The wind came up the Hudson River from the sea, whistling through the moorage of a retired World War II aircraft carrier—the *Intrepid*—just past 42nd Street. It would bend around the corner of 12th Avenue and force its way through sweaters, coats, and mittens. Protesters took turns holding up the banners, letting their hands thaw, then freeze, then thaw again. Tang would speak into a megaphone, and every once and a while the crowd would pick up a political chant, their voices carried off by the wind. Snow piled up on the sidewalks, and people stomped their feet against the cold.

The Monday before each scheduled protest, he would get a reliable flurry of phone calls from his members asking if he was canceling. Tang felt compelled to keep going—many of his members worked outside New York City. They traveled here in buses, rented a room for the night or took up floor space in a friend's apartment, specifically so they could attend the protest. They needed to take photos to support their asylum claims. It was not Tang's job to search for their motives; his job was to protest and to educate, to promote democracy.

In the winter of 2014, Tang's group was protesting the most recently detained pro-democracy activists, holding up posters outside the Chinese consulate, and listing their names during the educational meetings in his office. Tang makes a point of keeping his protests up to date. In 2011 he had talked about the Wukan protests. Now, three years later, Tang had a long list of new names and photos to hold up outside of the consulate. There were human rights lawyers like Xu Zhiyong, with his round head and buzz cut, and democracy activists like Liu Ping, a woman steel worker who had tried to run for office as an independent candidate. These pictures joined the ranks of people that Tang had been supporting for years: people like Liu Xianbin, who had been jailed after Tiananmen in 1989, again after organizing the China Democracy Party in 1998, and then a third time in 2010; or Zhu Yufu, another China Democracy Party founder, who had been imprisoned in 1999, 2007, and 2011. The founders of the China Democracy Party had a habit of getting arrested nearly as soon as they were released from jail.

• • •

By the mid-1800s, two Opium Wars and ripples of violence and unrest plagued China's final, flagging imperial dynasty. The warlords who ruled much of China invaded cities and slaughtered civilians. In 1850 religious fanatics staged a revolution so powerful that the followers of a man who claimed to be the brother of Jesus occupied most of southern China for more than a decade.

Men fled China, going wherever there was work. They traveled to Peru to harvest the bird guano that was a popular and expensive fertilizer in Europe. They found their way to Cuba and worked on sugar plantations. In America they became refugees and coolies, a cheap labor solution in the aftermath of the Civil War. Drawn to San Francisco by the Gold Rush, they took over gold claims that other miners had abandoned, in locations where the work was particularly hard or the gold scarce.

Most of the laborers fleeing China paid for their journey to the United States by way of a credit-ticket system. Agents would pay for their passage to California, later to be reimbursed with interest. A network of Chinese middlemen recruited immigrants from China for big U.S. companies. In San Francisco, family-based associations opened halfway houses close to the port, offering new arrivals a place to sleep, eat, and bathe. In exchange, the clan organizations required immigrants pay a fee before leaving town. Deals were made with shipping companies to ensure that any laborer who had yet to pay down the debt he had incurred for passage to the United States would not be allowed return passage to China.

Chinese immigrants were welcome in the United States as long as the economy was booming and their labor was needed. They went to work for larger mine owners, diverting streams to wear away the gold-bearing gravel, shifting through the sand and metal left in sluice boxes, working backbreaking hours for a fraction of the price of other laborers. Chinese immigrants, one San Francisco mayor commented, were well suited to the climate in northern California. They became preferred over recently freed slaves or Irish immigrants. "John," an article in the *New York Times* argued, using a common English name for a Chinese immigrant, "is a better addition to our society than Paddy."

As Chinese laborers—the miners, railway workers, and factory employees—spread throughout the United States, attendant communities of Chinese entrepreneurs followed. They built their own social support systems and established their own businesses. Chinese markets, laundries, and physicians served the community in San Francisco. Grocery stores opened in places like Evanston, Wyoming, and Ogden, Utah. Roast duck arrived in New Orleans in 1871. Chinese fishermen supplied U.S. fish markets and exported delicacies like abalone back to China. Other immigrants imported silk, tea, and porcelain to sell to Americans.

The networks the new immigrants built were complex and quasi-governmental. The same family organizations that opened halfway houses for recently arrived immigrants became centers of business—offering loans, settling disputes, and contracting with employers. They splintered and re-formed through internal conflicts that sometimes turned violent. One influential family-run organization, the Ning Yun Benevolent Association, got its start when a group of members defected from a larger, older company, instigating a bloody fight in front of a theater in San Francisco's Chinatown. That parent company further split when arguments broke out over leadership succession. Chinatowns were, from the start, self-governing, insular, and competitive.

Once the railways were built and the Gold Rush cooled, a wave of anti-Chinese feeling swept through the country and ignited into violence in California. Newspapers ran political cartoons that pictured the new arrivals as dirty, morally depraved, and threatening. In one cartoon, a Chinese man stands over a swooning white woman, a knife in his teeth, gun in his hand, his long braid whipping behind him. The caption reads "The Yellow Terror in all his Glory." In 1877 a protest in San Francisco turned into a two-day riot targeting Chinese businesses. The mob attacked laundries, stoned a Chinese church, set fire to a lumber mill, and left at least three men dead. The city's public safety bureau had to send out what it called a "pickaxe brigade" to stem the violence.

In 1882 the United States decided, for the first time in its history, to place a blanket ban on a single ethnic group. The Chinese Exclusion Act put into place a ten-year moratorium on any new working-class immigration from China. It denied naturalization for any Chinese person already living in the United States and required anyone leaving the United States with the intention of returning to obtain a "certificate of return." In 1888 another measure would cancel all the certificates of return, stranding nearly twenty thousand people.

The act had the desired effect. The rush of immigration slowed to a trickle. More laws followed, restricting whom Chinese immigrants could marry and where they could work. These limits initiated a tradition of slipping through loopholes, pushing people to use all the means they had to arrive and stay in the United States. After the Exclusion Act was passed, some immigrants paid agents to sneak them over borders with Canada and Mexico. Others exploited policies that granted citizenship to those born in the United States and allowed those citizens to sponsor the immigration of family members.

The loopholes in the Exclusion Act became easier to exploit in the aftermath of the 1906 San Francisco earthquake, when a huge fire destroyed most of the city's public documents. An industry in falsified birth certificates sprang to life. Chinese men with citizenship would claim that their wives had given birth in China, almost always to a son, opening up a space to sponsor a new family member. In reality, there was no new baby, and the immigrants with citizenship would sell the opportunity they had created to a hopeful immigrant.

The new arrivals were infamous; they were called China's "paper sons"—families built by immigration application, not by blood. Immigration agents in San Francisco became deeply suspicious. They grilled new arrivals on the precise details of their ancestry (or purported ancestry), the local geography of their claimed home village, and even the direction the windows faced in their childhood home.

The discrimination that led to the Exclusion Act also pushed the Chinese into ethnic enclaves, and the first real Chinatowns were born. People retreated into industries that would keep them out of competition with white laborers, in restaurants, laundries, and Chinese groceries. For many, the racism they faced in the United States, the restrictive laws and widespread discrimination, were not enough to deter them. The pull of the American dream—the thought they could change their fate and make something out of nothing—was too great.

· · ·

The dissidents who made up Tang's cohort were occupied with the same dream, for different reasons. "Of course, everyone wants to come to the United States," Tang says. "Even corrupt officials want to send their children to school here." Chinese dissidents first arrived in large numbers after the 1989 crackdown on student protesters in Tiananmen Square. At first, fleeing students escaped on their own or were spirited over Chinese borders by networks of sympathizers—Hong Kong's Operation Yellowbird, for example, sent fishermen to transport demonstrators by sea, smuggling more than four hundred people. American universities welcomed fleeing students. Chinese exiles already in the United States formed NGOs and started organizations aimed at helping bring democracy activists over, lobbying the government to welcome the student activists and provide them shelter from the persecution they faced in China.

As a result of their efforts, tens of thousands of Chinese students—those already studying in the United States and reluctant to return—and activists were allowed to stay. Prominent Tiananmen Square leaders like Wang Dan, Chai Ling, and Wu'er Kaixi attempted to piece together new lives, attending U.S. universities and doing their best to continue their activism. A Chinese proverb was passed around to try to make sense of their situation: the Tiananmen activists had "gained the sky but lost the earth."

If these dissidents were the predecessors of later activists like Zhuang, they set an uneven example of how to build a new life outside of China. Many left after seeing their friends injured or shot down at Tiananmen. Some had suffered torture in jail. Once in the United States, all exiled dissidents had to make their own decisions about the sacrifices they were going to make—whether and how they would go on protesting the Chinese government. Some started websites so they could keep publishing their ideas. Others started China-focused nonprofits or became leaders in human rights organizations. Wu'er Kaixi moved to Taiwan. Another famous activist, Li Lu, went into finance. Others moved to

South Korea or Thailand, and a few sneaked over the border back into China.

Tang Yuanjun was at once part of the events of 1989 and set apart from them. He was older than most of the students protesting at the square—old enough that his education had been derailed by the Cultural Revolution of the late 1960s and '70s, when schools were shut down and students encouraged to denounce their teachers. By the spring of 1989, he was working as an engineer at an automotive factory six hundred miles away from the capital city. Tang, however, had a long-standing interest in democracy and political reform. He had been running discussion groups in his spare time, and when the protests started in Tiananmen Square, he organized three different marches in his hometown, leading thousands of people in a protest supporting the students in Beijing. When the crackdown came, he was detained and sentenced to twenty years in jail.

Tang served eight of those twenty years before he was released. He suffered beatings and went on hunger strikes. When he got out, he found himself newly irrelevant, stuck in the past while everyone else had moved on. His wife, who had suffered for having a dissident husband, had divorced him while he was still in prison. Most of his friends cared little about the idealism that had sat static in Tang while he spent time in prison. The year after he was released, he joined a group trying to register branches of the China Democracy Party in municipalities throughout China. It was all legal, Tang argues, still frustrated by the technicalities. He was in the right and not just morally: strictly speaking, eight different parties are operating in China in addition to the Communist Party of China (CPC). The eight parties, however, cannot field candidates for public office, and all are financed by the CPC. The technicalities did not matter; the Communist Party began detaining the democracy leaders the day after they attempted to register their political party.

Tang avoided another jail sentence but soon found that he was detained wherever he went. He could hold a job for only a matter of months before the local authorities discovered him and forced him back to his home city. No one wanted to be responsible for keeping tabs on an activist. Tang moved from city to city, up and down China's coastline.

Finally, when he had been arrested so many times he was losing count, a man in an interrogation room was honest with him. "Do you know who we are?" the man asked.

"The police?" said Tang.

"No," the man said. "We're the State Security Bureau. You know, you're never going to be able to live anywhere in China."

Tang executes a practiced shrug at this point in telling his story. "They were going to arrest me no matter where I went."

After this, in 2001, Tang decided to swim to Taiwan. It was an escape plan worthy of a suspense film—he was still young enough to be foolhardy. He hoped he might swim to the closest island in the chain, a little patch of rocks that Taiwan fought for in 1949, just around fourteen thousand feet from Xiamen, a coastal city in Fujian Province in Mainland China. Dadan Island has an area of just under a square kilometer, with a stretch of beach on one side and rocky cliffs on the other.

Tang thought that if he made his home in Taiwan, he might be able to sneak back into China every once in a while. He could swim back, join whatever democracy effort was under way, and then escape back to safety. It was an outlandish dream, one in which he was safe but still relevant, an important member of an underground movement rather than a stubborn holdout.

Tang traveled to Xiamen with the barest outline of a plan. Xiamen is separated from Dadan Island by a strip of water that is not, to a man intent on escaping China, insurmountable. Tang took tourist boats around the bay, circling an island that was closer in, still part of Mainland China. He took notes on the coast guard patrols and realized they took a lunch break in the middle of the day. He contemplated jumping off the boat, swimming for the island outlined in the distance. It wouldn't work. It was too far—even if he was confident he could make the swim without drowning, the bigger boats could easily call in the coast guard before he reached the rocks. He needed another plan.

Tang walked Xiamen's docks for a few days before he decided his best option was to dupe a fisherman. He picked out a man with a little white boat, not too fancy but new enough that it looked capable of making its way out of the protected bay onto the open ocean. He told the man that he and his friends wanted to go out on a fishing expedition—the man might suspect him if he admitted he was making the trip alone. He offered a price that was high but not outlandish. And the next morning, when Tang's friends failed to materialize, he made a show out of it. "Well, you already have my money," he said, palms open in his retelling, eyes wide and innocent. "We might as well go out."

The boat chugged out past the near island and came to rest in a spot so close to the target island that he could see rocks breaking out of the water. It would be an easy swim. It was midday, and the coast guard would be eating lunch. Tang pretended to have a gun. He told the fisherman to stay behind the wheel of the boat. "I killed a man!" he shouted to him. "Don't come out here!" Tang had put all his important documents in a fanny pack wrapped in plastic, which he threw into the water ahead of him. He dove, grabbed the bag, and swam hard before he had the courage to look back—the fisherman was peering over the side of the boat curiously, checking to see whether Tang would drown.

The inlet that Tang Yuanjun aimed for in his swim was rocky, and he cut himself climbing out of the water. He lay out in the sun to dry and looked back at the coast of China. It was hazy and far off. He had never been anywhere else. Despite all his plans to sneak back in, he had a feeling that this first look at China from over the border would be his last. He sat there waiting to dry, · gazing back at the silhouette of his country. He baked in the sun for half an hour until a soldier spotted him from a ridge above the beach. "Who are you?" the soldier shouted. "What are you doing?"

Tang shouted his answer, explaining he was defecting. There was a slight pause, and then the soldier shouted, "Swim back!"

• • •

One of the first China Democracy Parties that Tang encountered in the United States was not so much a political organization as it was an immigration agency. The man running the party had approached Tang at a rally in Times Square, where exiled dissidents were commemorating the massacre at Tiananmen. The man had slipped through the crowd, half-protesting, half-networking. He shook Tang's hand and said he was looking for real, honest-to-goodness dissidents to come speak to his group of immigrants. Tang agreed to be a speaker.

He showed up at the man's office, and as the meeting progressed toward his planned appearance, he realized it was a sham. These people, in their asylum cases, would claim to be so dedicated to democracy that they would face persecution if they returned to China. They would back up their claim by documenting their attendance at these meetings. But here in this office, the discussion was focused on issues of immigration. These party members would get their asylum knowing barely more about the oppression, human rights activism, and political movements within China than they had when they walked in.

It was a disappointment, but the meeting in that office gave Tang insight into his own character. He did not mind working odd jobs, delivering food, fixing cars, and surviving in the fashion of an everyday Flushing immigrant. But it wasn't the life he had dreamed of. Tang was made to be a democracy activist. It was his *benzhi gongzuo*, his most essential work.

By the time Zhuang arrived in Flushing, Tang's office was attracting a steady mix of dissidents, curious young people, and hopeful asylees. In addition to the veterans of Tiananmen Square, the China Democracy Party supporters, and the other dissidents who had arrived in the 1990s and early 2000s, a new group of activists had started to trickle into New York in the late 2000s: people whose houses had been knocked down and who had moved (sometimes forcibly) to cheap housing on the outskirts of their cities. The process was so common in China that the new activists could efficiently sum up their stories of demolition, poor government compensation, and relocation in two words: *chai qian*.

In 2013 an activist named Ma Yongtian arrived in the United States and found a spot at Tang's folding table. Ma was a middle-aged woman with a short, practical haircut and the blunt, confrontational manner of a hardened businesswoman. She had been building her fortune in northeastern China by manufacturing funerary urns—Tang Dynasty style, an ancient and expensive-looking mix of yellow, brown, and green—when the local government sold the land under her factory, illegally, to a developer. They turned off the water and cut the electricity. They sent thugs to try to intimidate Ma Yongtian. She had fought for over a decade, joining the ranks of China's petitioners—people who traveled back and forth to Beijing in a Sisyphean attempt to alert China's central government to local injustice. Ma sued the developer in a local court, and won, but nothing was done to enforce the court's ruling. When she tried to petition in Beijing, agents from her hometown intercepted her on multiple occasions, throwing her into "black jails"—extrajudicial detention sites set up to thwart petitioners like her—and forcing her to return home. By the time she arrived in New York, Ma's lips were frozen in a line of grim determination.

The *chai qian* activists, all with stories similar to Ma's, had been content enough as Chinese citizens until their local government bulldozed their homes in the name of new developments, roads, rail lines, and real estate profits. Together they were an outraged and confrontational group, one time even marching into the Chinese consulate and getting into a shoving match with one of their guards. Ma Yongtian had, by 2014, established a reputation for throwing herself in front of the cars of visiting Chinese dignitaries.

She and her friends wore their convictions on their sleeves, but Tang's office had also become a center for immigrants who were still wary of protest. They were economic migrants who had arrived at Tang's doorstep out of curiosity or opportunism. A number came on the instructions of their asylum lawyers, looking to build a case of persecution. While this group had, at first, disillusioned him, Tang had come to regard educating these asylum seekers as one of his most important duties. Some came to their first Democracy Party meeting having no clue about what had happened to the students at Tiananmen Square. It had been wiped from China's history books. It was not, Tang realized, the dissidents in exile who needed to learn about democracy. It was the regular immigrants, people who might not understand that many activists were still being jailed, who might not know the real hardships of China in the twentieth century—the famines, political purges, and corruption cases. He hoped that after a year or two, his members would be able to look past propaganda and hope for change. Asylum was a side effect, the great gray area of running a Democracy Party.

Not everyone understood the way that Tang embraced these members. It was not his business, he explained, to pick apart their motives. "People are complicated," he said. "If you say they are here just for their asylum case, that's not true. But if you say there are not here for their asylum case, that's not true." Even if the people who showed up in his office did not face persecution in China, even if they couldn't care less about democracy, they would attend his meetings for months. And if they took what he said to heart, they could face persecution in China all the same.

• • •

Zhuang Liehong was interested in the question of democracy in China, but he had arrived in the United States determined not to join anyone else's movement. He was dedicated to one cause, and that was Wukan. He didn't trust the other dissidents in Flushing; he was wary they would use his story to promote themselves.

Zhuang did strive to befriend anyone with a connection to his old life. When the Chinese assistant of a German journalist he had met in Wukan arrived in New York to attend graduate school, Zhuang invited her out to Flushing and gifted her with tea. A Chinese documentary filmmaker came to New York, and Zhuang offered her a foldout cot on the floor of his single room. He kept up persistent contact, e-mailing, texting, and inviting his few friends to tea. Through these efforts, he established a small network of students and journalists—but there were drawbacks to such friends. None of them lived in Flushing. Some were immigrants, but they lived differently from Zhuang, passing through New York temporarily, showing up at Zhuang's apartment for a few days and then moving on. One woman, a Chinese-American translator named Sophie, grew concerned that Zhuang was too isolated. She suggested that he introduce himself to Tang Yuanjun.

Zhuang protested, privately, that he was not interested in joining anyone else's group. But he had only so many friends, and Sophie was one of them. He decided it would be rude not to take her advice. So in June of his and Little Yan's first year, Zhuang took Little Yan out to the China Democracy Party headquarters. He located the space on Google Maps, tucked into an aging, stout office building not far from the entrance to the Flushing Library and just past a sidewalk that was wet and cluttered with wooden boxes of grocery store bulk items.

The office Tang had rented on the second floor of the little building was accessible by two tiny elevators or by a stairwell with doors that slammed shut with a loud, violent clang that reverberated through the halls of the floors below and above it.

• • •

Zhuang and Little Yan trudged down their street in the cold and caught a city bus, a mode of transportation they were still adjusting to, memorizing stops as they went. Despite his protestations, he entertained the idea that he might find a community of likeminded people at the China Democracy Party. At least, he hoped people would give him the kind of reception he had envisioned before coming to the United States. Little Yan slipped after him quietly, in winter boots that added to her height with a few inches of platform heel, her ability to negotiate the icy sidewalks one of those little miracles performed by determined women.

They pushed past the mail center on the first floor and into the little elevator. Zhuang took in the space: a nice office with big windows that looked out onto the snowy street. He saw the scores of folded-up plastic and metal chairs lining the walls, the plastic folding table for visitors, the rolled-up years of protest banners stacked against the windows.

It was an off day, and Tang Yuanjun was there alone. He was puttering on a computer under a poster of Abraham Lincoln that read, in English, WHEN I DO GOOD, I FEEL GOOD. WHEN I DO BAD, I FEEL BAD. THAT IS MY RELIGION.

Tang stood up and greeted Zhuang and Little Yan warmly. "Sit down, sit down," he told them. "Would you like some tea?" He poured into paper cups from a glass carafe in the center of the table. He sat down on one of the folding chairs and asked Zhuang, "Do you need help finding a lawyer?"

Zhuang said he didn't. He had his own lawyer already.

"Do you need any help with your case?" asked Tang.

"No," said Zhuang.

They talked a little bit about Wukan. They talked a bit about Zhuang's plans, and Zhuang was evasive. He was waiting until his asylum claim was settled, he said. He wasn't worried about work.

Tang nodded, quietly. It was still early days. Zhuang was still expecting America to accommodate him. He was still full of bold ideas. "He had a lot of plans," Tang would say later. "He was still a little unrealistic."

It was not the reception that Zhuang had hoped for. Tang was warm, but he had seen his fair share of newly arrived dissidents. Zhuang did not get the sense that he was a celebrated visitor. A few people came and went, mostly to ask about their asylum cases. After about an hour, Zhuang and Little Yan took the rickety elevator back down, feeling doubtful. He didn't need Tang's help. He had his own network. He had the same sense Tang remembers from his first Flushing Democracy Party experience—that the people attending Tang's meetings were not there for democracy at all.

Zhuang did not want to get caught up in someone else's problems. He had his own asylum case to make, but he wouldn't need anyone to help him prove his devotion to freedom and democracy. He had his own plans, his own glory to chase down. He would make a life in the United States and send money back to friends and family. He would write a book and start a company. He was determined to go it alone.

7

Sanctuary

避难所 / *Bìnànsuǒ*

Sitting on the corner of Kissena Boulevard and Main Street, an off-kilter intersection that requires multiple street crossings just to proceed in a straight line, an older woman spends most days standing underneath a traffic signal, peering out from under a visor and repeating a message over a bullhorn. "Green card! Marriage license! Immigration! Visa! Asylum!" The metallic-sounding voice has the same lilt that street vendors in China use to advertise a cart of fruit.

Zhuang's agenda, on his very first day in New York, started with obtaining a green card. Over years of researching land sales and drawing up petitions, he had developed a preoccupation with documentation. He wanted official recognition for his own sense of security and so he and Little Yan could apply to bring their son over to join them. The first step would be an asylum application for himself and Little Yan. On his second morning, he sat on my sofa in Brooklyn and asked me for help.

My own understanding of the U.S. asylum process was not much better than Zhuang's. With him looking over my shoulder, I Googled "asylum lawyer New York" and came up with a handful of offices in Flushing. I called one, and a secretary answered the phone in Mandarin. "I have a friend who is looking to apply," I told her.

"No problem," she said, switching to English. "We generally charge eight thousand dollars for an asylum case." The cost might go up, she explained, if Zhuang needed to appear in court to defend his case. I thanked her and hung up.

When I told Zhuang the price I had been quoted, his jaw dropped. He had expected to file the papers himself. He thought it would be cheap or even free. He wondered if he was missing something. "I bet Chen Guangcheng didn't pay for a lawyer," he said, mentioning a famous Chinese exile, a blind human rights activist who spent years in prison and under house arrest. Chen had grown so famous in his government-enforced isolation that even the actor Christian Bale had attempted to meet him, arriving with a film crew from CNN that captured Bale getting pushed around by a potbellied man in a long green army coat. In the end, Chen had escaped house arrest and taken refuge in the American embassy, causing a brief diplomatic crisis. Zhuang was always comparing himself to Chen Guangcheng.

I told Zhuang I would look for organizations that provided legal aid while he asked around in Flushing. A few weeks in, all the organizations I called had no space to take on any additional clients. Zhuang came back after investigating his for-profit options—the law offices that operated out of Flushing and Chinatown and catered to Chinese customers. He confirmed the price I had been quoted. Asylum, in all of Manhattan's Chinatowns, was a booming business.

• • •

New York City is estimated to have more undocumented immigrants than any other metropolitan area in the United States. It is a "sanctuary city"—the police force does not arrest individuals because they lack documentation, and they do not cooperate with Immigration and Customs Enforcement when it comes to tracking down and deporting immigrants. A mix of local organizations offer free legal services to recent arrivals. A quick, incomplete survey included Catholic Charities, Cabrini Immigrant Services, Human Rights First, UN Local, the Legal Aid Society, Safe Horizon Immigration Law Project, and the Hebrew Immigrant Aid Society. I filled out intake forms, called branch offices, and asked friends if they knew any immigration lawyers. One organization would get back to me nearly eight months later—a spot had finally opened up.

Zhuang did not have to wait that long. Through a chain of connections that crisscrossed two universities and someone's ex-girlfriend, I was put in contact with a lawyer named Alexandra Goncalves-Pena, working at the Hebrew Immigrant Aid Society (HIAS). She spoke no Mandarin—Zhuang would need a translator at all his meetings—but she agreed to represent him at no cost. The rest, he said, he could figure out.

For his first meeting, Zhuang would have to make his way to Manhattan on the subway, walk past a handful of Chinese restaurants and a Starbucks, sign in on the ground floor, and buzz at the entrance to the office. He called and told me not to worry—he knew the subway better now. He and Little Yan could make it on their own. For the first couple of meetings, the two of them would wait in the lobby of the building for their interpreter before approaching the doorman and going up.

Goncalves-Pena opened the door to the HIAS offices and grinned. She was taller than Zhuang, with unruly hair, and she had an artful, disarming way of chattering only when there was space to fill. She listened to the story of Wukan Village, rapt and unhurried. In her office, Zhuang answered every question at the length he felt it deserved. He was brimming with names and dates. He had gone over the details so many times that they came to mind faster than he could speak them; he stuttered trying to get them all out.

Zhuang held out the hope that, once their asylum case was settled, opportunities would finally open up for him—he had to be more employable once he had papers and a Social Security number. He befriended anyone who was willing to work on his case. Sophie, the woman who had introduced him to Tang Yuanjun, helped him recruit people to translate his documents, and Zhuang invited them all to tea. When Sophie gave him the number of a woman working at the Congressional Executive Commission on China, Zhuang leaped at the opportunity to visit Washington, D.C., and booked a ticket on a Chinatown bus. He paused for a photograph in the lobby of Congress. He was welcomed into an office and told his story while a researcher took notes. He kept the phone number of everyone he met.

Zhuang's case file grew thick with the documents he provided. He handed over pictures, petitions, and news articles. He waited patiently for everything to be translated and filed. He explained that Lufeng bureaucrats had changed his birth date, and his lawyer offered to change it back—to give him a start in the United States that was entirely based on fact. Zhuang was skeptical. He'd grown comfortable with the wrong date on his passport.

It was June by the time Zhuang and Little Yan were scheduled to get fingerprinted in preparation for their asylum interview. They struggled to understand the directions of the security officer at the door, and were nearly kicked out of the waiting room for using their cell phones. The office initially turned him away because of the mix-up with his birth date. He had to return the next day, his lawyer in tow. Any bureaucratic delay could require months of sorting out. Nothing was simple.

In its annual data, the U.S. Department of Homeland Security distinguishes between "defensive" and "affirmative" asylees. More than half of the successful asylum cases from China are defensive. In these cases, applicants who were denied asylum in their first interview are given a court date where they are expected to defend their claims in front of a judge. Getting asylum this way, according to Tang, can take nearly three years. Members of his Democracy Party spend years attending protests, documenting their actions in order to convince a judge of their dedication to democracy. People cry in their hearings, whether the news they're getting is good or bad. Tang thinks it's because they have caught the American dream like one catches a cold—it spreads from family member to family member and passes through the air vents during the plane ride over.

To pass an initial interview and avoid the years of court hearings, an asylum seeker must follow a few rules of thumb: *Look your interviewer in the eye. Answer quickly, even when you're not sure of your answer. Never look at your lawyer or your translator for help. Look confident.* None of these were a problem for Zhuang. Instead, he talked too much. In the weeks leading up to the interview, when he and Little Yan met at the HIAS to prep, he answered every mock question at length. He talked excitedly about the people he knew in the village. He grimaced when he mentioned the village chief, while his interpreter looked on helplessly.

Finally Little Yan kicked him under the table.

"What!" he said. "I'm just telling them what they asked."

"They only asked you for a yes or no," said Little Yan. "They can't translate that quickly."

"Okay," said Goncalves-Pena, who was overseeing the exercise. "Why don't we have your translator hold up her hand when she needs you to stop?"

The woman nodded in appreciation.

"Oh," said Zhuang, switching into his unsteady English. "I'm sorry."

When Zhuang plunged back in, answering the next question, the interpreter's hand flew up, and Zhuang gave a grunt of surprise.

• • •

Nationwide, more Chinese people apply for and attain asylum every year than any other group. Every year Chinese asylees outnumber those from the next three nations (Guatemala, El Salvador, and Egypt) combined. For a working-class Chinese immigrant with no existing family in the United States, asylum is one of the only pathways to citizenship. And yet for the most part, Chinese asylum seekers have avoided New York's ecosystem of legal aid services; Zhuang and Little Yan's path was rare. Spanish, Arabic, and French speakers are common at aid organizations, but when I began inquiring on behalf of Zhuang, I found very few pro bono lawyers available who spoke Mandarin. Chinese immigrants, instead, had created a network of their own. In Flushing, the signs cluttering the sidewalk included multiple offices for immigration lawyers. People exchanged their lawyers' phone numbers while lingering around employment offices or waiting for customers in nail salons.

Asylum claims from China are so successful, in large part, because of the specific types of persecution Chinese citizens face. To be granted asylum in the United States, an individual must prove that he or she faces persecution based on race, religion, nationality, political opinion, or social group. The persecution must have been carried out by government forces or else involve violence the government is unable to prevent. Immigrants fleeing gang violence in Honduras or El Salvador are hard-pressed to fulfill all these requirements—it is difficult to prove that the violence is targeted and that governments are doing nothing to prevent it. In Chinese asylum cases, however, the government is typically behind the persecution.

In Flushing, three types of asylum cases dominate. They center on China's limited religious freedom, its one-child policy, and its intolerance for political dissent. Immigrants who have converted to Christianity tell stories of unsanctioned churches raided by officials. Women asylees might face forcible abortions if they try to have a second child. And then, like Zhuang, some dissidents are not free to express their political beliefs.

While asylum claims in Flushing tend to meet all the required criteria, stay long in Flushing, and you will begin to hear near-identical stories told over and over again. Lawyers in Chinatown have a reputation for manufacturing or embellishing on their clients' stories. Democracy Parties are not the only enablers: churches in Flushing offer slips of paper that confirm an immigrant's weekly attendance. In 2012 an FBI raid on lawyers in Manhattan's Chinatown merited the headline "Asylum Fraud in Chinatown: An Industry of Lies."

• • •

Zhuang imagined his case would move quickly. He had documented everything so well and was speaking honestly. There were no embellishments for him to memorize or outright fabrications to fret over. The interview was scheduled for both Zhuang and Little Yan at once, but Zhuang would be taking the lead. The office was in Long Island, and the pair caught the train early in the morning. They met their lawyer and their interpreter and went into the building together, moving through security. Zhuang and Little Yan had been warned they might have to wait a long time, but the interview started quickly. The interviewer, if not friendly, was not combative. Zhuang answered questions about his village. She asked about the protests, the beatings, and his fear of future violence. He paused for his interpreter and tried his best not to stutter. He looked his interviewer in the eye. He covered every detail he could remember. He spoke for two full hours before the asylum officer closed the file and shook his hand. She told them that she thought the case was well documented.

There was, however, a wrinkle in Zhuang's case. Because he had been interviewed by a number of international media outlets, it would require an extra layer of review. He fell into an uncomfortable middle ground: he was not famous enough to receive special, expedited treatment but was notable enough that the U.S. Immigration Bureau needed to make sure it wasn't stepping into any larger international disputes. The interviewer didn't offer Zhuang or Little Yan a time frame, but Zhuang understood that any delay might expand incalculably, lost in a shuffle of papers in New York, Washington, and Texas. Goncalves-Pena optimistically estimated the review would last three months. If it ran longer than that, she explained, Zhuang and Little Yan would be allowed to apply for a work permit while they waited, a stopgap that everyone in Flushing called the A5 card.

For months, Zhuang had been marking time by his asylum interview. He felt frozen on the threshold of the city, waiting for it to open up to him. He had told Little Yan not to worry about money. They had argued at night until she turned over on their hard, thin mattress, facing the wall and willing herself to fall asleep. Then the interview came and went. It took Zhuang and Little Yan a few days to realize what had happened. When they walked out into the summer morning, they had felt triumphant. He would find work soon. They would apply together to bring their son over. Their rocky transition period would be over.

In the days that followed, however, Zhuang realized that he had not received the welcome he had hoped for. He had not been commended for his bravery or recognized for the sacrifices he had made. The interviewer had been polite but distant. And then the decision had been delayed. His son would remain in China; his life would remain the same. He woke up in the morning on the same mattress as always, the clutter of Little Yan's things stored in two stacked plastic crates near the head of the bed. Zhuang showered and made his way from the house down an uneven sidewalk. He cut behind a defunct Korean karaoke bar, hopped over the spot where the concrete crumbled into a puddle, and then crossed a parking lot toward the McDonald's, where he could order a hamburger and a coffee like any real American. And he could sit at one of the plastic tables just past the counter and consider his situation.

• • •

In the spirit of making the best of his reality, Zhuang decided to look for a new apartment—something cheaper and closer to the center of Flushing. Most of the available housing was informal: rooms rented without contracts, bunk beds stacked in the living rooms of small apartments, single-family houses split to accommodate four or five families. The Flushing housing market was not the stuff of commission-seeking rental agents or online photo galleries. There were two unofficial housing markets near Flushing's center. One was located alongside a glass wall just outside a bubble tea shop, the other along one wall of a local supermarket. Here people could pay a small fee and pin up a handwritten note describing what they offered and how much it cost. For many people subletting rooms in their apartments, the process of advertising on a supermarket wall was more navigable than trying to set up an ad on one of the Mandarin-language websites.

It was early fall when Zhuang decided to hunt for an apartment. He visited the supermarket and gazed up at the wall of papers, some scrawled quickly in pen, others written out attractively in different-colored markers. He wondered how he was supposed to tell a good landlord from a bad one. He had started to get the feeling that everyone in Flushing was out to take advantage of him.

He was busy looking at the advertisements when a squat, gravel-voiced woman sidled up next to him. He didn't see her until she growled up at him, loud and up front: "Hey, are you looking for a room?"

Zhuang jumped and looked down. He was.

Chen Tai was a stack of spheres, round-faced and round-bellied. She did not pay anyone a fee to advertise her room. She did not like to give out her phone number. Instead, she lingered near the wall, pretending to be picking out fruit, until she saw someone she liked. Then she led them down the street and showed them the room for rent—a run-down but spacious bedroom with a little window and a closet. The rest of the apartment was a jumble of temporary walls that she had erected to carve the living and dining rooms into three additional bedrooms. The only common area was the dark entryway outside the kitchen, just large enough for the square card table that Chen Tai had stuck in the corner. She puttered around the apartment, opening doors so Zhuang could see everything. He stuck his head into the bathroom, where Chen Tai kept a bucket and a mop and clothes hung above the bathtub. He turned on the water in the galley kitchen. He went home feeling optimistic.

On that first visit, Chen Tai had explained to him that there were two other people living in the little temporary bedrooms— Chen Tai's own daughter, and a man everyone called Uncle. There was a child in the apartment as well, a boy who slept in the section of the living room Chen Tai had reinvented as her own bedroom. He was the son of some relatives who were working outside New York City, and Chen Tai had agreed to take care of him in their absence. She picked him up from school and made sure he did his homework. At night they shared the makeshift room. His parents paid her a small fee for the favor but not enough to make her rich. "I have been here for years, and we're still poor," she told Zhuang. "This is a good country, but it's a hard one." She told him to forget about himself and think about his children.

The apartment was not luxurious, but the bedroom that Zhuang and Little Yan occupied was larger, even, than the place they had rented in Wukan. They purchased one new table, and then another. They filled the closet up with their clothes. Zhuang liked his new landlady, who called him "Little Zhuang." She was quick to point out that she had very little education but no shortage of opinions. She kept to herself most of the time, but she liked to offer wisdom on poverty and hard work, her rasping voice filling up the tiny common area of the apartment. She wasn't too different from some of Zhuang's aunts back in Wukan.

Chen Tai worked pushing a dim sum cart at a banquet hall not far from her apartment. She bustled out in the morning, her back straight and her stocky legs moving in a clipped, rapid stride, heading to the East Buffet. Dim sum is traditionally a morning and afternoon meal, and service at the East Buffet ended by three. She could work the lunch rush, change in the bathroom, and leave in time to pick up her charge from school. She invited Zhuang to stop by sometime—if she could, she would slip him a few extra egg tarts.

• • •

There were few community spaces in Flushing. Old men hung out in a park off Maple Avenue, playing cards. Students and older aunties filled up the seats in the Flushing Library, but Zhuang was no scholar. He did not like to gamble. He had invited his handful of friends into his small room and served them tea on a makeshift tea table he had constructed, with a pink plastic bowl and a flat sieve laid across the top, pouring hot water and brewing the tea the traditional Chinese way. But compared to the village, it was a lonely way to socialize. Zhuang liked the feeling of community; he liked a little commotion, a little background noise. And then he found the East Buffet.

The complex where Chen Tai worked did not serve the best dim sum courses in New York or arguably even in Flushing. The skins on the steamed shrimp dumplings were not the delicate, paper-thin wrapping that a diner might expect from a top chef in Hong Kong. The menu was, however, comprehensive. Taken in its entirety, the business operated on two floors. The first was cramped and humid, with an LED sign in the entryway that scrolled the characters 欢迎, or "welcome," over and over again in orange lights. The front doors opened next to a cafeteria-style takeout counter, offering four dishes and a soup to customers in Styrofoam boxes. A small à la carte restaurant, sticky and expensive, was tucked in the back. These were the low-rent alternatives to the main attraction, the banquet hall, which could be found up a sweeping, curved staircase. Zhuang called it simply a "teahouse."

Dim sum, in many ways, is the antithesis of American Chinese food. It is difficult to make and meticulously presented. Most dim sum restaurants offer a long list of dumplings, steamed buns, rolls of shrimp and meat, cakes, congee, and more. The kitchen in the East Buffet was massive, stretching the length of the banquet hall, half-filled with the cooks who tackled the buns, soups, and dumplings that would replenish the cart. Other cooks, the ones who took orders for individual dishes, cooked whole fish or fried up noodles and rice in massive woks, tossing the contents with two hands, the muscles in their shoulders tightening against their white chef's coats.

Zhuang loved the banquet hall as soon as he saw it. The East Buffet was decorated with just enough flourish to suggest opulence, but the dumplings were priced well. The servers spoke Cantonese, and so did Zhuang. He brought his own tea leaves and asked the servers to brew it for him. He understood the rhythm and the culture of the teahouse—the long mornings of drinking tea and eating snacks; the bustle of a cavernous hall filled with people pushing carts and customers plucking steamed dumplings out of communal baskets. Zhuang liked to sit by the windows, whose edges were draped in gold fabric, and chat amicably with the servers. He would order a selection of bamboo baskets and insist on pouring the tea for everyone. Against a far wall, waiters were constantly changing a backdrop for nighttime weddings, taking down a flowered heart and putting up a giant gold character for "happiness."

Inevitably, Chen Tai would round one of the tables with her two-tiered cart and shout with surprise, "Hey, Little Zhuang, you've come!" She offered her customers a selection of turnip cakes, egg custards, and sweet buns, her voice gurgling and breaking like an adolescent boy's. She would push her cart back and forth, slipping Zhuang some free buns if she could, stopping to pick up turnip cakes and wheeling toward the back.

Zhuang had found the first place in Flushing where he felt truly comfortable. Anyone who came through Flushing now was invited to the banquet hall. He brought in the interpreters who had helped him with his asylum case and the journalism student he still kept in touch with. When a German reporter he knew, Yang Xifan, came through New York on holiday, she brought a friend—a dissident with a perpetually moody look on his face. Yao Cheng placed spectacles on the tip of his nose when he needed to read something, and he had a knack for exaggeration. "I thank the United States for taking me in!" he told Zhuang. "But I am not planning on staying in the United States forever." Yao Cheng was waiting for the regime change he thought was inevitable.

Yao Cheng had worked, he said, for the Chinese military. He had been disavowed and thrown in prison after following orders and stealing the plans for a military helicopter from Russia. The veracity of his backstory was hard to confirm, but later in his life Yao Cheng had worked with Chai Ling, a leader in the Tiananmen Square movement, rescuing girls who had been kidnapped (to be sold as brides) or abandoned. He provided assistance to the abandoned girls, sometimes placing them with guardians, and he did his best to reunite girls who had been kidnapped with their families. He was outspoken and passionate. The existence of kidnapped children in China was a sensitive issue. All this had landed him in jail a second time, and then a third.

Zhuang welcomed the man into the neighborhood with a basket full of chicken feet as Yao Cheng launched into a story about the coming collapse of the Chinese government. Zhuang wasn't sure what to make of the man. A journalist he respected had introduced them, but Zhuang worried the man's exaggerations were a sign of instability. Eventually, over the following year, Zhuang's judgment would soften. Yao Cheng was to become the first fellow immigrant whom Zhuang really trusted.

• • •

In the aftermath of his immigration interview, Zhuang knew that he could not put off finding a job any longer. He was just starting to understand Flushing, trying to adjust to the limits his lack of education and English would impose on his life here. "If I had known that someday I would be moving to the United States, I would have kept studying," he said. "It wasn't that I was a bad student. I liked studying! It was just that in China, it didn't matter. Going to school would have been a waste of my time." He cycled through a series of short-lived jobs at Chinese restaurants, busing tables and frying food in the kitchens. It was thankless work, and the meager salary he brought home offered little consolation. Little Yan moved from one nail salon to the next, complaining that the fumes gave her headaches.

Every two weeks, almost on the dot, Zhuang would send me an e-mail asking about their asylum case. He knew someone would contact him if a decision had been made, but his patience ran out again and again. I would call his lawyer, and then, after the next disappointing answer, Zhuang would hold his breath as long as he could, waiting to hear. Two weeks later he would find himself at his wit's end. He stayed up late, adding music to a series of photos and videos he had taken on a summer trip to Coney Island with Little Yan. He would send it to his friends.

Zhuang waited the exact number of days he had before he and Little Yan could apply for work permits, then asked me to contact his lawyer. He had been assigned a new lawyer at the Hebrew Immigrant Aid Society, a man whose office walls were occupied almost entirely with bookcases of asylum cases in manila folders. Zhuang arrived at his first meeting with a tray full of coffee from

Starbucks. The man clipped his and Little Yan's passport-size photos onto their applications and spoke with gravity. The immigration offices, he warned, seemed more backed up than usual. It was good they were applying for work permits, because it might take months, maybe even a year, before their case was processed.

Zhuang was prepared for this news, and he had come up with a plan. As soon as the lawyer started talking about further delays, Zhuang suggested that he contact the Congressional Executive Committee on China (CECC)—the group he had traveled to Washington months earlier to connect with. "I can ask a member of Congress to write a letter!" he said. He wasn't sure who would write it or how it would be submitted, but he was confident he could get it done. He had sat in a room with a researcher and told his story; although he couldn't read it, parts of Zhuang's testimony had been included in the annual report the CECC distributes publicly. Surely they could instruct the immigration bureau to speed up the process. "They can tell them that everything I've said is true!" Zhuang said. "What do you think?"

The new lawyer looked at his client with narrowed eyes, sizing him up. "Let's wait," the man said. If, in fact, a letter was really possible, it was a delicate matter. If it was sent by the wrong person or arrived at the wrong time, it might cause Zhuang's case to get pulled temporarily from the queue of waiting cases. It could delay it further. "He thinks a letter would make things slower?" Zhuang asked. "*Aiya.*" He looked to Little Yan, who was still clutching her purse in her lap. They returned to Queens to do more waiting.

November slid into December and then the New Year. Zhuang and Little Yan celebrated the anniversary of their arrival in the United States with no word on their asylum case. She kept working, doing her best not to think about their immigration status. He spent every day thinking about it, pouring every last ounce of his optimism into the waiting. The friends he had made came in waves, visiting often, then not at all. Zhuang tossed cigarettes at the men, as he had done in China. He grinned relentlessly.

At night, when he called home, his friends and family offered him respect. He was sending money back to his family, and everyone assumed he was working in a restaurant. According to

Zhuang, even if he told them how difficult life was in New York, they wouldn't have believed him. They didn't understand that his feet were still not planted firmly on the ground. He had clung to regulations as a protest leader in China; he had collected piles of evidence for his asylum case; and now he had nothing. He had no documents or laws to tie him to the country where he was living. There was no official proof that he even existed in New York City.

8

Wukan! Wukan! A Death

死亡 / *Sǐwáng*

When the rioting started in Wukan, and villagers took turns breaking windows and shouting at the police, a little family-run restaurant had pulled the shutter down on its storefront. A heavy-browed man named Xue Jinbo closed shop for the day and went to join the protests. He made his way to the square where people were gathering and marched with them to the Lufeng government headquarters. He grabbed a bullhorn from someone in the crowd and shouted into it. "Return Wukan's land!" he shouted. "Justice for Wukan!"

Brother Xue might not have recognized Zhuang, but Zhuang knew him. He had eaten at the man's family-run restaurant. In Zhuang's worst years, when he barely had enough money to get by, he would go to the Xue family restaurant and enjoy generous portions of spareribs and cured meat. Xue's wife would ladle large mounds of rice onto Zhuang's plate, offering it to him for free.

At one time, before the protests and the scandals, before Zhuang had even imagined a life outside China, Brother Xue had been a model of everything Wukan, and Zhuang, might have been. Xue had a reputation for generosity and openness. He ran his restaurant out of the first floor of his three-story home, and he made villagers of all stripes feel welcome. He was like Zhuang—if his friends were in trouble, he would give them his last penny. He listened to people's problems and did his best to help. He loved his family. He loved his village. And Wukan loved him. Some village elders, Zhuang explained, had required convincing before they joined the Hot Blooded Youth. But Xue had been different. "We did not have to go find Xue Jinbo," Zhuang told me. "Xue Jinbo came and found us."

On the first day of the protests, after Xue and Zhuang had joined in yelling slogans at government buildings, a handful of protesters had been detained and taken to the local police station. Other villagers had gathered outside and demanded their release. By the evening, the husks of overturned police cars sat abandoned in the road. The next day the rioting continued. Schoolchildren walked out of their classes and ransacked the three-story village council building. They smashed chairs and desks and threw ripped-up papers out the windows like confetti. The wrecked police cars from the previous day still sat in the streets like overturned bugs. The streets were littered with broken glass. By the third day, when things had calmed down, the world looked different. People were out in the open, talking about their land. Xue Jinbo approached Zhuang. "I knew you were petitioning!" he said. "I would have helped, but I had no idea how to join up with you young people."

• • •

Not everyone was so enthusiastic. In addition to Brother Xue, the Hot Blooded Youth had sought out a man named Lin Zulian, who everyone called Old Lin. The young protest leaders had marched right to Old Lin's door and asked him for help. He professed reluctance—Old Lin was sixty-seven and, having made his fortune, had recently returned to the village to start a quiet retirement—but he was one of Wukan's most upstanding villagers. He was the closest thing that Wukan had to an aging scholar: a successful businessman with a rattling voice, glasses, and hair that curled up from his forehead in a thin, gravity-defying frizz. He told them that he was too old and too tired, that they thought too much of him. But after a few minutes of pleading and flattery, Old Lin agreed to help. He joined Yang Semao and Brother Xue at the head of the movement Zhuang had started.

There were signs, in the days after the protest, that Wukan was the extraordinary village Zhuang had envisioned. Zhang Ji-anxing had posted photos of the riot online, first on his own QQ account and then, after being blocked by online censors, using the accounts of his friends. He posted videos on a site called Weibo, which functions similarly to Twitter, and amassed thousands of followers nearly overnight. By the second day, a handful of jour-nalists from Hong Kong found their way to Wukan. The atten-tion had helped, Zhuang thought. In a village just hours away from Wukan, riot police had arrived at the scene of local protests, throwing punches and canisters of tear gas and jailing protesters. Wukan had not been similarly cowed, and violence had been kept to a minimum.

Their demands, too, had not been ignored. Wukan had stood together until the officials in Lufeng City had been forced to offer them a solution: they were welcome to appoint a council of thir-teen people to negotiate for the return of Wukan's land. The vil-lage selected its champions: Yang Semao was chosen, along with Hong Ruichao, Brother Xue, and ten others. The Lufeng govern-ment, Zhuang was sure, would be impressed. His little revolution had been successful, and the village waited for the negotiations to begin. Lufeng, however, intended to keep them waiting. The officials under the golden dome sent no word.

The second official protest of Wukan Village was held on November 21. It was orderly and somber. Even the march was organized—each villager assigned a place in line. Old Lin was adamant that this march would be by the book, just a little ges-ture to remind everyone that the villagers were still there. They would not sit and wait forever. Zhuang and his friend used Weibo to inform the world about the protest. He documented the march and set it to music. The weather was good, the marchers waved the red flag of the People's Republic of China. People talked about holding village elections and insisted they weren't challenging the government. They were just asking for everyone to follow the law. According to Yang Semao, it was so well organized that the Lufeng government was scared. "They saw a dangerous future in the forty-five hundred people marching in line," he told people, later. "They couldn't solve the problems we wanted them to solve, so they decided to crack down."

In China, it was always difficult to tell when a line had been crossed. The Wukan riot had made news: photos had circulated on social media, newspapers in Hong Kong had run stories. The event was big enough that someone in China's central government might have noticed, but even then there was no hard and fast rule on how Beijing reacted to protests. Protests that were national-istic in bent—riots protesting Japanese war crimes or American imperialism—were tolerated. Protests that targeted local govern-ments in discrete matters—against planned-for power plants or instances of local corruption—were often resolved peacefully. In other instances, however, leaders in Beijing would allow local gov-ernments to crush protesters ruthlessly.

The line was blurred even in daily life. People in Wukan oper-ated in the same semilegal gray areas that allowed the village land to be sold out from under them. They were smugglers, gam-blers, and ticket scalpers. Many of the villagers were everyday small-scale lawbreakers, their businesses unofficial, their homes erected without permits. When Zhuang started petitioning, he knew the danger, in theory. But he had been doing it for three years with no reprisal. And over three years, he had invented him-self as fearless and outspoken. He had no intention of stopping.

The day Xue Jinbo was kidnapped, the negotiating team fi-nally received word that they would be meeting with government officials from Lufeng. He had attended a village meeting earlier that morning and was scheduled to meet with officials in the af-ternoon. He invited Zhuang's friend Hong Ruichao and one other representative to eat at the People's Cafeteria, a three-story res-taurant a few blocks from the ocean. They sat inside while the restaurant's parking lot filled up with unmarked cars. The people who got out of them were wearing street clothes. They walked up the steps, into the restaurant, and grabbed all three men. Everyone in the village was confused about who the kidnappers were. The men accused Brother Xue of collaborating with a foreign power and organizing an illegal gathering. They dragged the three villagers out of the restaurant, stuffed them into a car, and drove off.

It is not uncommon, in China, for a local government to outsource violence to plainclothes thugs. In Beijing, the business of crushing dissent has got so big that the system of black jails that ensared Ma Yongtian does brisk business, running off money provided by local governments trying to prevent petitioners from registering their complaints. Local thugs might monitor a dissident under house arrest. Or as in Wukan, they might be sent into an unruly village to deliver troublemakers to a jail in another town. The Lufeng government may not have wanted to risk another mob outside the local police station.

By the time Xue Jinbo and Hong Ruichao were taken, Zhuang had been arrested himself. He and Little Yan had left Wukan to attend a wedding and were staying at a friend's house when, in the early hours of the morning, the police arrived at the door. They twisted Zhuang's arm and dragged him into the precinct, where they strapped him into a chair and left him in a freezing-cold room. The first thing the interrogators did, Zhuang remembers, was attempt to have him sign a piece of paper confessing to selling fake cigarettes. He refused. When they asked his name, he said, "You have my ID card—why don't you go and look!"

• • •

In retrospect, Zhuang had been fortunate. When a group of police speaking his local dialect showed up, he suspected they had been sent from Lufeng. If they had been in Wukan rather than Shunde, with the Shunde police around them, Zhuang felt sure they would have beaten him up. As it was, they could only interrogate him. And when Zhuang refused to sign their papers, he was transferred to a Guangzhou prison where he was treated gently. Every few days he would be interrogated, but otherwise no one bothered him. The meals included meat and eggs.

In the two months of organizing that had occurred since

the first protest, Wukan's villagers had developed a protocol for emergencies. They would announce a crisis by banging on family gongs that had been in the village for generations. This would alert people that an emergency meeting would be held in the village square. With Zhuang gone from the village and three other village leaders kidnapped, it was up to Yang Semao to act. He had noticed the number of police cars in the village increasing. He suspected that something would go wrong with their negotiating meetings. "Coming events," he said, "always cast shadows before them."

Yang told people to stop what they were doing. He warned them the kidnappers would come back to take more village leaders. He guessed that the thugs were targeting the entire thirteen-person negotiating team. Brother Xue and his companions had simply been at the wrong place at the wrong time—a restaurant off Wukan's largest road, and with a parking lot, was easy to drive in and out of quickly. As if to prove Yang right, local television stations broadcast news of the warrants issued for the three people who had been taken from the restaurant, for Zhuang, and for Yang himself. If the outside world was dangerous, Wukan Village had always been safe. So they set up some makeshift barricades with felled tree trunks, stones, and gathered branches. Teams set up checkpoints at all the possible entrances to the village and required identification of anyone on the road. No one who wasn't a Wukan resident could get into the village.

The village had been blockaded for two days when Xue's family got a phone call from an official in Shanwei, a prefecture-level city an hour's drive from Wukan, one rung above Lufeng in the local administrative hierarchy. Xue Jinbo was critically ill and in the hospital, the caller told them. The police would send a car to pick up Xue's wife and daughter on the outskirts of Wukan. Not knowing what to do, the two women collected his medical records and walked out to the street. A car pulled up, and the pair got in.

The road from Wukan to the county seat is indirect and full of potholes. And when the car carrying the two women finally got to the city, it did not take them to the hospital. It took them, instead, to the Meilihua (Beautiful Flower) Hotel. Mother and daughter were led into a hotel room with a circle of couches. A camera was rolling, and they seated the pair in the center of a circle of officials. The only person Xue's daughter recognized was the mayor of Lufeng.

"Xue Jinbo has been charged with organizing an illegal gathering," said an official from one side of the camera, reading off a sheet. "He has been charged with colluding with foreign powers." They asked his daughter, Jianwan, questions about her father's background, his interests, and his friends. It was a full half hour before Xue's wife spoke up. She asked what had happened to her husband.

One of the officials took out a timetable. At such-and-such an hour, he read, Xue Jinbo was struck by an illness related to his heart. At such-and-such an hour, he received emergency treatment. At eleven p.m. on December 11, 2011, Xue Jinbo had died.

At first Jianwan didn't believe them. Next to her, her mother started to cry, but Jianwan took out her cell phone to call her relatives in Wukan. When an official made a move to snatch it from her, she held it close to her body. "If you touch me," she shouted, "I will sue you!" The videotape was still rolling. She called her relatives and told them to come to the city. It was one in the morning when they got there. It was two by the time the officials agreed to let Xue Jinbo's family members view his body, as long as they handed over all their cell phones and cameras. They drove in a caravan to the mortuary. When they arrived, they found it surrounded by police cars. Inside, the number of police thinned out and were replaced by young people in street clothes, some of them armed with knives, some of them clutching brass knuckles.

It was three in the morning. The family were led into a back room of the mortuary, and the thugs filed in behind them. The room had a huge refrigerator in it. Someone opened a small door and pulled out a slab with a body on it, wrapped in plastic. When they unwrapped her father's body, even from across the room, Brother Xue's daughter could see the blood on his face.

•••

The standoff in Wukan went on for thirteen days. On December 10, the day after Xue Jinbo was kidnapped, police cars came with water cannons and tear gas, but the villagers blocked the road. On the twelfth, the news about Brother Xue's death made it back to the village. They set up teams to watch the roads, day and night, and alert the others when the police approached the village. Villagers contacted journalists who had visited Wukan in the past and did their best to sneak them past the police barricades. Everyone gathered in the square, outside the small pagoda with a tiered red tile roof, and cried. Led by Yang, crowds chanted about land and free elections. Banners asked the central government to help the people of Wukan, and village leaders were careful to emphasize the village's continuing fidelity to the Communist Party. They demanded the return of the village land and focused their complaints on the corrupt local government. And then people started demanding the return of Brother Xue's body. The protest turned into a wake.

Reporters from the *Telegraph,* the *New York Times,* Reuters, and the BBC all broke through the barricades. They set up a media tent and a communal kitchen as more people trickled in. Just down the road from the Wukan barricades, police set up checkpoints of their own. Fleets of boats prevented fishermen from leaving the bay, and police blocked any food or water from being transported into the village. Residents of neighboring villages started to carry in supplies on their backs.

The media coverage made Wukan a particularly hard case for local officials. In an internal speech that went viral on social media before it was censored, the party leader in Shanwei, Zhen Yanxiong, blamed foreign influence. "If you trust foreign media, then pigs can climb trees," he said. "There's only one group of people that really experiences added hardships year after year. Who are they? Government officials, that's who." But the attention worked. A few days into the siege, Yang Semao reported receiving conciliatory phone calls from the Lufeng government. Zhuang's initial aim had been achieved—higher levels of government were starting to pay attention.

In the final days of protest, the deputy party secretary of

Guangdong—the second-highest-ranking party leader in the province—was dispatched to negotiate with the villagers. According to the state-run media, he had called the demands of Wukan villagers "reasonable." Their "extreme actions" would be forgiven if the villagers would agree to sit down with the government in good faith.

The standoff ended on December 21, and negotiations began. According to the villagers present, the deputy party secretary agreed, in the meetings, to release the village leaders still held in jail—including Zhuang—and to drop all charges. He agreed to return Xue Jinbo's body and to launch an investigation into his death. The surviving twelve members of the negotiating council were given the authority to govern the village until an election could be organized in February or March. It was the first time in modern Chinese history that a protesting village had won this kind of compromise. Online, Western observers and hopeful Chinese activists spoke, tentatively, of a "Wukan Model." Villagers started considering whether they wanted to run for election.

Zhuang had not been there for the barricade. He had spent twenty-one days in the Guangzhou prison, and by the time he got out, the siege of Wukan was over and his friend was dead. The village had won. Zhuang found it was possible to feel elated and brokenhearted all at once. He figured it was simple luck that while Brother Xue had been beaten, he had escaped unscathed. Maybe Brother Xue had run into a particularly sadistic prison guard. Maybe someone had paid the other inmates to rough him up and things got out of hand. Torture, in Chinese prisons, wasn't unheard of. The Guangdong deputy party secretary had agreed to investigate Brother Xue's death, but nothing would come of it. Zhuang, and Xue Jinbo's family, would never find out what happened. Zhuang supposed that Brother Xue had sacrificed himself for the dream of what Wukan Village might one day be—its orchards restored, waters clear, and its villagers free and unified. He did not worry, yet, that the dream had died in that prison alongside Brother Xue.

9

Little Yan

小燕 / *Xiǎo Yàn*

1986–2013

When Zhuang's friend Hong Ruichao was kidnapped, his girlfriend promised, in a moment of passion, that she would wait for
him however long it took. Little Yan had no such inclination. She
had been there when Zhuang got arrested. She had watched the
police drag him out of the hotel room kicking and yelling. She sat
in the police precinct and answered their questions. When they
finally agreed to take her home, she called through the door to
her sister in their home dialect, and one of the men had growled
at her, "Speak Mandarin." They had tromped through her little
home in heavy boots.

Little Yan had known Zhuang for less than a year. She respected his resolve, on the one hand. But she was practical.
Women, she thought, can't dwell on injustice or past humiliations. They are responsible for day-to-day survival—getting food
cooked and children taken care of. Women aren't allowed the
same amount of outrage.

When Zhuang got out of jail, he heard about Hong Ruichao's
romantic moment. He asked Little Yan if she would have done
the same as Hong's girlfriend. "I told him, well, if he had been
inside for a long time, I wouldn't have waited for him. My family

would have opposed him," Little Yan told me. "I was just telling the truth! It didn't sound that good, but it was honest."

Little Yan had grown up in a village even smaller and more impoverished than Wukan. She had been born on a farm in Guangxi Province, a neighbor to Guangdong. She was tiny from the start, and pretty, with an exceptionally flat face, clear eyes, and a jaw set in a determined but almost imperceptible underbite. Her parents named her Xiao Yan, or "Little Sparrow."

Little Yan was the fourth baby girl in the family; her mother had wondered, as she gave birth to daughter after daughter, if the family was cursed. She had stacked her first four pregnancies one after another, each new birthday not much more than a year after the last. But after Little Yan, Chen Fengxian slowed down, waiting until the eldest could be more helpful on the farm. Her last three daughters were all born with the barest amount of breathing room between pregnancies, two years apart. She had seven girls in all—and no boys. The other women in the village were kept busy giving her pitying looks.

Girls, in Guangxi and Wukan alike, were undesirable. Thousands of years of tradition lay behind the distaste. Girls would eventually move in to another household, and it would cost money to get rid of them. It didn't matter what the government said, girls would not be there to look after their parents when they grew old. Boys were more helpful. A boy was responsible for his family. A grandchild would belong in the home of his paternal grandparents. The preference was so strong that both Little Yan and Zhuang grew up with aunts and female friends who had been marked with names like Zhao Di, "Looking for Little Brother," or Lai Di, "Little Brother Is Coming."

It was no one's fault, Little Yan thought. The preference for men was society's fault, and she accepted the reality. And her household full of sisters had its advantages. Although she had been brought up to feel no claim on her home—women usually left when they were married—no brother was born whose status outstripped her own.

Little Yan was in the curious position of being a woman in a rural village where women had little value, but in a family dominated by women. Growing up, it was always Little Yan's mother who dictated what was grown on the family's land. Her mother, in fact, dictated almost everything in the household. If Chen Fengxian (whose given name means "Fresh Breeze") told you to do something, you did it quickly and without complaint. Little Yan liked the pace of the countryside, but she never felt completely free. She was always bending her will to accommodate her mother's. Chen Fengxian was *laoda,* the boss.

Little Yan's mother was a model of practical womanhood. She insisted her daughters learn the imperative of *eating bitter*—a Chinese phrase for an ability to endure hardship. She operated according to the subsistence logic of a lifelong farmer and made sure everything, including her daughters, was put to its best use. After Chen Fengxian realized how much they could save if they didn't buy vegetable oil, the family started cultivating peanuts. With a family peanut crop, Chen Fengxian could cook for all nine family members and not spend a penny on oil. The girls would pick the pods off the plants and hang them around the farmhouse, drying them. Then the peanuts, shells and all, would be spread outside in the sun, drying again before the family would shell the peanuts and press them into oil. At certain times of year, the little Guangxi farmhouse was draped and drowning in peanuts.

In addition to peanuts, the family grew its own vegetables. If there was excess, Little Yan's father would take it to the local market, biking the uneven roads down the mountain. The only purely commercial endeavor her parents undertook was the raising of pigs. At any given time on the farm, a few enormous pigs were eating trash and getting fat enough to be taken to market on the outskirts of a nearby city. The money from pig sales went to pay the girls' school fees, at least until the eldest went to work in the city and started sending money home.

• • •

Little Yan's father was the softer of her two parents. He had gone far enough in school to be a village teacher, but Little Yan's mother had no patience for that—a teacher could not make enough money to support and feed their growing family. And with her growing tribe of females, Little Yan's mother could not manage the farming by herself. So Little Yan's father stayed home, working in the fields until his skin was cracked and leathery and dark from the sun.

Even as the rest of the village shook their heads at the long line of daughters, Little Yan's father loved them. He insisted that all seven go to school. He did not expect to turn out seven doctors and lawyers, his imagination did not stretch that far, but he hoped for someone to follow in his footsteps and become, maybe, a teacher. He did not want his daughters to work in the fields. He did not want to marry them off to other people's families and never see them again. So he sent them to school. The village was so small that, by the time they reached middle school, they were sent to the closest town. They lived in dorms and walked two hours home on weekends. The family ate vegetables and rice most nights, but on the weekends Little Yan's father would buy meat. He worried about the meals the girls were getting in their school dormitories.

Little Yan's hometown lies near the city of Hezhou in Guangxi Province, which, in turn, lies to the west of Guangdong, bordering Vietnam. It is mountainous and wet, a frontier with a reputation for beauty and wildness that runs hundreds of years back into imperial Chinese history. She grew up on a green slope, the land below threaded with rivers and punctuated by karst rock formations that rise inexplicably out of the landscape in Seussian, forest-covered peaks. At the time of Little Yan's birth in 1986, Guangxi was almost entirely devoid of industry. People in the province farmed or worked in manganese mines; even today Hezhou's biggest industry is forestry. China's economic miracle didn't make it to the province until Chinese tourists with disposable income started showing up in Guangxi's more pristine corners. Places like Guilin, where the Li River meanders around rounded peaks, grew rich on tourism. Little Yan's village, where fields were planted into the side of a mountain, had no such luck.

News of China's economic changes arrived in the village in rumors and gossip. Land there would never be worth much—

although the village was almost the same distance from Guangzhou as Wukan, it was a world away from the sprawling influence
of the Shenzhen Special Economic Zone. Her parents' lives kept
to the same rhythm it had had in her childhood. Little Yan's eldest sister left in the late 1990s, looking for work in a nearby city
and making the family's first tentative steps into the wider world.
Some of the sisters would leave for good and send money home
when they could. Others would end up back in the village. No one
from the village expected to turn out a factory boss or successful
entrepreneur, and no one came back truly rich.

Out of all the sisters, Little Yan believed she was the least extraordinary. She spent her childhood lost in the din of her three
older siblings. She did not excel at school the way her younger
sisters did. She was tiny and quiet; she didn't fight with her sisters. She was helping clean, cook, and pick peanuts as soon as
she could take direction. She started working so young that she
cannot remember what her earliest responsibilities were. Later
she did everything. She carried water, tended to pigs, picked peanuts, hung peanuts up to dry, pressed peanuts into oil, and studied
in her spare time. It sometimes seemed as if half of Little Yan's
childhood was spent preparing peanuts.

If Little Yan shared Zhuang's sense of predestination—that
she would live a different life, somewhere far from home—she felt
none of his pride of origin. She didn't grow up wanting to impress
anyone. She felt no drive to rebel against the realities of her life;
rebellion wouldn't get her very far anyway. There had never been
any question that her mother and father would make all her most
important decisions.

That didn't mean Little Yan was weak. She had her own, quietly kept opinions. She was not dumb or easily swayed when she
had made up her mind. She had grown up taking care of herself. She hoped for a small life that was more comfortable than
her mother and father's, with children and some small amount of
money. She kept her expectations reasonable but resolute.

As Little Yan finished all the available school in the area, the
family received pamphlets for newly opened vocational schools.
She tested into a handful of schools, and they vied for her tuition,

promising secure jobs and good salaries in the future. Her parents sifted through the choices and considered what would suit her best. Her father decided that she would follow in his footsteps and study to become a teacher. Little Yan was not scholarly enough to become a good teacher for older children, but she could take care of younger children. She was reliable and hardworking. She could teach preschool. It would be her best use. So they signed her up for a program that would prepare her to play educational games, sing children's songs, and keep everyone safe. At the beginning of the semester, her parents put her on a bus heading out of the village.

• • •

In Guangxi Province, vocational schools have become big business. Subsidized by state government, the schools train rural students to work with military-style precision. They take orders from industry in coastal cities and offer a supply of laborers trained in whatever jobs are in demand. The schools focus on practical skills and "moral development." In Guangdong, the students of certain vocational schools—those aimed at factory work—were in high demand. A vocational school graduate was considered cheap, efficient, and more manageable than a migrant worker who had arrived on his or her own. Guangxi Province was sending tens of thousands of graduates to factory towns every year.

In Little Yan's classes, she studied languages and the basics of child care. Her teachers warned female students to stick to themselves. They were advised not to meet with men they had encountered on the Internet or to waste too much time on their phones. Little Yan was taught how to listen to her future bosses, how to clean up efficiently, and what kinds of games to play with young children. During the week, she slept in a dorm with other women.

Little Yan's most serious courses were language courses. She worked on English and Cantonese. Everyone in her school knew that the best jobs were in Guangdong Province, and Little Yan would leave Guangxi able to have simple conversations in Guangzhou's dialect.

At the end of the year, Little Yan boarded a bus with a handful of other graduates. It drove her out of the mountains toward China's coastline. When the bus arrived on the streets of Guangzhou—a city of some eleven million, nearly five times bigger than the most populous city in Little Yan's home province—it made no big impression on her. It was noisy and dusty. Her parents had given her three hundred yuan for a bus ticket in case she didn't like the city, but she didn't anticipate using it. She felt ambivalent about leaving her village and her home life. She did not spend her evenings worrying about her family reputation or imagining a triumphant return home, wealthy and successful. She would not have the time to miss home, anyway. She was planning to spend most of her time working.

Her first job was at a preschool in an outer district of Guangzhou, where the buildings were still low-slung and banyan trees hung heavily over the street. She spent twelve-hour days chasing the four or five children she was charged with supervising. She prepared their meals, played games, and learned more Cantonese. The children helped her. When she didn't know a word, one little boy in particular would explain. He knew the Cantonese slang for "boss." Little Yan learned. At night, after sending home the latest group of children, she and the other teachers would push aside the tables and chairs and sleep on the floor.

In the early 2000s, a job at a preschool was not hard to come by. When people grew tired at one job, they would leave. They would go home for Spring Festival and spend a week or two lounging, eating their mothers' cooking, then head back to Guangzhou. There were newspaper advertisements and recommendations from friends. There was the reliable knowledge that some other preschool teacher had also gone home for Spring Festival, leaving a vacant position in her wake.

There wasn't much Little Yan needed in Guangzhou. Even though she had no bedroom, she kept herself neat. All the teachers did their washing on the weekends and hung their bras on lines strung up in the bathrooms. Little Yan liked to dress nicely, if she could, and on her occasional day off, she would go out with the other teachers and spend a little money on clothes. She bought approximations of Western luxury brands and shoes that boosted her height by several inches. The shoes, in the end, weren't that useful. In the classrooms, she mainly wore rubber slippers. Little Yan bought herself a cell phone and put in all her contacts: her friends from school, her sisters, her parents, the other teachers she had met. Connections were useful, they kept her from feeling lonely, but she knew she was transient. She didn't take her friendships too seriously—she already had six sisters to keep up with—but she made them easily. She had learned from a big family to keep her opinions largely to herself. She could gossip without offending anyone. She could disagree with someone and still consider them a friend. She threatened no one and made no one uncomfortable. It was her particular talent.

Despite the stereotypes prevailing in her Guangxi village, unmarried daughters, according to Little Yan, are a more reliable financial resource than sons. Most of her salary she sent home. If she didn't go home at Spring Festival, she sent gifts. Men, on the other hand, had love to think about. Little Yan was learning the basics of Guangzhou courtship. You always went on dates with a friend, and the men were required to pay. They were required to buy gifts and provide dinner. The most attractive man had a car, or at least a motorcycle. He had to be saving. He had to offer some promise of a future home. A man who sent all his money back to his family would never find himself a girlfriend.

Little Yan did not date much in those early days in Guangzhou. She chatted online a bit—meeting people through QQ or playing popular games that had her keeping a little virtual farm. She chatted about nothing, mostly, and rarely met anyone in person. In those early years, she heeded her teacher's advice and did not look to meet men online. She was taught to be wary. Most of the men in Guangzhou were suspect, looking to have fun but not make a commitment. Village values did not apply.

After two years, Little Yan grew tired of her first job. With four or five children to look after, she was exhausted. She didn't want to sleep in the classroom anymore. She had kept up with job opportunities by cell phone, reaching out to friends and former colleagues who had moved away. One of the jobs she heard about, in a city just sixteen miles outside Guangzhou called Foshan, sounded easier than the one she had. The school matched a single teacher to only one or two children, so she would not have to run around as much. The pay was good. She packed up her belongings, got on a bus, and went.

By the time she met Zhuang Liehong, three years later, she wasn't teaching at all anymore. One of her phone acquaintances had called her one day and asked if she wanted to open a shoe shop. She knew of a place, she said, in Foshan, where they could open two shops nearly side by side. Little Yan's friend showed her where to purchase her shoes—wholesalers gave them good deals in Sanyuanli Market, a packed five-story free-for-all in Guangzhou. She took what she bought back to Foshan and stacked the shoes wherever she could fit them. It was not a beautiful store. The single aisle was barely wide enough for two people to squeeze past each other. She sold shoes during the day, and at night, she unfolded a cot in the back of the shop and fell asleep looking up at the jungle of boxes tucked in every corner, stacked in impossible towers always threatening to fall down.

• • •

By the time Little Yan met Zhuang Liehong, he was already Patriot Number One. The kid who had slept on park benches and sneaked into his aunt's apartment for showers had repurposed himself as a village hero. He had made friends on QQ and in Shunde. The shop owners who purchased cigarettes and other goods through him thought he was reliable. He invited people to his apartment for hotpot—communal meals over a tub of spicy, bubbling soup broth. He lived a double life through his alias. Little Yan thought he was honest and brave, even if Wukan Village was not her fight.

The pair met on a service called True Marriage. Zhuang had set up a number of dating profiles. He had filled his account up with fifty yuan and sent out a bunch of canned messages, at two yuan (about thirty cents) each, until it ran out. Little Yan spent some evenings managing her own online accounts and sent him back her own rote message—*nice to meet you*—although this service was free for women. Two weeks later Zhuang was on his scooter, heading toward her shop in Foshan.

Zhuang didn't think he could marry a girl from Wukan. They were just as bull-headed as he was. And for the most part, women from Wukan knew his family's reputation. Most parents would not have wanted to match their daughters with someone from Zhuang Songkun's family.

Zhuang was not good-looking, but he was reliable and honest. And by the time he met Little Yan, he had been living in Shunde for a few years and had a good job delivering supplies to local corner stores. Marriage decisions in Wukan Village were often made quickly; there are few reasons to delay. To wait, particularly for a woman, is to risk aging out of the popular dating pool, and having children early makes it easier to enlist the help of grandparents who might otherwise grow too old and frail.

Before Little Yan, each one of Zhuang's near misses looms large in his imagination. He was rejected on two notable occasions. A year after joining his friend's business, he branched out on his own, running his own delivery service. One of his clients, a woman named Yu Huang, was very close to his own age. She was from Zhuang's home county but had married a man from Sichuan Province. He made a handful of deliveries to the shop Yu Huang ran, when one day she stopped him before he left, waving him over to the concrete steps that led to her store.

"Hey, brother Zhuang!" she shouted as he wandered toward her. "Are you married?"

"Not yet!" he shouted back. He suspected she was setting him up for a joke, so he grinned.

"Do you have a girlfriend?"

"No!"

"How's your work going?"

"Not bad," said Zhuang. He was earning a little more than a thousand yuan every month, about $150. It was respectable.

Yu Huang must have thought so, because the next thing she

did was make him a proposition. "I've got a friend I want to introduce you to," she said. She had a little sister who was working in a factory not far off. "When she gets a break and comes to Shunde, I'll give you a call."

"Okay!" Zhuang said. If it was a real offer, he would take it. But he wouldn't get his hopes up. He had never gotten an offer like this before. He rode away on his motorcycle, heading to make another delivery, still not sure whether Yu Huang had been making a joke.

About a week later a call came. "Brother Zhuang! Come to my shop tonight!" Yu Huang shouted. Zhuang put on new clothes and got onto his motorcycle. He drove to her shop and found a pretty, neatly dressed younger woman waiting for him on the dusty sidewalk outside. He swung his leg over the scooter and walked up and introduced himself. He spoke in Mandarin.

Yu Huang's little sister quickly turned to her sister. "He has buckteeth!" she said in her home dialect, no one realizing that Zhuang could understand. Zhuang stood to the side, pretending he didn't hear.

"What do his looks have to do with anything?" Yu Huang answered. "Looks don't matter! It's what is in his heart that counts! He's honest. He's a good person."

Zhuang took Yu Huang's little sister out to dinner and then shopping. He spent more than three hundred yuan on a coat for his date—overdoing it a little. Three hundred yuan was more than he would have spent over several weeks of living in the park in Shenzhen. He spent more money than he would have if his teeth had been straight, or if he hadn't spent the last few years halfway homeless. And then he drove her back to the corner store. He knew she wouldn't call him, but he told himself he was better off. He didn't have too many requirements for a wife, he thought. He wanted someone who was good-looking, loyal, and nice. Someone who would respect him.

Although Zhuang didn't find a wife quickly, he was a reliable businessman now. His dogged petitioning had earned him respect from other villagers. His status was changing. He met another woman online and took her and a friend on a weekend getaway to the beach, but nothing came of it. He met the woman who worked at the print shop where he first learned to use a computer, but she was from Sichuan Province, which he suspected contributed to her bad temper. And she was unfaithful.

When he drove his scooter to Foshan and saw Little Yan for the first time, he was surprised at his good fortune. She was beautiful. And quiet. And she didn't look twice at his crooked teeth. He was sincere and enthusiastic. He took her out to dinner. He went out of his way to buy her things. And as the pressure built in Wukan, she saw him as he hoped she would: he was fighting for what was right. When he explained the situation, the stolen land and corrupt officials, she nodded in sympathy.

Little Yan was surprised by Zhuang, as well. His personality was so forceful and unguarded. She had no interest in protesting—she had long made it a point to avoid conflict—but she respected his resolve. He knew so much more about the situation than he did, she would later say. It was his area of expertise, and she trusted his judgment. And on top of all that, he was honest. He was the opposite of what she had come to expect from a Guangdong suitor.

Little Yan was twenty-six when she met Zhuang, old enough that her parents might start wondering what she was doing with her life. Still, she was not as eager to get married as Zhuang. She was happy to get to know him and to get swept up in his life. She met his friends in Shunde, and he included her in plans to open up a clothing shop. She wasn't a romantic; she had never expected to hit it rich or marry a movie star. She liked the idea of settling down in Zhuang's village, having children, and living quietly.

The night Zhuang was arrested in Shunde, Little Yan watched the police twist his arm behind his back and force his head down. Two visions of her life were laid out in front of her: Zhuang would be released, or he would not. Little Yan was her mother's daughter. For two weeks she went about her days selling shoes as if her life hadn't changed and wouldn't change, wondering what would happen. And then when Zhuang got out of prison, he called her before anyone else. He called her before he called his parents.

Little Yan knew her shoe shop days were over: she was going to marry Zhuang Liehong.

The couple took their engagement photos not long after that, along with Hong Ruichao and his fiancée. The four of them dressed up in rented finery and climbed out onto rocks on Wukan Bay. In one photo, Little Yan poses in a white dress, pretending to play a white violin. In another, the four friends are walking down the beach, barefoot, grinning at the camera. Little Yan was practical, but she was happy to be marrying a hero. She was not immune to the triumph that coursed through Wukan Village. She believed, with the rest of the village, that they had accomplished the impossible. Zhuang Liehong had an unconquerable spirit and a warm heart, and Little Yan loved him.

Little Yan didn't feel that she fit in Wukan Village, but she didn't mind. The people in the village were blunt and opinionated. They hadn't learned, as she had learned, to eat bitter, and to do it quietly. They spoke before they thought. She befriended Hong Ruichao's wife, the woman who had promised to wait forever for his return from jail, and their husbands both ran for election when, in January 2012, the village set up ballot boxes in the elementary school courtyard. Little Yan thought she might go back to Foshan eventually and open the clothing shop she and Zhuang had been planning before the Wukan revolution. In March, however, Zhuang was elected to the Wukan Village Council. By the end of the year, both Little Yan and Hong Ruichao's wife were pregnant.

While Zhuang was struggling with his new position, Little Yan let pregnancy take over her tiny frame. She took long walks and ate carefully. She decided, against trends in China, to give birth naturally. She wanted to nurse her baby for at least a few months rather than move to milk powder. The couple bribed a doctor to tell them the sex of their baby—a practice that is illegal in China—and Little Yan went into labor early, on one of her walks. She made her way back home, and Zhuang rushed her to the hospital in Lufeng. On May 8, 2013, she gave birth to a calm, blinking baby boy. Little Yan loved him more than she could have anticipated. She had always been her mother's daughter, prag-matic and ingrained with a work ethic born in scarcity. But now that Kaizhi was in the world, Little Yan wanted nothing more than to stay home and take care of him. So that was what she would do, for now.

10

Brewing Tea

泡茶 / *Pào Chá*

In January, nearly a year after they arrived in the United States, work permits arrived in the mail for Zhuang and Little Yan. Zhuang pounced on the letters. He saved the envelope and the papers and put the card in a thick plastic sleeve. It was a sturdy card, with his photo printed, his birth date and his address right there. It was heavy enough to serve as an anchor, or at least the first stable foot planted on the ground. To work legally, Zhuang needed a Social Security number, so his next step was a trip to the Social Security office (or rather two—he had schemed to avoid lengthy wait times by going to an office farther out on Long Island, where he learned that as a resident of Queens, he could only apply for his card in Queens). Once he had that card in hand, tucked safely in with his asylum documents, he applied for every other kind of card he could think of. He opened new bank accounts. He studied to take his driver's exam and enrolled Little Yan in classes. "Someday," he said, "we are going to live somewhere that you can't just walk everywhere."

Zhuang was brimming with pride when he passed his written driving test, in Chinese, on his first try. He added a driver's license to his collection. "Little Yan will need a little more practice, I think," he said. "She's not as quick a study as me!" For the most part, she agreed. On the first day of her own driving class, the instructor scolded her for wearing high heels, saying, "It is dangerous to drive in high heels!" She came home and looked at her closet. If she couldn't wear high heels, she didn't have much to go on. The next class she opted to wear her house slippers and got scolded again. She would have to go out and buy driving shoes.

Zhuang applied for Medicaid cards for the both of them, then insurance cards on top of that. He sat in the Flushing Library for three hours waiting for his appointment to get a New York City ID. As Zhuang's collection grew, he would take out his cards and spread them on the folding table they had placed in the corner of their room. Zhuang would blow cigarette smoke into a little fan he had set up in the window, to avoid stinking up the apartment, and list them, each one a little affirmation of all the decisions he had made. "I have so many IDs," he would tell visitors proudly.

• • •

While Zhuang was collecting IDs, Little Yan's list of regrets was growing. Her parents complained, on their phone calls, that their grandson was poorly behaved. He didn't listen to them. She worried that her son would become set in his ways before she had the chance to meet him again. She worried that asylum would never come and she would remain a stranger to her only child. During the days, when she was busy, it was easier for her not to think about him. During their occasional video calls, he looked like a child from her village, a little bowl cut mushrooming off his head in a style reminiscent of Kim Jong-un, the plump new leader of North Korea.

Little Yan was beginning to find her husband frustrating, sometimes even embarrassing. He was now insisting that they find jobs together or not at all. They had worked together briefly at a Chinese restaurant, and then, expecting their asylum to arrive in the predicted three months, Zhuang had insisted that they quit. He took Little Yan out to lunch at the East Buffet to discuss, as usual, their next steps.

As they ate, a call came in on Zhuang's phone from an old

colleague who was opening up his own restaurant. He asked for Little Yan, and Zhuang handed the phone over to her. "He's very hardworking," Zhuang explained. "He left his wife ten years ago and never got papers—he can never go back." The man had paid a friend to sign all the paperwork for the new restaurant.

Little Yan was nodding at the phone. "Where is the restaurant?" she asked, then paused, nodding. "You will have to ask Liehong," she said, handing the phone back. He was offering her a position at the counter in his new restaurant.

"Are there two positions?" Zhuang asked. He frowned at the answer. "No, no, she can't take it. We'll only do it if we can work together."

Little Yan gave a tiny sigh. "Liehong doesn't want me to work by myself," she said, addressing her plate of chicken feet. American values were well and good. He was open to friendships with women who were fiercely independent, with men who were shy and studious; he was interested in all kinds of people who were unlike him. But in his marriage, he was still a man of Wukan. "Zhuang doesn't think a woman should be smarter than her husband," she said. And she was fine with the arrangement, as long as he took care of his family and let her be.

She was learning things about her husband in the United States that had lain dormant in Wukan. She had not been blind to their differences—his natural inclination was to run toward a fight, while hers was to keep her head down. She wanted comfort and financial security, whereas he would always put friends, and respectability, above money. He had asked her to stop working even before she was pregnant, since it was considered a loss of face for a married woman to work outside a family-run business. In Wukan, however, she had not thought these differences too important. He had not needed to lean so heavily on her there—they had their roles, his in the tea shop and with the village leaders, and hers at home.

But in the United States, under the pressure of building a new life, both of them were under stress just walking down the street and neither had friends or family to lean on. Here the little differences between Zhuang and Little Yan seemed to turn into chasms. She complained to her parents, "He loves to talk, but sometimes he should speak a little less." Everyone had to work hard, but Zhuang had trouble accepting the realities of life as an immigrant. "For example, a customer will come in, and the boss will say, 'No time to eat! Eat fast!' And Liehong will say, 'I'm still eating!'"

"You can't be like that," Little Yan said. "Everyone has to eat bitter."

Zhuang saw her growing discontent. On his days off, as his own optimism was wearing thin, he would sit at their little card table and offer Little Yan the comfort of his own self-reflection. One day he cooked a meal, chunks of meat in a thin soup, and stared at some photographs they had inherited from another former co-worker. They were photos of Washington, D.C., in the early spring, cherry blossoms framing the White House. "I think it is because of my father," he said. "He was not a good man. I spent so much of my life trying not to be bullied that I can't let myself be bullied by these Chinese bosses."

He sighed and dabbed at his eye with a tissue—he had a blocked tear duct that grew more bothersome in winter. Since he had started working in restaurants, his eye had gotten worse. "When we get asylum," he said, "I'm going to go to the doctor and get this fixed." The operation was simple—a matter of a few specialists and less than twenty-four hours in a hospital. It was something his family should have had done when he was still a child. But they didn't know to do it, and villagers had a tendency to ignore the problems they couldn't fix themselves.

Once his work permit was in hand, Zhuang decided once and for all to stop working for overbearing bosses. He brought up the idea to Little Yan while sitting on the edge of their mattress, village style, with his knees folded down so they were touching the floor. She could keep working, he didn't mind, but he wanted to start his own business. He would get some investment from family, take a month or two to figure it out, and open his own store on Main Street. He would make sure it was profitable right away.

There were a million reasons for Little Yan to say no. People who opened stores in Flushing, for the most part, had more money than she and Zhuang did. And if he failed, if they lost all the money and owed their investors, she worried, they would end up deeply in debt and still struggling to find jobs.

On the other hand, she felt relief. It would be quieter to work a job without Zhuang there to police her. And if what he said was true, he would be happy to let her keep working. There would be no arguments when she got home, nothing to keep her up at night aside from her own worries. So she put up no resistance. Zhuang enrolled in English classes at the Flushing Library and set about studying for yet another permit—one that would enable him to open a food stall. "Did you know," he asked Little Yan one night, "that you have to cook an egg to at least one hundred forty-five degrees? Or else it's illegal!"

Zhuang's first plan was Beef King. No one in the United States made smoked beef quite right, he said. In Wukan they made thick strips, smoky and covered in grease. He did reconnaissance on the corner where the kebab guy set up shop every day. He dreamed of logos in his sleep. He would start with a cart, then expand. He would franchise. And then he would take his Beef King money and help his family back in the village. He would use the rest of the money to buy land somewhere in Upstate New York or maybe Florida. He would help others from Wukan make the jump to the United States. They would not be so isolated when they arrived, because Zhuang would be generous with his time and money. They could join him on his land, creating a new community. He had even decided on a name for the homestead he envisioned: New Wukan Village.

After researching, Zhuang decided, instead, to fall back on what he knew. He had been taking stock of his strengths and weaknesses. One of his strengths, he decided, was tea. Opening a tea shop was not a novel idea. With the arrival of more young people in the neighborhood, a handful of bubble tea shops had opened in Flushing. There was CoCo Fresh, a popular Taiwanese chain, with a mascot that looked like a bug-eyed marshmallow. There were a few family-run kiosks on Main Street, one in the basement of the New World Mall, another in the basement of the Golden Dragon Mall—less of a shopping spot, but the little store had the advantage of low rent, low prices, and a rolled breakfast crepe, with egg and cilantro, called a *jianbing*. And these were all in operation before the advent of Kung Fu Tea, a Brooklyn-born franchise that had inspired Zhuang's own ambitions.

A new outlet of Kung Fu Tea had opened just behind the Flushing Library, and Zhuang slipped in with me one day, ready to size up the competition. He ordered a basic green tea and carried it back to a little wooden table. The shop was more modern than the kiosks down the street—it had music playing, cashiers in uniform, and free Wi-Fi. Across from Zhuang, the old lady who spent her days on the sidewalk holding up the "Green card! Marriage license!" bullhorn was meticulously unwrapping a steamed bun, all her supplies tied up in a little plastic bag stored under her stool.

Zhuang set down his tea and took a sip. It had been sweetened. "This doesn't taste much like green tea," he said. He strode back over to the kid behind the counter. "Are you using real custard apples or syrup?" he asked. "Syrup," said the kid, standing very erect in his paper cap. Zhuang nodded and returned to our table. "They all use these syrups," he told me. "They aren't real fruit— they're fake. It's bad for your heart. It'll block an artery and give you a heart attack."

He hoped to open a high-quality option, a place where the tea leaves would be sourced, personally, by himself, and the fruit would all be fresh-squeezed. He would be a strict but amiable employer. He wouldn't mind if they talked or chatted with customers. He wouldn't let them sit on their cell phones at work, but he wouldn't boss them around constantly. He had been reading the Starbucks employee manual. "It doesn't matter if you've served one hundred people in a day, to the hundred and first person, that's the only time they've been in Starbucks," he recited. "You should treat them with as much courtesy as you did the very first."

Zhuang had a deep, lasting love of tea; that was not the issue. His challenge lay in developing his own recipes—healthy versions of the popular sweet teas that incorporated mangoes, lemons, and tapioca balls. He decided to invest in a kit. He boiled fruits down and chilled them in the refrigerator, much to Chen Tai's dismay. An uncle in China had offered to invest ten thousand dollars in the business, and he tried to work practically with the numbers he had. He spent a morning camped out at the CoCo's near the subway station on Main Street, counting customers and estimating how much he would have to charge to turn a profit. He would need, he thought, around six hundred customers a day. He considered it was doable. Just one customer for every minute of a ten-hour day.

It was lonely work, researching and testing things all by himself. Zhuang spent the afternoons brewing tea and then, having drunk too much caffeine, stayed up late into the night and called China. Around midnight, when the busy streets of Flushing had cleared almost entirely, he went walking, listening to the tinny echo of his friends' voices over his phone. He joked about the weather and caught up on village gossip. He brought others into his vision, making his optimism relentless. Now when a journalism student or documentary filmmaker visited, he would show them the logo he was trying to design himself, a ship's steering wheel imposed over the name of his tea shop. He changed fonts and color schemes and sought their advice. He educated himself on the differences between design and video editing programs on his computer, and he asked his visitors for their opinions.

Zhuang wanted to call the shop the Wukan Chinese Tea Bar, then decided that the words *Chinese* and *bar* might discourage some potential customers. He opened a Facebook page for an entity called Wukan People Tea, and a bank account to hold the funds he expected from his uncle in China. The woman at the bank suggested that Zhuang give her husband, a CPA, a call and register the business. So Zhuang made an appointment, gathered his IDs, and wrote the name he liked down on a piece of paper, both in characters and in his wobbly written English.

The CPA worked in a high-rise just off Main Street, in a quiet building with an airy lobby and an escalator that seemed out of place in an office building. It was raining, and Zhuang carefully set his umbrella down on a section of newspaper so as not to get the carpet wet. He was still debating about the name. He had written down Wukan People, but then someone had suggested Wukan Village, and now the latter was starting to appeal to him. When the CPA arrived, he explained the business and the benefits of healthy versus unhealthy bubble tea. "Well then," said the CPA, across from Zhuang in a black suit and red tie, "you will definitely be successful!" He suggested he register the company name as Wukan Village Inc., and Zhuang agreed.

"This is just the business," the CPA said carefully. "When you actually open a store, you will have to fill out more applications. You will have to have the health department come and check the place. And they do it after you've remodeled."

"After?" Zhuang asked. He wondered about pouring all that money in if there was still a chance he might get rejected by the health department.

"They have to check to see if the ventilation is good," said the CPA. "And that everything is safe. If you work with a construction company that knows restaurants, then you shouldn't have any problems."

Zhuang took all this in while the CPA typed furiously at his computer. A piece of paper started making its way through the printer, and the CPA looked up. "I charge five hundred dollars to file the business name." Zhuang reached into his back pocket and tossed a wad of cash onto the desk. Silently, the CPA counted the bills.

On the walk back from the appointment, Zhuang kept up his spirits. He gazed into the window of a store selling Rolexes, a sign announcing their last seven days. He liked the white granite in the display cases and the bright lighting. He had asked a real estate broker, however, and he had said the shop would rent for at least $25,000 a month. It was too much. But Zhuang didn't want to open a little mom-and-pop kiosk in a basement. He drank too much tea again that afternoon and tried to work out the money in his head, walking up and down Main Street in the middle of the night.

• • •

Zhuang was holding himself together with the idea of his tea shop. It saved him from embarrassment, giving him a project to tell people about, something impressive and respectable. He had discovered a new phone application called WeChat and left voice messages for his friends. "Hey brother, hey brother," they inevitably started, "I miss you." He didn't have to lie to anyone about his vocation. He was an entrepreneur in a land of entrepreneurs.

Little Yan can't put her finger on the day it all fell apart. For weeks, Zhuang had been talking about the investment that would arrive from his uncle, never wavering in his faith that it would come in. And then he grew quiet. And then one day he told her that his uncle had to buy an apartment somewhere in Shenzhen and needed money for his son. "Or something," Zhuang said. "He wasn't totally clear." And then, around the same time, Chen Tai told the couple that she needed them to leave—her daughter was getting married, and she and her husband were going to take over Zhuang and Little Yan's room. Chen Tai invited them to the wedding, at the East Buffet, but they would have to move out soon.

Zhuang gave Little Yan a day or two to digest these bits of news before he sprung another surprise: he was going to buy a car. "It will be easier for me to find work," he explained. "And we can find a cheaper apartment, farther away from Main Street." He could buy it on a payment plan, he assured her. It wouldn't cost too much right now.

Little Yan was exasperated; they were soon to be without a home, and Zhuang was spending money faster than she could earn it. He had been planning his tea shop for more than six weeks, had been out of a job for longer, and Little Yan had not yet learned to drive. Her instructor kept them on the streets nearest Main Street, narrow strips of pavement between apartment buildings that were technically two-way but that were so tightly packed with parked cars that two drivers could not actually pass at the same time. She hated driving.

Zhuang went to a Chinese-owned car dealership not far from Flushing's center and tried to take out a loan. The salesman looked at Zhuang's finances and quickly told him he would not qualify for a loan. "You have no credit history," he told Zhuang. "You can't get a loan with no credit history." It was another humiliation; the scaffolding of Zhuang's optimism was starting to fall away.

Determined, he answered an advertisement for a secondhand, two-door Honda that a Chinese student was selling. It still had a UNIVERSITY OF MICHIGAN sticker in the passenger-side window. It cost him seven thousand dollars, but the transaction was quick and respectful.

Then Zhuang set out to rent a new apartment and found a place for little money—a sublet of a sublet—a short drive from the center of Flushing. It was a second-floor apartment with a big kitchen, two occupied bedrooms in addition to their own, and a shared bathroom. He had stopped worrying about adults sharing their bathrooms.

On the day they moved their small collection of belongings into the new room, a woman came out of the apartment downstairs and confronted them. "Who told you you can move in?!" she asked, screeching. "You can't move in! She can't rent it to you!"

Zhuang was at a loss. "You should talk to her about it," he said. "We already gave money, and we already have the key!" Zhuang's fuse was shorter than usual. He heaved his little mattress up the stairs and went back down as the woman watched from her doorway. "If you have a problem, you should not yell at us!" he yelled at her. "This has nothing to do with us! We are paying renters!"

The woman slammed her door. It was not an auspicious beginning.

Zhuang had promised Little Yan that he would look for a job, but he was brooding. He thought about the money they were spending on Little Yan's parents, and the money he was sending to his own family. He worried that she wasn't listening to him as she used to. When he tried to assert his authority, she resisted. She had changed jobs—moved to a new nail salon—without even telling him. He didn't know her co-workers, and he didn't know why she had moved. He asked her to quit, and she refused. She didn't like a fight, but she was not going to give up the last piece of security she had.

Zhuang turned their interactions over in his head too many times. He had made so many concessions and compromises. He helped cook and do laundry. He had suffered so many humiliations and worked jobs he never would have accepted if he had been on his own. He had done it all for her!

He decided that he wanted to teach Little Yan to drive. On her day off, he sat her down in the driver's seat and took the passenger's seat. It did not take long for him to lose patience. As she paused in an intersection, he snapped at her. He confused her by telling her to turn one way or another. When she moved her hands from the proper position on the steering wheel, he chastised her.

"She doesn't listen!" he told one of his visitors, a woman who had translated during his asylum preparations. "*Aiya*, she doesn't understand anything! She's impossible to teach."

"When you yell at me, you make me nervous!" Little Yan told him. "And then I make more mistakes!"

"I've taught other people," he said. "It's not so hard to understand! You don't pay attention!"

The lessons did nothing to stop old arguments from coming up again, and Zhuang did his best to put his wife in her place. When at dinner their former translator turned to chat with Little Yan about Chinese politics, he interrupted their conversation. "Don't listen to her!" he said. "She doesn't know anything!"

The old arguments were, in fact, growing more heated. Zhuang, in his idleness, was worrying about Little Yan's working conditions again and the bad attitude they were giving her. She came home with stories he didn't like. Her boss had been dating one of the girls working for him, and then, one day, his wife had shown up from China. Little Yan would rarely tell Zhuang directly, but on occasion she would let the details slip. At the same dinner, Little Yan had launched into the latest gossip. "She doesn't know, and nobody dares to tell her!" Little Yan giggled. "And the girlfriend, she keeps trying to make friends! She says she's teaching the woman about the business!"

The stories cut Zhuang deeply. He worried that his wife would follow in the footsteps of her co-workers, treating her marriage as lightly as they did theirs. When they argued now, she questioned his ability to take care of her and his son. He complained that she was selfish, unable to think of anything but money. The possibility of divorce, a shameful thing in Wukan Village, hung over the little room where they had just moved.

• • •

When Zhuang called me in early June—his second summer in New York—he invited me to meet him at the East Buffet and mentioned that he had found a new job. He had paid two hundred dollars to get an extra brake installed, pasted a second rearview mirror onto his windshield, and taped a yellow piece of paper to his back window that read STUDENT DRIVER. He had gotten certification as a driving instructor and found a job with a company called Union Driving School. The school was matching him with students, at twenty-six dollars for each hour-and-a-half lesson. He still had to pay for his own gas, and his students were scattered enough that he had to allow at least a half hour between each lesson, but he thought he could make decent money this way. "I had six students yesterday," he told me over the phone. "Six is too many, though, you barely get time to eat lunch." Five, he explained, was ideal.

When we made a date for lunch, I asked him whether Little Yan would have the day off. "I haven't talked to her in three days," he said. "We've been fighting."

He picked me up at a little playground he had initially discovered on Google Maps. He eased into the conversation, talking first about his new job. Most of his students, he explained, were people who had been in the country for some time. Maybe they were looking to move out of the city or start a new job. "If you live in New York without a car," he explained, "there are lots of inconveniences."

He was proud of his mastery of the vocabulary. "Parallel parking!" he recited to me on the way to the restaurant. "Pull in here!"

His lessons started out in the busy, narrow streets around Flushing center—there was no gentle initiation in a parking lot. He was a stickler for keeping his students' hands at ten and two o'clock on the steering wheel, and he made sure all his students used their turn signal and looked both ways at every stop. He did not like sudden stops or jerky driving. He took all the rules very seriously.

By the time I met him by the playground that summer, Zhuang had worked himself up to blaming Little Yan for almost everything. He hinted at their problems at lunch and then invited me back to tea at his apartment. We walked past the suspicious landlady and into their latest room, much smaller than the last. He set two stools out around his little table and tried to explain. He was worried that Little Yan was getting harassed at her job, that her boss was flirting. It was embarrassing to have her working at a place with people like that. He had raised the idea, again, of the two of them working together, but she had resisted. It made him suspicious. "I know she is texting with someone else!" he told me. "I see her hiding it from me." As for the job, "she says it's about the money, but she just wants the freedom to do whatever she wants." She's naïve, he said. If it hadn't been for him, someone would have already taken advantage of her.

He leaned over his electric kettle and wiped his bad eye with a tissue. "It is like I am not a man here," he said in a hoarse whisper. "You don't understand—even my wife no longer respects me. She doesn't listen to me. I am afraid to say out loud what I am thinking!" His wife was supposed to be the one person who stood with him when things were difficult. He should be able to trust her not to disavow him as his family had, back when he was living on the streets in Shenzhen. She was supposed to remember who he was when he was at his best. "I don't want to fight with her, so I have stopped talking to her," he told me. Little Yan, for her part, had returned the silent treatment. She didn't want to argue about quitting her job again.

There were only two ways Zhuang could imagine resolving their problems. "Either we go back to China, or we get a divorce," he told me. If he went back, he ran the risk of being thrown in jail, he said, "but sometimes I think jail might be better than this. At least in jail, I would be a man." He shrugged and turned toward the window, looking miserable. He couldn't grin his way through it. It had been nearly a year since his asylum interview and more than a year since he had arrived sure that the United States would recognize his worth.

He heaved a sigh, looked down into the empty maw of his electric kettle, and decided to go to the kitchen for more water. "I'm sorry," he mumbled. "I shouldn't be bothering you with all this." And then, just as he disappeared, my phone buzzed with an e-mail. It was from Zhuang's lawyer, copied to me.

"Asylum APPROVED," it read, and then included the date. And that was all there was to it. I stared at the message as Zhuang came back in and sat down across from me. I handed the phone to him and started to explain.

Zhuang understood before I had finished my sentence. He leaped off his stool, sloshing the kettle water. "Oh!" he said, frozen on his feet. "Shake my hand!!" He looked left, and then right, then out the window, then back again. "Do you mind if I smoke a cigarette!!" He scrolled through his phone and called both his interpreters. "Hello! I just wanted to tell you that I got asylum!! *Yes! Yes!* I just heard now!" He tried to call his friends in China, but no one was answering. He called an old restaurant co-worker, someone he hadn't seen in months. When he looked up at me, his grin was plastered back across his face.

Zhuang's contact in Congress had come through. She had put in a request to the CECC in April, and the congressman who had been in charge the year Zhuang was interviewed—Chris Smith, a Republican from New Jersey—had signed his name to a letter of support. The sudden reality of the letter took Zhuang's lawyer by surprise, but he seized the opportunity, coordinating with them to send a second letter inquiring after the status of the case. And then, Zhuang had assumed, the letter had disappeared into the maze of immigration offices that had, up until now, seemed to have swallowed all his documents, all his applications, evidence, and testimony, and never spit it out again.

"It was the letter!" he told me joyously. "I knew that the letter would help! *Aiya*, I should have insisted on it earlier!" He sat on his stool, then stood up again, then sat again. He rubbed his hands along the sides of his jeans, unable to keep still. This was the confirmation of everything he had believed. Zhuang was important enough to grab the attention of Congress! And Congress had made a difference! The man of Wukan was no longer just *in* New York; he was *of* New York. "Thank you, America!" he said in English, to the air. He looked at his phone for a second, then leaned forward in his chair, slowly.

"Do you think you might text Little Yan and tell her?" he said.

• • •

That night, after hearing about the asylum case, Little Yan returned home and started talking to her husband again. She agreed to quit her job. Their new status changed things. The couple still argued, but they had begun having conversations about their future together in Flushing. Zhuang was feeling like a man again. And as a man, he would make plans for his family. "Go to school!" he told Little Yan. "I wish I was good at studying, but we both know I'm not."

The schedule would be hectic. Little Yan would be exhausted. But she saw the logic of Zhuang's thinking. Certifications were Zhuang's specialty—taking tests, amassing IDs—but some were more suited to Little Yan. She would have to take English classes first, and courses would take time. But all of a sudden, she had time. And eventually, if the classes led her to a job working in an office or behind a counter somewhere, Zhuang would feel that she was safely in a respectable environment. She would not have to spend her days breathing in the fumes of a nail salon. She could make more money, and Zhuang would not lose face among his friends back in China. And her family would be proud. An office job was respectable.

"You can learn!" Zhuang told Little Yan. "You can study English. We need to invest in our future!"

11

Fortress Besieged

围城 / *Wéichéng*

2013–2015

It would be years before Karen Xie learned Little Yan's real name, and when she did, she would have a difficult time remembering it. To her, Little Yan would always be Angel, the name she used to introduce herself at the Long Island Business Institute (LIBI), the vocational school where they had both enrolled. Karen was eight years younger than Little Yan and had arrived in the United States six months earlier. She was talkative and friendly, with rectangular glasses that she pushed up her nose when she was nervous. Karen worked in a print shop on Main Street. Little Yan was working as a home health aide but told everyone in class that she worked the front counter of a Chinese restaurant.

In some ways Karen was Little Yan's opposite: she had come to the United States alone, without the support or hindrance of a husband, and in possession of a university degree. Born in 1991, she was part of a generation that came of age alongside China's economic miracle. She was not a villager; she had grown up on the outskirts of a city of six million in Henan Province, a place where a university education was a realistic goal for women and men alike. While Little Yan was selling shoes in Foshan, waiting for Zhuang to get out of jail, Karen had been studying computer design.

Whatever the differences in their ages or family histories, Karen and Little Yan met on equal footing. They shuttled between ESL classes with names like "Life Skills" and "Aspects of Communication," remaining at LIBI until ten p.m. most weeknights. Students brought in tea eggs and little plastic-wrapped cakes and ate them together during breaks. They passed their homework back and forth, checking answers. In shaky English, they introduced themselves to their classmates over and over again. Little Yan and Karen found they had the exact same schedule, and they began to talk.

• • •

When Karen was a university student in Henan Province, she had come across one of China's most famous novels, first published in 1947, *Fortress Besieged*. The book had been recommended by her college boyfriend, a skinny, studious upperclassman with glasses that nearly matched her own. It opens with a boat trip: the student Fang Hongjian returns home after years of study abroad. Fang is carrying a fake diploma that he had purchased from an American con man, expecting that no one in his hometown would know the difference. Returning to China, he hoped, would be as natural as water evaporating and then raining back down, making a splash as it returns to the ocean.

Karen had found the book funny. She laughed at Fang's guilelessness and his bumbling attempts to gain wealth and recognition. He lies constantly, aping sophistication by criticizing everyone he meets. He leans heavily on the cachet of his time abroad but often misreads social cues and is at sea in a mix of cultures and class divisions.

By the time Karen met Little Yan, she had reevaluated the book's dark humor, seeing similarities between Fang's life and her own. Her friends dealt in half-truths to make themselves feel more comfortable, and she in turn lied to her roommates about her immigration status and to her friends about the salary she would be earning in a new job. She saw herself buffeted by forces in both China and the United States, pushed along in life by friends and family members. By the time she had a green card and the money to go back and visit her parents in Henan, Donald Trump was president, and she was afraid she wouldn't be allowed back in.

The fortress in the book's title was a metaphor for marriage, more attractive from the outside than from the inside. Karen's fortress, however, was New York. Everyone on the outside was trying to get in, while she had spent her first year in the city desperate to find a way out.

• • •

Karen had come to the United States when Zhuang was still considering travel by boat. While he was weighing the viability of Guam, she had reserved a place at a language school in Ohio. Her mother had put her on the plane in Henan Province—her hilarious, outgoing, and fashionable mother who by rights should have been making the trip herself. All the women in Karen's family were better suited to an adventure in a strange country. Karen was quiet and plain. She was not bawdy or tough like her mother or grandmother. Her younger brother better reflected their charm and wit. Karen didn't like to wear makeup or fuss about clothes. She worried sometimes that her head was too large to be attractive. She sat on the plane, heading toward Ohio, surfing through movies and feeling dismayed by the turn her life had just taken.

Henan is a dusty, landlocked place with a dense population, bisected by the silt-filled, changeable coil of the Yellow River. Karen and her mother had lived with her maternal grandparents, tucked in a low-slung old house on the outskirts of a midsize city. In the winters her grandfather wandered the streets selling sticks of candied fruit, a treat called *tanghulu*. He harvested the fruits himself, little red berries that grew on hawthorn trees, and dipped them in sugar. In the summers, he sold peaches. If he came back with leftovers, he would slip Karen a treat to tide her through her studies.

Karen's grandfather is a kind presence in her memory, but it was her mother who, despite their differences, shaped her. Her mother was not relentlessly practical like Little Yan's. She had an expansive imagination. She had raised Karen on stories about her one adventure: a trip she had made to Beijing in the late 1970s. The worst of the Cultural Revolution had passed, and the country was making its first few steps toward normalcy, reopening universities and reviving industry. Karen's mother had boarded one of the old slow trains that cut north through Henan into Hebei Province and up toward Beijing. She had sat up alert and imagining her life in China's capital city. She found it bustling and full of young people. Karen's mother was ambitious, and she wanted to stay in Beijing indefinitely, but her parents called her back. She was the eldest of five children, and they needed her help at home. By the time she was twenty-three, Karen's mother was pregnant. She would never say she regretted it—her missed chance at a different life—but she told it as a cautionary tale, one that Karen never completely understood.

· · ·

The call came through while Karen was at work, sitting at a computer in the storefront graphic design business where she was employed shortly after graduating from college. Her mother was on the line, chattering to her about a family friend she had just run into, and about the friend's child who had traveled to the United States and stayed there. It was safe, she said, and people were friendly. Her friend had bragged about the opportunities in the United States and the money her kid sent back. Karen's mother had asked, and the friend had recommended an agency that placed students in U.S. schools. It would cost money, but Karen's mother would find a way to raise it. It would be a great opportunity for Karen to have a new and different life. Her mother was not giving her an option, really, but Karen told her that she would think about it.

"The dream," Karen told me later, "was my mother's." Her mother had a relative living in Long Island—the two rarely talked, but Karen's mother had heard about the woman's accomplishments. In the United States, you were able to act boldly, to take any opportunity. You were free of family obligations, free to take risks and jump the class divides that seemed so insurmountable in China. In China, Karen's mother worked hard every day and still lived in the same house with her parents. There were no opportunities, just daily responsibilities. New York represented everything Karen's mother had ever desired.

Karen, on the other hand, thought of the United States as just another place, one where people happened to have bigger noses. She had learned much of what she knew about the country through a hit television series called *Prison Break*, in which eight hard-boiled convicts escape from a prison called Fox River. She wasn't so naïve as to assume *Prison Break* was an accurate representation of American life, but she hadn't bothered to give it much thought.

Karen suspected that the timing of her mother's suggestion had to do with her dislike of Karen's boyfriend. She had met him during her freshman year of college, and they had been together ever since. He was three years older and a good fit for her, smart and decent. They were both quiet people, and he was eager to get married. After graduating, Karen moved to his hometown, where she got a job at the same company as him and where they talked about opening a graphic design shop of their own. Her mother complained it was too far away—two hours by car.

Now when she looks back, Karen can imagine a shadow life, one in which she is pregnant by the time she is twenty-three or twenty-four, just as her mother had been. She would have worked hard during the days and let her mother-in-law watch her children. She would have eaten dinner with his family every night. Her days would have stretched out in front of her, uniform and expected. It wouldn't have been an easy life, by any means, but it would not have been a bad one. And she had been happy with the future she imagined. It was her mother who was not.

Karen, true to her word, spent days considering the United States. She tried to imagine blond people speaking English and living in big houses with green lawns, but she didn't like the idea. All Karen's friends were in China. Her family was in China. And her boyfriend disapproved. She resolved to tell her mother no.

It didn't work. Her mother persisted. She scolded and cajoled.

Karen would finish a phone call with her one day and find herself having the exact same conversation again the next. Her mother never said a word about Beijing, never mentioned her own shadow life, but it hung over their phone calls all the same. Generation after generation of women would have babies young and work into old age, the pattern spinning out and repeating itself over and over. "Sometimes you have to stop and listen to your elders," Karen says. "Even if your own instinct is to say, no, no, no."

. . .

At the end of the twentieth century, Chinese immigration picked up speed. The wave that would pave the way for Karen, Little Yan, and Zhuang was built in equal parts on U.S. immigration policy and on changing realities in China. In 1965, after years of exclusion, the United States finally changed its immigration policy. The new quota system limited immigration based on nationality, not ethnicity, and it provided two paths into the United States: family reunification or professional preference. Students from Taiwan and Hong Kong trickled in and attended universities. Flushing's modest Chinese population grew. By the 1980s, the decades of slow, cautious immigration to the United States were over. The Chinese economy was opening up, and people who had been trapped by restrictive residency systems could move from province to province. They were no longer stuck on their farms or in their fisheries. People could acquire travel documents and earn money. And they could, once again, pool their resources and send family members out over the ocean.

In addition to an increasing number of Chinese immigrants who arrived and lived legally, old Chinese networks of people-moving reestablished themselves in the 1980s, frequently piggybacking on channels run by human traffickers in Mexico or Canada. Chinese agents called snakeheads kept other routes entirely in Chinese hands, transporting people cheaply on rickety boats that could spend months in international waters. The path to New York was indirect, depending on the availability of boats and safe houses in other countries. Some emigrants waited months in apartments in Thailand or Russia before they received the fraudulent passports they would travel on. Once they landed in the United States, they were instructed to rip up their documents and tell immigration agents that they were there to apply for asylum. Others spent months on boats or moved from city to city on airplanes, making stops in Africa, South America, or parts of Europe, finally approaching the U.S. coastline at night.

This new network was focused on the cities and villages in Fujian Province, a few hours' drive north of Wukan, on the coast closest to Taiwan. Around the city of Fuzhou, entire villages emptied out. And once one village was gone, and the path toward immigration had been established, other villages followed. Most of the former inhabitants went to the United States, but some villagers followed other routes, moving to Japan, Italy, or Canada.

Karen was lucky and unlucky at once. Her visa came easily. Her mother paid an agency 100,000 yuan, about $16,000, to help her obtain a student visa. The agency followed the letter, if not the spirit, of the law. It provided Karen with a document that cleared her to study in an expensive English-language school in Ohio. She received some coaching from an agent on what to say in her interview, and a letter from the school appeared with her name on it. She held out hope that the visa would not get issued, so she could stay with her boyfriend and her friends and so the decision to remain in China would not be her own. But the visa arrived, the money was paid, and Karen was issued a plane ticket.

The money her family collected represented a small fortune in Henan, in a year when the average family income in China was around 14,000 yuan, or $2,083. The family borrowed from some distant relatives already living in the United States, scraping together enough to send Karen over with a little bit of cash in her pocket. Once she was in the United States, Karen was expected to start working, paying down the debt the trip had incurred. No one in her family had seen 100,000 yuan all at once before. Still, they had no idea how expensive life in the United States would be. No one had any idea where Ohio was. And they had only the testimony of their friends to go on that the agency wouldn't kidnap Karen or take her money and then leave her friendless in an airport somewhere.

The cost of passage to the United States varies widely depending on geography, age, and luck. Karen's cost only a fraction of what some pay. In Fujian, where huge numbers of people left for the United States in the 1980s and '90s, U.S. visas were more difficult to obtain. Visa officers were more suspicious of travelers coming from Fujian, more willing to turn down applications, and human traffickers in the region could charge as much as eighty thousand dollars for their services. In the 1990s, it was not unusual for an immigrant from Fujian to make a months-long journey by boat. But after boats repeatedly proved uncomfortable and dangerous, they slowly fell out of fashion. In 1993 a boat called the *Golden Venture* sank in very public fashion off a Far Rockaway beach in New York, and a report issued by the U.S. Coast Guard in 1996 described repurposed fishing boats as "in danger of sinking," their human cargo "packed into hot, poorly ventilated, and confined spaces." Today Fujianese are more likely to travel first to Mexico or Canada and to make their way secretly over the border.

For hopeful working-class immigrants from other parts of China—from Henan or Guangdong, for example—the options are cheaper and more obtainable. Some, like Zhuang and Little Yan, manage the feat of arriving and staying in the United States by simply joining a tour group. Others pay agencies to help with their applications. Older people will apply for tourist visas, making their case with false documents, provided by their agent, that attest to the applicant's steady employment or property holdings in China. Younger people will apply for student visas, enrolling in schools in cities or towns scattered across the Midwest, many of them switching their plane tickets after the fact and flying straight to New York.

Karen was not one of them. She was neither savvy nor well informed enough to skip Ohio. She had a three-month visa and a ticket to Columbus International Airport. She left China as summer was drawing to a close, the peaches her grandfather picked sweet from the spike in summer heat. In Ohio, the day of her arrival was hot and clear, the sky blue with big clouds hanging low and heavy. Karen wandered out of the baggage claim holding a bag stuffed with three outfits and a backpack containing a new laptop computer—she had promised her boyfriend that they would chat online every day. Another student had been on the airplane with her, unknown and sitting in some other row, and they found themselves wandering in parallel, looking for a man holding up a sign in Chinese. They didn't say much. They didn't chatter on the walk to the van that the man was driving, and they didn't talk much on the highway. Karen watched scrubby green trees speed by the windows, the blur dipping down over the pointed roofs of the occasional low-slung warehouse. She wondered where the people were. Cities in America, she thought, were emptier than the Chinese countryside.

The school Karen had enrolled in consisted of a block of classrooms in a nondescript high-rise. The Chinese students were housed in a nearby set of apartments that had been turned into dorms and Karen arrived to a room furnished with three little metal-frame beds and three desks, a comforter folded at the foot of her bed. Her roommates, Karen would find, had flown in just days before. She can barely remember what her classmates looked like, she was so occupied with chatting to her boyfriend back home.

In China, Karen had prided herself on her friendships. She had close friends from as far back as middle school, women who, unlike Karen, were brave and opinionated—hardly ever quiet. In their company, Karen might even imagine that she had a wild side. She was not convinced that the United States had anything better to offer in terms of people.

Her arrival in the United States had been even more disorienting than Little Yan's. She was alone and in debt. Little Yan might have been limited by Zhuang's expectations, and by his pride, but he had provided a safe center in Flushing. Karen had a total of two acquaintances in the country. She had the relative on Long Island—the woman her mother admired so much had contributed a good deal to the cost of getting Karen to the United States. And there was a girl her own age somewhere in New York.

Karen had met the younger girl through the agency in China. She called herself Isobel and had arrived at the office in Henan in full makeup and heels. It was not a good first impression; she was too dressed up and too aloof. When the agency made the two girls exchange contact information, Karen had promptly forgotten it. She didn't care about Isobel. And once she was in the United States, she didn't care much about her classmates.

Karen made the walk to school every day and tried to keep up with her studies. But she learned nothing. She barely talked. She spent two months pretending her situation in Ohio was temporary, messaging her boyfriend at night and lamenting her decision to come to the United States. She was earning no money, and the days on her student visa were running down uselessly. She complained to her mother and thought about coming home. But she still owed her auntie (a term used in parts of China for any distant relative around your mother's age) 100,000 yuan. And she still had her mother's full, hopeful heart to consider.

So Karen decided to leave school and do what everyone had expected of her in the first place. She phoned the woman she called Auntie, borrowed one last sum of money, and booked her ticket to New York.

• • •

This auntie, whom Karen had never met, had kindly offered to let Karen stay with her. This was not uncommon; in China people went out of their way even for distant relatives. If Karen's family members had visitors, they would squeeze together in beds. They would stack on top of one another to make guests feel comfortable. If they had food to eat, they would be happy to offer it to anyone who happened to stop by.

There was another side to this politeness, however, and as Karen knew, family life was not uncomplicated. Keeping up appearances might mean someone said yes as a stopgap, when their real meaning was no. She assumed she knew an uncomplicated yes from a false one. But now she found that something had recently gone askew with her sense of propriety, or else something had gone wrong with her relative during her years in the United States. Her auntie looked wealthy, but she was specific about money from the moment Karen got into the car. She informed Karen even as they left the airport that she would be expected to pay rent. Then she leaned around from the front seat and warned Karen that she should be careful in New York. "You don't know anything about this place," she said. "People will take advantage! Don't go outside without me."

The auntie had moved to the United States nearly two decades before Karen. She had opened her own takeout restaurant, divorced her husband, and dated an Italian man. They all lived together—the auntie, her children, the Italian man, and his—in a big house on Long Island. To Karen, driving in from the airport, the neighborhood looked rich. They house had a yard where the children could play. It had multiple bedrooms and floors.

Karen's auntie had a plan for her: she would stay in the house in Long Island indefinitely and work off the money she owed. She would work as a maid and a babysitter, and her monthly rent would be added to the debt and taken out of the opaque, unspecified salary that she would be earning. When she arrived at the house, the older woman took her passport and told her it was for safekeeping. Maybe, Karen thought, her relative had just become American. Maybe the preoccupation with money, the cold reception, and the suspicious looks were part of a more dangerous world.

Karen still had the look of a student. She still pushed her glasses up her nose when she was nervous. A renegade pimple or two would still pop up on her cheeks when she felt stressed. But she also had some of the hard edges that her mother had hoped to instill. She found them in Long Island, when she went into the room she would be sharing with her auntie's son, flipped open her computer, and found a message she had been ignoring on QQ. It was from Isobel, writing from Flushing, a neighborhood that Karen knew to be somewhere in New York. Karen had felt her passport slip out of her fingers with alarm. She knew enough to see that her auntie was trying to take advantage of her. She knew enough to get out of that house as fast as she could.

Karen replied to Isobel, and she was lucky again. Isobel, despite her makeup and high heels, answered her message warmly. She assured Karen that Flushing was safe and that Karen's auntie was exaggerating the dangers of the city. She even offered Karen a place to sleep while she figured things out. "Everybody does it," she texted. She sent Karen an address. Isobel was Karen's first friend in the United States

After just a few days in Long Island, Karen Googled how to get to Flushing. She told her aunt she was going to meet a friend and walked to a bus stop, the correct change already in her hand. As she got closer to Main Street, she noticed jet-black heads on the sidewalks and realized she could understand more of the people who boarded the bus, talking to their friends. Flushing was loud and crowded and overwhelming, but at least Karen knew how to ask directions.

That week in Flushing, Isobel saved Karen. She knew someone who was looking for a roommate in the building where she lived. She knew where the cheap food stalls were in the food courts—the Shanghainese place that would give you a deep-fried cube of rice for a dollar, the cafeterias that would stretch five dollars into an enormous meal. She walked Karen up and down the sidewalks and introduced her to friends. She showed her the newspapers and the classified sections and left her alone to find a job. Karen still owed her auntie money, but with a job, she could pay the woman back on her own terms.

After nearly a week Karen took the bus back to Long Island. Her belongings were already stashed in her new shared room in the shared apartment off Main Street. She walked up to her auntie and told her she needed her passport back. The older woman sighed, acting as if Karen had misunderstood, and handed over the document. It would have been a loss of face, Karen later explained to me, for the woman to admit she had been trying to take advantage of a young relative. So they parted, still pretending that the woman was a benefactress and that Karen was grateful.

• • •

In Flushing, LIBI advertisements were everywhere—on banners hanging on lights along Main Street and posters in the cars on the 7 train. The school, founded on Long Island in the 1970s, had moved its headquarters in 2008, having discovered a lucrative opportunity in Flushing. By the time Karen and Little Yan enrolled, the hallways were filled with Chinese immigrants. LIBI was headquartered in a narrow office building off Main Street, the lobby entrance unattended and located between a regularly shut garage door and a pharmacy, across from a Paris Baguette. During class breaks, some of the younger students would stock up on sticky pastries, mounds of bread somewhere between a Chinese sweet bun and a real croissant.

The classrooms at LIBI were, for the most part, windowless. The hallways, two on each floor extending from the elevator bank to the front of the building, were painted blue and decorated haphazardly with scheduling announcements, signs about student IDs, and a handful of airbrushed drawings of sports cars. Before enrolling, Karen met with an administrator who explained what the school offered. In Long Island, LIBI had become well known for its program in court stenography, but in Queens, students could choose from programs in accounting, hospitality, office technology, and homeland security. Very few LIBI students, the woman explained, had to take out loans to cover the tuition, partially because many of them qualified for federal financial aid and partially due to the low cost of tuition. Karen filled out the forms for financial aid and put down the initial two thousand dollars for her first semester of ESL classes. At the end of the semester, she would choose her specialty. On the evening of the first class session, Karen walked into a windowless room and picked a seat just behind Little Yan. By the end of the semester, the pair had become friends.

• • •

Karen does not like to discuss her first year in the United States. Little Yan had the flexibility to quit her jobs and look for new work, but Karen was terrified of failing to pay off her debt. She worked long shifts that stretched from ten to twelve hours, trying to fill daily quotas. She walked home along Main Street, barely daring to buy food. She cried quietly at night, her head smashed into her pillow, or under her pillow, or facing the wall. She was sharing a room and didn't want to disturb her roommates. She cried because she was lonely and because money was impossible to keep in her pocket. She was beginning to realize the change was permanent. She cried while texting her friends, pretending not to be as unhappy as she felt. She cried after she hung up the phone with her mother.

In her first few days in Flushing, Karen found a job working in a sign-making shop that abutted Flushing's Botanical Gardens. She had called a few stores in advance, and no one had wanted to hire her. So she went to Flushing's center and walked into shops to ask if they were hiring. She walked the length of Main Street and spotted a sign for a print shop, with an arrow pointing toward the basement. She made her way down the steps and pushed open the glass door. She had experience with graphic design, she told the owner of the print shop, bending the truth only slightly. He couldn't pay her much, the owner told her, but she could start the next day.

Karen spent her first two years in New York working in that print shop, ironing logos and lettering onto T-shirts, one after the other, over and over. Every once in a while, she would use the computer and design a banner herself, but for the most part, her boss did the creative work or people brought in their own files. The money was bad, but she could not afford to risk any time unemployed. She saved every penny she made, paying back her auntie in installments. She washed her three outfits—one for each season—in a basin at night and took care not to break the single pair of glasses she had brought with her.

For months, Karen told herself stories about how she might return to China. She spun out scenarios about paying off her debt, making some money, then traveling home to the life that had been waiting for her. And then one night during her first Chinese New Year holiday in New York, her phone buzzed, and her boyfriend's face popped up, with a short little message next to it.

Karen doesn't remember how it started, but it was something in-nocuous like "Are you there?" or even just the character for *hai*, an approximation of the English. She is also unclear about whether she saw the breakup coming. She remembers feeling shocked and heartbroken. Afterward her tears came louder, less self-aware, more exhausted. They became a necessary preamble to sleep. Her roommates did not complain about the disturbance. Every young person ended up crying at some point.

Karen at least understood the subtext of the breakup. Her boyfriend had lasted for nearly six months before going home for Spring Festival. His family wanted him to settle down and start a family. So they had put pressure on him, and he had not stood up to it. Whatever he felt for her—the vision of their future to-gether—it had been strong enough for only six months and one holiday's worth of separation.

Karen cried every night, but she also erased every trace of her boyfriend from her phone. She deleted his number, blocked him on all her apps, and removed him from her contacts on QQ. She gave herself no room for any moments of weakness. It didn't mat-ter anymore whether coming to the United States had been the right decision. It had happened. It was the only decision. Karen would not plead with her old life.

12

Paper Sons

契约儿子 / *Qìyuē Érzi*

When Little Yan heard that she had been granted asylum, the rock of tension she had been holding somewhere behind her eyes softened. She didn't think women needed to dwell on things as men did. She felt confident in her ability to compartmentalize. But morning after morning she had been waking up to a single thought: she wanted to see her son.

It was common, in Flushing, for a family to leave their children behind in China for some years while they focused on making money. But that didn't make it easier. It had been eighteen months since Little Yan left her son behind in her parents' village. In call after call, they told her he was difficult to handle, which made her worry.

"Your parents don't know how to discipline a boy!" Zhuang told her unhelpfully.

"He's only two!" Little Yan kept repeating. "He can't be that bad." But she didn't know, because she didn't know her son anymore.

Now that they had asylum, they could finally apply for Kaizhi to come over. But this gave rise to a new worry: how would he get here? Little Yan did not want him to travel with someone she did not know, and she did not want to be a stranger to her son when he arrived.

Zhuang told her he had been thinking: she was not the democracy activist in the family. She would not be in danger if she traveled back to China. Zhuang thought that after they applied for their son's travel permit, Little Yan could return to China. She could spend a month with her son, get to know him in the only village he could remember, with her parents nearby. And then she could ease his transition to New York, serving as his bridge from one world to the other. It was a plan designed to put Little Yan's fears to rest, and she agreed without hesitation.

If the plan worked, if Little Yan went to China and brought their son back to the United States, Zhuang wanted to make a home for them. He had been working hard as a driving instructor, booking five or six lessons in a day, speeding from one pickup to the next, skipping meals when he had to. With the cost of car insurance and gasoline, his profits were slim; he relied on tips and a packed schedule. He thought he might have found the right job to sustain him and provide for his family. He was hopeful, again, that life was moving forward.

From the moment he gave her the option to return home, Little Yan had the trip planned out in her mind. But she was still her mother's daughter, still cautious and tactical. Even before their asylum letters arrived, she had decided on a career change. One of her colleagues at a nail salon had told her about a nursing school that, for five hundred dollars, would certify you to work as a home health aide. In Flushing, a home health aide was only slightly more respectable than a worker in a low-end nail salon— there was something distasteful about working in other people's homes. Zhuang would have preferred that she get a job as a secretary, where she could spend her days dressed nicely and sitting at a desk. Little Yan told him he was unrealistic. Her English was not good enough, she had no experience, and no one would ever hire her.

Zhuang complained about the cost of the nursing school, but he did not stop her. She took a six-week class, and for another small fee, an agency associated with the school placed her with a family not too far away. The job was not as difficult or competitive as a nail salon. She was paid over the table (the agency was responsible for handling payroll), and Little Yan didn't get headaches after long days of breathing in fumes. Her employers were an elderly couple from Hong Kong—Zhuang would hardly worry about their possible bad influence. The pay was not good—Little Yan took home around fourteen hundred dollars her first month—but it was enough to make do.

It took a few weeks for the pair's official asylum letters to arrive, and before they could schedule another meeting with their lawyer, they needed to collect a list of documents for Kaizhi's application: birth certificates, residency booklets, immunization records, and passports. Once they gathered them and friends helped translate, they set up a meeting for early fall. Little Yan dressed nicely in a pink cardigan, put on lipstick, and hooked a leather backpack over her slim shoulders. They arrived fifteen minutes early so Zhuang could stop at the Starbucks and buy coffees to hand out.

The lawyer's office was in the back of the floor, past a sea of cubicles. Their lawyer led them back to his office, still cluttered with files, and pulled up the forms they would need on a computer screen. Zhuang handed over the coffee he had brought and looked on attentively. Little Yan considered the separate case files lining the wall, each one thicker than her fist. She was already exhausted by the turns her own life had taken. Her lawyer, she thought, must have had a hard time keeping it all in his head. She wondered how many times he had filled out those forms. He was busy making a valiant effort at her son's Chinese name, saying "Kaizhi-zee" when the name, pronounced properly, sounds like "Kai-jur."

Little Yan waited patiently as they went through the application to bring Kaizhi over. They went over her parents' address five or six times—there was no house number, only a street corner, and it didn't fit properly in the form. They listed phone numbers and e-mail addresses (her parents didn't have one), and they photocopied Kaizhi's passport and his vaccination records. Little Yan waited nearly an hour before asking what she wanted to ask. She looked at Zhuang, to see if he would raise the question, then spoke up: "Can I go back and visit my son?" She waited patiently for a translation. "Can I apply for a travel permit?" She had looked it up—she knew which form she would need and how long it usually took.

The gravity of the moment had escaped the lawyer, and he held his hand up distractedly, staring at a blank that the computer wasn't letting him fill in properly. "I don't think that's a good idea," he said quickly.

Little Yan pressed her lips together and looked across the desk. "If I can't go back, how will our son travel to the United States?" She looked at Zhuang.

"It will be no problem for Little Yan to travel back to China," Zhuang cut in reassuringly. "All the problems are my problems. She won't have any trouble."

"No, no, no," the lawyer said. "I would not advise that she go back. It will look bad, going back to a country that you just got asylum from." He was still distracted by the forms, moving through them as fast as he could. "You should have a family member accompany him." This, he said, was what many immigrants did.

Zhuang and Little Yan exchanged glances. "We don't have a family member who could take him, I don't think." None of her family members had ever traveled on an airplane. They would have to get a visa and a passport. They would be terrified. Little Yan didn't think it would be possible.

"Well, if you don't have anyone to take him, maybe we can reach an arrangement with an airline," their lawyer answered, rolling his chair back from his computer screen with a half-sigh.

"The airline?!" Little Yan's eyes widened with alarm. She was speaking to Zhuang now. Her voice, usually even and calm, practiced at avoiding conflict, was expanding its range. "He's only two and a half!" she said. "He's too young to travel alone. Would they even let him? He'll be scared." Even if he didn't travel until he was three, she repeated, it was too young. She looked at her lawyer, her eyebrows knit together. The month-long visit home, the gentle transition that she had planned for Kaizhi, was falling apart. She had been so excited about the proposition, and so sure that things would work out now that they had asylum.

The pitch of her voice finally captured the lawyer's attention. He rolled his chair closer to his clients. He looked at Little Yan and said more gently, "You don't have anyone who could accompany him?"

She shook her head, looked at her hands, and blinked angrily.

"I don't think you should go back," he repeated. "It might be okay, but if it catches the attention of an immigration officer on a bad day, they might make it an issue. It looks bad for someone to apply to travel back to the country they were granted asylum from right after they were granted asylum."

She nodded miserably.

"Look," her lawyer said. "Here's what we can do. Even after Kaizhi gets approval to come to the United States, it will take some time to process. He will have to visit the consulate in Guangzhou for an interview. He will have to get his travel documents in order. Let's wait until he gets permission to come and then think about getting you permission for travel."

Little Yan and Zhuang nodded in unison, Zhuang giving her a water-eyed, apologetic smile. He had been so sure of this plan. He had intended to send her back and heft all the pressures of making a living onto his own shoulders. In China, he had mobilized an entire village with a few sheets of paper; in the United States, it didn't seem to matter how many forms he filled out, it was impossible to put plans into action. In the lawyer's office, going over the last few details of Kaizhi's papers, it took Zhuang a few moments to recover himself.

Their lawyer finished the forms, his tone still gentle and unhurried. When he finally closed his computer Zhuang managed to smile again. "Drink your coffee!" he admonished. "It will make you strong." The lawyer grinned back and pretended to flex a muscle. He walked the two of them out through the maze of cubicles. "It shouldn't take too much time," he said, shaking their hands warmly at the door, handing them a packet of papers about their benefits as asylees. "We'll be in touch. And congratulations on your asylum."

Zhuang doubted that first part. On the elevator ride down to street level, he turned to Little Yan, who was holding her elbows. "It will probably take a little while to get done," he said. "If we have green cards by then, we can travel wherever we want. We can go to Hong Kong together and pick up Kaizhi."

Little Yan nodded. She walked down the sidewalk in her favorite pair of platform heels. She looked at the magazine kiosk they were passing as if it interested her greatly. "I don't want to talk about it," she said. There were too many twists and too many opportunities to get her hopes up. Zhuang could change course in the middle of a conversation and feel like he had always been headed that way anyway. Little Yan needed more time.

• • •

The marital peace that had returned with their asylum was disrupted by the news that Little Yan would not be traveling to China. Zhuang was still giving driving lessons, but some days were busier than others. In the winter, he complained, nobody wanted to sign up for lessons. When he sent money back to Wukan to help a cousin fund a wedding, he and Little Yan argued about finances again, which made him chafe at the money they were sending to Little Yan's village. The more his pride was hurt, the more he felt that a man's children belonged with his own family. And the more they fought, the more hostile Little Yan's parents were to Zhuang. He didn't want Kaizhi's maternal grandparents badmouthing him to his son.

Zhuang decided he wanted to send Kaizhi back to Wukan. "The food in Wukan is better," he argued. Kaizhi would eat fresh fish every day. He told Little Yan that his father would do well as a grandfather.

"I don't know why you think that," she said sharply. "Did he do such a great job with his family?" She did not have to say, outright, that one of Zhuang's brothers had been crippled and the other was addicted to drugs. It was in the tone of her voice, which Zhuang ignored.

"He doesn't consider that his grandchildren are his to do whatever he wants with," Zhuang explained. "He treats them better." At the same time, Zhuang's father was tough and wouldn't let Kaizhi get away with being naughty.

Little Yan disagreed. Both families were poor, a poor farmer was different from a poor fisherman with a tendency to gamble away his money. "Have you seen his parents' house?" Little Yan whispered to me later. "It looks like it would blow over in a strong wind."

In the end, though, she agreed. She couldn't argue with Zhuang about everything. "It's like beating your head against a wall," she said. Her parents took Kaizhi to stay with Zhuang's parents. But sending Kaizhi to Wukan would give rise to other complications. For the first time since Zhuang left the United States, his father had influence again. After a few months of looking after Kaizhi, he asked Zhuang for about thirty thousand dollars to build himself a house, something suitable for a man with a son in the United States. Zhuang tried to tell him that he didn't have the money, but his father didn't believe him. Everyone who went to the United States had money, Zhuang Songkun said. What kind of thankless child would refuse his father—who raised him and who was raising his child, who had spent his life breaking his back pulling crabs out of the bay—the consolation of a comfortable home in which to live out his old age?

When Zhuang refused to pay, his father threatened to borrow money in Zhuang's name.

"I can't call people and tell them not to lend him anything," Zhuang explained to me. "And I can't pay them back if he takes out a loan." He finally sent his father a little money, chipping away the last of their savings.

With Kaizhi in Wukan, Little Yan couldn't talk with her son over video chat. They talked on the phone occasionally, but mostly she got updates through the filter of Zhuang's parents. "They tell me that Kaizhi is really naughty," she said. "He was so good when he was a baby. I don't know what happened to make him change."

She comforted herself that it was just a phase. Kaizhi was three; kids were more difficult at three. Kaizhi had been a wonderful baby.

Zhuang had promised Little Yan that he would keep working at the driving school for six months, but she could see him getting restless by the end of the summer. Their most recent sublet room had turned out to be a bust. The woman who yelled at them on the day they arrived had persisted, and they eventually learned that she had cause. The woman who had rented them the room had cheated them: she had been subletting from the woman downstairs, who had forbade her from renting the room to anyone else. She had charged Zhuang and Little Yan more than she was paying herself, then disappeared. "This is a terrible environment!" Zhuang told Little Yan one evening.

Two days later he located another room even farther out, in a tiny Tudor-style house in a neighborhood called Fresh Meadows. It would be their fifth home since arriving in New York a year and a half before. Little Yan would have to wait for a bus to take her to the 7 train, which would take her to her job, just a few stops west in another neighborhood of Queens. But the room was spacious and had two sets of windows—enough to get a cross breeze in the summer. The backyard was a snarl of watermelon vines that the landlady cultivated.

The new house was also the most family-friendly place they had lived. Across from Zhuang and Little Yan, the landlord's young son and daughter shared a room, doing their homework, arguing, and playing games. The landlord, a man from Fujian, spent nights working in a Japanese restaurant, doing tricks over a big grill in the middle of the restaurant, chopping up noodles and setting onions on fire for effect. During the day he drove a fancy black SUV for a local car service. He owned a home but worked three jobs and rented all but two of the rooms to make ends meet. "I respect him!" Zhuang said. "He's really been successful in New York!"

• • •

After their first semester at LIBI, Karen and Little Yan had both picked the specialty that sounded the most respectable and the most practical. Little Yan didn't remember making the decision herself—she had attended an advisory meeting, and her career adviser had simply told her. In the LIBI catalog it was listed as "medical office." They would have to take classes from other specialties, like business, computer, and office technology. They would learn record-keeping, insurance billing, and medical terminology. And they would have to do it all in English.

In the first few weeks of their second semester, Little Yan and Karen worked themselves into the same evening schedule again. Some classes were easy—language classes that focused on everyday life, or classes that focused on computers or math and didn't require any language. On Wednesdays, everyone filed down the blue-painted hall for a class called "Keeping Financial Records." Little Yan and Karen agreed that this class was one of the most confusing and difficult on their schedule. Computers lined the walls of the classroom and were bunched on two round tables in the center of the room. Those tables, and all the chairs, made the classroom nearly impassable. Students parted office chairs with their arms as they made their way to their seats. The Chinese students clustered to one side of the room as the other students— four women—spread out their things expansively in front of the computers on the far wall.

In the classes Little Yan and Karen shared was a young man named Jerry, thin and nattily dressed in button-down shirts featuring geometric shapes or squiggly lines running across them. An older woman named Carol came dressed neatly and took photos of the whiteboard with a new iPhone. Everyone but Carol was working full time and stumbling into the classroom at night, trying to keep up with the homework. They studied all weekend in the lead-up to midterms and finals. The classes moved quickly, and even Karen, with her university experience, found herself cramming on weekends, posting emojis on her WeChat feed of faces crying.

On a night in early January, Little Yan walked into class with her books neatly tucked in her leather backpack, the weather just warm enough for her to wear her blue suede shoes. "I looked at the homework," she said, sitting down next to one of the computers, "and then I made the decision not to do it. It was going to take too long." Jerry, a few seats away, was taking photos of his own homework and loading them onto the computer. Across the room, a similar conversation was going on in another language. "This class has *way* too much homework," one woman commented. "I'm gonna complain."

Karen had stolen Little Yan's regular seat that night, seeing as another Chinese student had stolen her own regular seat. The pair grinned at each other, then opened their textbooks. Carol dabbed at her face with a piece of blotting paper and wrapped a scarf more tightly around her neck. She was there because she was interested in *learning*, not out of necessity, she had told them. She was of the opinion that the most recent round of Chinese immigrants were lazy and unimaginative. They were not so interested in learning or bettering themselves. They were just taking jobs and driving down salaries for everyone else. Carol herself hadn't arrived long before, but her husband had been in the neighborhood for years. She got out her iPhone.

The professor was an African immigrant, although Little Yan had never determined from where. He rushed in, dressed in a sweater and slacks, and spread out his books. "Today we're going to be talking about a general ledger," he said, speaking quickly. "Can anyone tell me what a general ledger is?" When no one answered, he drew diagrams on the board, imagining a business selling shoes or T-shirts. He motored through all the basics of a general ledger. "What's a proof of payment?" he asked the silent class. "Check stubs," he answered himself. "Check stubs are a proof of payment."

The instructor took them through credit, debit, and cash accounts, drawing graphs on the board and selling thousands of dollars' worth of imaginary shoes. The woman who had occupied Karen's seat closed her eyes. Then she slumped onto her desk. Jerry poked her in the ear with a marker. "Jerry, leave her alone," said the professor, not missing a beat.

Karen and Little Yan spoke up whenever they could answer

in numbers, an easy way to use English in class. Their instructor plowed ahead, offering three different definitions of "net" versus "gross" income. "Some people say your net income is after costs," he explained. "Other people mean after taxes." He segued into Social Security taxes. "Your book says eight percent, that's wrong. I'm going to use six point two percent, but on the test you're going to have to use eight percent." The Chinese side of the class, struggling to follow his quick English, knitted their eyebrows together. Carol took a picture of the board.

The instructor's final stretch involved the question of buying a new car. "Who here knows anyone who has purchased a car recently?" he asked, to a silent room.

"I know," said one of the non-Chinese students, confident and joking. "You bought a car. Don't think I don't see you looking at cars all the time." The student imagined the instructor purchasing a BMW X5.

"Okay, if you were me, would you buy it with cash or use credit?" asked the instructor. "Which one would be better?"

There was a lack of consensus in the class. If he bought with credit, then he would have to pay interest. "But then you could turn in the car," said one of the non-Chinese students. "And get a new one!" Others thought cash was the safer option.

Little Yan took the opportunity to speak. "I would use credit," she said.

"Really, why?" asked the instructor.

"Because I don't have enough money."

The whole class laughed and nodded. That's why they were all here in the first place.

• • •

The breaks at LIBI were short. At the end of their second semester, as the second frigid winter that Little Yan had spent in New York was finally giving way to spring, the school took a two-week break. Karen enjoyed them, feeling suddenly free. Her life in the United States was more straightforward than Little Yan's—the more she worked, the more her situation improved. And after two years, she didn't feel so desperate. She had paid off her debt and saved some money. She was no longer wearing just one pair of pants per season.

Little Yan, on the other hand, felt the pressure of her life building. She spent the break busing to her most recent job as a home health aide, looking after two elderly immigrants and their little grandson. She cooked, cleaned, played with the child, and hoped they needed her for the full forty hours every week. If she didn't work, she didn't get paid.

Zhuang had run out of driving students recently and seemed to be losing interest in the job anyway. He was cycling through alternatives, unable to find anything that would pay well enough to make it worth his time. He parked cars outside a karaoke bar, then delivered food for a restaurant in Long Island. Nothing stuck. He spent his days reading the news on WeChat, thinking about Wukan and his son.

Zhuang did not worry about Kaizhi as much as Little Yan did. His own childhood had been difficult and itinerant, but he had survived it. Children were resilient, he told her. The delay was even, now that Zhuang thought about it, a bit of a relief. He was convinced that it would take at least a year for Kaizhi's papers to arrive. He would have time to try a few more jobs and business ventures. A year was enough time to find something more secure. They would apply for a green card in the summer, and by the time Kaizhi was ready to come over, they would be free to travel. Little Yan could still go get him herself.

Zhuang was occupied with his own set of worries. His life in New York might grow more stable, but the peace in Wukan, he felt, was temporary. He hoped the village could hold on for another year.

13

Wukan! Wukan! Land and Committee

土地和村委会 / *Tǔdi hé Cūnwěihuì*

The first election in the history of Wukan Village was held on a sunny day in early March 2012, not long after Zhuang and Little Yan's marriage. A month earlier the village had voted on a commission to oversee the election and had decided on a two-day process in which villagers would choose from over twenty different candidates. The villagers would be able to select any name from the list of candidates for any of the seven spots on the village committee. The village election committee had also decided that the best spot for the event was at a local school, where rainbow-colored umbrellas were set up for shade on the athletic fields and pink sheets strung up in the classrooms for privacy. Wukan's villagers were buoyed and hopeful as the day approached. People discussed the election in open-air mahjong parlors and over games of dice on the street corners. Fishermen moored their boats for the day, and villagers working in factories scattered throughout the Pearl River delta took time off to travel home.

Everyone who had been prominent in leading the protests felt optimistic about the future—and nearly everyone put their name forward in the election. Those who ran campaigned openly, talking about freedom and democracy but thanking the Communist Party all the same. The wounds of Xue Jinbo's death and the thirteen-day standoff were deep, but the time for revolution was over. Criticizing Beijing, or suggesting that Wukan could be a model for other villages, could jeopardize the progress Wukan was making. When Old Lin stood up in the village square and announced his candidacy, he kept his remarks generic, telling the crowd of enthusiastic villagers about the hard work and hopeful days ahead of them. "I'm an old man, without much ability," he told them. "But my heart is close to the villagers."

Zhuang's friend Jianxing decided he was too young to run, but Xue Jinbo's daughter, Jianwan, put her name forward. She had asked Zhuang to her house in advance of the election to discuss it, and he told her to follow her instinct. After the first day of voting, however, which put Jianwan in a runoff election, she withdrew. Her grandmother had threatened to drink poison if she continued.

Newspapers around the world, meanwhile, speculated that Wukan's election marked the beginning of a trend. "Wukan offers democratic model for China," ran one headline in the *Financial Times*. "Rebel Chinese village prepares to run extraordinary elections," declared the *Telegraph*. Even China's Communist Party–run media outlets praised the way officials had resolved the village protest. A commentary in the party-run *Global Times* praised leaders for "putting the public first and helping them fulfill reasonable interests." In the *South China Morning Post*, a Hong Kong newspaper, prominent democracy activists expressed hopes that events in Wukan marked the beginning of a sea change—a foothold for democracy and rule of law.

All these reactions ignored a simple truth: Wukan was betting on a political reform that had already failed. The first village elections in China were held in the late 1980s, when a trial run of the proposed national Organic Law on Village Committees was launched. The law laid out a basic structure for governance, with a village committee of seven to nine people (depending on population) selected to administer the affairs of the village. Shortly after it was formally passed into law in 1998, at the peak of the village election movement, nearly 40 percent of Chinese villages had elected their own councils. The European Union and the

Carter Center in the United States provided money and expertise to help train the new village committees. Scholars came to observe the elections. Farmers were convinced that China's central government was serious. And then, in the second decade of the experiment, village elections started to fail because of land.

As was the case in Wukan, these village committees were "overseen" by town- and county-level officials—party leaders from places like Lufeng City. When land became more valuable, and elected village officials began asserting their rights over it, elections became more fraught. County-level officials needed control over the land to balance budgets and line pockets. They started rigging elections and detaining candidates. And when villagers tried to take their complaints to a higher level of government, petitioning and protesting as Zhuang had, they were ignored. China's central government had already come down in favor of land-grabbing officials. In this sense Wukan's election was less a model for future liberalization than a holdout from the past.

As the villagers saw it, that Wukan had never before had an election was both result and cause of the corruption that had been chipping away at their land. Yang Semao, in particular, had used the 1998 law to anchor his argument in favor of elections, and he had found a receptive audience in the village. People in Wukan clung to China's written laws the same way Zhuang had done while petitioning. They were uneducated villagers. They didn't have money or influence. If China's laws meant nothing, then they would have to admit they were exposed, poor, and inconsequential.

Around 80 percent of the village showed up to the polls. Old Lin was elected village chief, winning 6,200 out of 6,800 votes cast, and Yang Semao earned enough votes to serve as his deputy. After two days of voting, Zhuang, his friend Hong, and three other people were elected as council members—Zhuang having received 4,115 votes. The village celebrated late into the night. They had fought off wealthy developers, corrupt leaders, and armed thugs. They had been kidnapped, imprisoned, and beaten. But on election night, the whole village was hopeful and naïve all over again.

• • •

The council held its first official meeting in May, all seven of them seated at a long table in the biggest room at Wukan's village committee headquarters. It was a three-story, salmon-pink building a few dusty blocks east of the village square. Old Lin, as village chief, occupied his own office on the second floor of the building; everyone else shared.

The meeting room was on the third floor, filled with benches and infrequently used. Most often it could be found strewn with plastic bottles and pamphlets on good governance, the relics of previous events. For the first village committee meeting, however, they cleaned it up. The event was going to be photographed and recorded: a new day for the village. The council members took their seats along the benches. They grinned and joked and divided responsibilities—Zhuang Liehong would be in charge of village security, civil mediation, and funeral reform. He asked if Hong Ruichao might help him with some of his tasks. There would be no training sessions. "You need to have a deep understanding of your responsibilities," Old Lin told the new committee. "And you need to have regulations in place that are clear and keep things functioning."

Old Lin was the only one among the protest organizers who had previous experience in village governance. He knew how to organize people, although he described himself as a simple man who likes to keep to himself. "How the stomach feels is real," he once told me, nearly a year after the election. "Everything else is illusion."

Lin had worked as a cadre—a low-level official in the Communist Party—in the village from 1969 to 1974 after serving as a soldier in the People's Liberation Army. Lin was appointed to serve as a village leader under Xue Chang, the man who would go on to steal most of Wukan's land. The pair did not get along, and Old Lin left quickly. He was one of the first people to leave the village and go into business, opening up a grocery store and then going into clothing manufacturing. He had done well for himself.

His relative wealth, people theorized, would make him a virtually incorruptible village leader.

When Lin moved back to the village in 1997, he intended to retire. He was ill; his children were grown up. "I am a loner!" he says. "I don't gamble, and I've quit smoking and drinking, so there is no place in the village to socialize." On top of this, he says, he had no interest in politics. The protest leaders and the Lufeng government pushed him into leading. "The government was afraid if I didn't lead, the village would fall apart," Lin said.

• • •

Zhuang Liehong knew he wasn't well suited to government. He was too loud and brash and lacked a talent for compromise. Enthusiasm, however, was not one of his shortcomings. People in the village had pushed him to run. They looked to him for leadership, and Zhuang wanted to execute his duties well. He wanted to bring Wukan's management up to unimpeachable standards. In the days following the first committee meeting, Old Lin was walking to work when he passed a pile of garbage. Trash is a common problem in Chinese villages—there are barely enough dumps and incinerators for China's cities, so villages tend to just wing it, dumping in empty lots if they are organized. No one in the new council had yet thought to organize the village trash collection. A few yards past the trash pile, Old Lin came upon Zhuang, trotting down the street, a camera in his hand.

"Where are you going with that camera?" asked Lin.

"I'm going to photograph the trash pile as evidence." Zhuang was planning to post the photos online to push the committee into action.

"You are part of the committee!" said Lin, blinking. "If there is trash, you should clean it up, not put it on the Internet!"

Zhuang began thinking of ways to improve the village through his own role as the head of village security. He stayed up nights and looked for advice online, taking a full week to craft a proposal to present to Old Lin. He wanted to establish a strict on- and off-duty schedule for the security team, with incentives and penalties for people who did not show up on time. He wanted to score each team member's performance in a monthly report. He wanted to replace the current head of the security team (who happened to be Zhuang's cousin) with someone new. He handed his suggestions to Old Lin, written up and printed out in a folder.

The old man balked. "If the team members can live up to these requirements, they can work for the United Nations!"

Zhuang, Old Lin said, was overestimating village resources. These were fishermen, not highly trained police officers. And Zhuang's cousin would not leave his position quietly. "Things need to be realized gradually—step by step," Old Lin said. "Zhuang Liehong just wants everything to happen immediately." He advised slow, careful consideration. Zhuang wanted action.

Zhuang attacked all his tasks with the same swashbuckling energy. He could not photograph the trash, so he made an enemy out of the bus companies that left a trail of litter along their path through the village. The buses picked up villagers by the side of the road and delivered them to Lufeng and other neighboring cities. One of the other council members proposed that they pay a fee for operating in Wukan. When the companies refused, Zhuang took the matter into his own hands. He led his security team out into the streets and began blocking buses. In retaliation, the bus services decided to skip Wukan, take an alternative route, and force villagers to walk a long way if they wanted a ride. Villagers were upset.

"There are a lot of trivial things that occupy a village committee," explained Zhuang's co–council member, a woman who had discovered a talent for the minutiae of bureaucracy. Zhuang had no patience for the slow, repetitive work. He was an unpredictable colleague. Everything with Zhuang, people complained, was a fight.

• • •

Little Yan arrived in Wukan in late December, not long after Zhuang had been released from detention. She had been glad when Zhuang called her before anyone else—before his parents, she liked to remind herself, who must have been worried. She presumed the rocky days of protest were behind her husband-to-be. She closed her shop in Foshan, left her sister in their shared apartment, and came to settle in Wukan.

The village took Little Yan by surprise. She had never spent much time there while she and Zhuang were dating. She had not realized what a peculiar place it was. Married women stayed home but could crack jokes that were just as dirty as any man's. People weren't polite, they were direct. Villagers were openly nosy and did not hesitate to offer their opinion. And they made Little Yan uncomfortable.

The money Zhuang was making as a village committee member was negligible—a spare few thousand yuan each month. So while he was crafting his plans and waging a small-time war with the bus companies, Little Yan looked for work. Her options were slim. Most of the villagers worked on fishing boats or ran their own small businesses—hair salons, tea shops, restaurants, and mahjong parlors. One morning she wandered down the main strip and into the pink complex of the Haiyun Holiday Hotel and found that they were hiring. She started work within days, welcoming rich businessmen from around Guangdong Province, people there to invest in the surrounding area or to take in the scenery. In their Mercedes and BMWs, they would cut past the village, drive down a lane of abandoned two-story buildings that were intended to house a shopping strip, and pull up in front of the hotel. The hotel, Zhuang said, was part of the problem. Little Yan worked there three months before he made her stop. He may have been a bad bureaucrat, but he had a handle on what constituted a conflict of interest. "People will use you to pressure me," he told her. Plus, in Wukan, respectable men could support their wives at home, and Zhuang, finally, was a respectable man.

• • •

It was Old Lin who was tasked with managing the question of Wukan's land. In his second-floor office, he stacked his desk with papers and stuck metal filing cabinets in the corners. He put out a tea set for visiting officials and folded himself up in his chair, trying to sort through a mountain of paper, adjusting his glasses and running his hands through his frizzy hair. Old Lin had envisioned a year or so of getting things in order, of setting up his filing system and paving the way for a village that followed China's laws and functioned like a well-run factory.

But none of the documents he was given made any sense. Maps of the village were inconclusive, and Lufeng officials kept changing what was legal. "I'm old," he told visitors to his office, his feet tucked under him so his knees practically hit his chin, his plastic slippers still on the floor. "Sometimes I think the earth will still rotate if I'm not around." He was now sixty-eight. He considered stepping down only a few months in but worried how the village would fare without him.

There was no official map of Wukan. No one had taken the time to approve the boundaries of the village's residential or farmland, because everyone had simply known what belonged to who. And then there was the land that had been illegally taken. The map of Wukan that was initially drawn up by the township officials was of a village with a total of about 9,000 *mu* of land, or some 1,483 acres, a fraction of the size Old Lin knew the village to be. When he protested, they revised the map and Wukan clocked in at 21,000 *mu*, or 3,459 acres. Still, the land on the negotiating table was much smaller than the land Wukan had started out with in the 1990s.

In addition to land, Wukan's money had disappeared. If Xue Chang, the old council leader, had amassed any fortunes by way of the Wukan Port Industrial Development Company, it was long gone and inaccessible. Officials from Lufeng City—the men complicit in years of corruption—were in charge of the council's budget. If Old Lin needed a few thousand yuan to pay the salaries of the town's trash collectors, he had to put it into a budget and submit it. Even his own salary came from above. And the villagers were impatient for results. They, like Old Lin, had expected to wait a matter of months before they started to see their land returned to them. Old Lin felt he was getting squeezed from both sides. "There is a conflict," he said, "between being reasonable and being legal."

Zhuang first tried to quit the village committee during the summer—only months after his election—when he felt unfairly blamed for the bus incident. He finally did quit in October, following the first meeting of the village representative assembly—a group of about a hundred villagers also elected earlier in the year, intended to give the entire village a say in Wukan's most pressing matters. The representatives were technically required to vote on any decision involving village land, and the discussion at the meeting focused on two strips of land straddling the road. Villagers asked the council to distribute the land to the villagers and let them use it as they wanted. Yang Semao, who was heading the meeting, admitted the option was not on the table. He spent a few hours getting yelled at. "They were like a pack of wild horses—I couldn't control them," he reported back afterward. "They started yelling at me the moment the meeting opened." This kind of thing, he supposed, is going to happen in a democracy. The villagers had been suppressed for so long; now they wanted to speak up about everything.

Zhuang didn't see things in such a positive light. He saw the Lufeng government clamping down—the slow creep of corruption and authoritarianism returning. When Zhuang suggested releasing regular reports to the villagers on land, he was rejected. He decided to release a letter announcing his resignation. "The village committee is not the right platform for me," he wrote. "I still believe that I am a child of Wukan, and I still stand with the masses to work together toward Wukan's new paradise." Privately, he thought that the village committee was like a house balanced on weakening stilts—one well-placed blow could send the whole thing tumbling down.

• • •

By the time the village erupted in protests, Wukan was no longer stuck in abject poverty. Enough money was coming in from family members working in the cities that no one went hungry and no one lived on the street. Villagers who came back with money built new houses so fast, they no longer fit along paved roads. (Yang Semao's house was reachable only by wending through a maze of new construction off a gravel road, an empty lot occupied by a legion of bullfrogs, and an alleyway.) Some villagers, however, were being priced out. They lived in run-down houses forced to accommodate several generations. Newly married couples could not move into homes of their own—they had to rent or squeeze in with someone's parents. The remaining village land was, according to law, communally owned, but with the success of the protests, the villagers wanted that land for their own private use—measured and meted out to individuals. The party officials in Lufeng, Old Lin found, would never agree to it.

The items on the negotiating table were more limited than he could have imagined. Over the first year of negotiations, the Lufeng government offered two mediocre parcels of land. One was an undeveloped spit that protected Wukan Bay. The other was being rented by a wealthy villager and run as a pig farm. This was scheduled to be returned to the villagers in April 2013, and the day of the farm's handover was expected to be triumphant. The villagers had yet to determine what they would do with the land, but it was the only thing Old Lin had to show for his year of leadership.

On the day of the handover, the villagers set out to the pig farm in a happy parade of scooters to see what they were getting back. When the gates were opened, they rushed in to find a rutted road, smashed windows, uprooted trees, and rubble everywhere. The family leasing the land had destroyed everything as they left—ripping up roads, demolishing buildings, and crushing plants with heavy machinery. No one had realized what was happening because the gates had still been locked. Now a group of angry villagers decided to block a road in protest. ("It worked once," explained Zhuang. "And it's the only thing they know how to do.") There was a standoff, protesters were carted off by police, and a crowd at the village committee building hounded Old Lin until his hoarse, wavering voice nearly gave out. He shouted at the crowd that, once and for all, he was quitting. No one could convince him otherwise. His threats, however, were hollow. Quitting wasn't an option.

It was after the incident at the pig farm that Zhuang started considering his escape routes. The village could not block roads again. Every day from his vantage point in the tea shop, he watched the village and observed paranoia building among his friends. People were sure their phones were being monitored. Hong Ruichao hadn't felt comfortable traveling outside Wukan since Xue Jinbo's death. Zhuang worried about Little Yan and their newborn son. His moment of heroism had passed; he had run out of plans to help his village. So he started planning something else entirely.

14

The Moon Represents
My Heart

月亮代表我的心 / *Yuèliang Dàibiǎo Wǒ de Xīn*

SPRING–SUMMER 2016

According to Tang Yuanjun, most immigrants, Chinese and otherwise, come to the end of their lives telling two stories: one set in their country of origin, and one set in the United States. Nearly always one story dominates. Tang's story, of the first kind, is recounted in vivid detail. The story is so familiar, so well-worn with retelling, that it takes over his body as his tells it. He executes well-timed hand gestures and dramatic pauses, the most painful parts—of abusive prison guards, hunger strikes, and detentions—delievered with a pleasant expression on his face, sometimes even a smile, as if he is trying to reassure his audience that he is okay, that he survived it.

When Tang arrives at the moment when he walks out into the sunlight at JFK airport, however, and first sets foot in the United States, his stories grow fragmented and diffuse. He is less willing to volunteer details. The people in his office are less interested. Years pass in single sentences, wiped away with brief references to jobs and apartments. "I edited an online magazine," he told me when we first met, waving his hand over his early years in the United States. (The "online magazine" that Tang mentioned was actually *Minzhu Luntan,* or Democracy Forum, an influential publication among China's democracy activsts.) "Then I worked in a restaurant. Then I delivered food on a bicycle. In the United States, you have to work. You have to be realistic."

If engaging with life in Flushing was difficult for the majority of Chinese immigrants, the pro-democracy activists who made up Tang's supporters and friends struggled more than most. The min yun, a shorthand term used frequently in Flushing for China's pro-democracy activists (from the words *minzhu*, meaning "democracy," and *yundong*, meaning "campaign"), taken as a whole, were a stubborn group of people: Tiananmen Square activists, China Democracy Party members, human rights defenders, and grassroots organizers. They might have had comfortable lives had they ignored government corruption or stopped agitating for democracy. The simple fact of being in the United States did not often shake their resolve; their interests and obsessions were firmly planted in China. Their bodies were New York, but their thoughts were elsewhere.

• • •

For the min yun in Flushing, the unreality of living in the United States meant that they celebrated life milestones—a birth, a marriage, the arrival of a relative—with relish. These moments pulled Tang and his friends back, grounding them in Flushing with the consolation that, exiles though they might be, they were not alone. Tang Yuanjun might have subsisted forever on this arrangement—no one was more determined to keep protesting; to keep his inner life grounded in China. But then two things happened to plant his feet more firmly on American ground. His daughter arrived in New York on a student visa. And Tang fell in love.

Tang's daughter came to New York City in the late 2000s, despite the objections of her mother, his ex-wife. Tang's wife had divorced him while he was in prison—she had lost her job because of his political activities, and she didn't want to lose the life she had carved out for herself and her daughter during the years he was away. And she didn't want her daughter to follow in his footsteps and find herself barred from ever returning home. Eventually, however, Tang's daughter convinced her that the education she would get in the United States would be worth the risk. It was an opportunity to reconnect with her father. Even after she graduated from university and then law school, Tang's daughter would continue sharing an apartment with her father.

By the time his daughter arrived in the United States, Tang had already met his second wife, an American woman named Jen, while wrapping cabbage and pork dumplings at a dinner party. She had brown hair and an easy, slow-moving smile that put Tang at ease. He had been invited to the party by a mutual acquaintance, another exiled democracy activist, and their host had introduced Tang in a single sentence. "He's a northeasterner," she told Jen, pinpointing Tang's origins in China. "He's a *dongbei ren.*"

Jen spoke Mandarin fluently. She had been fascinated with China for nearly two decades. She wasn't the type of person who needed shared friends or events to make conversation; she had a talent for finding common ground. At the dinner party where they met, Tang set to work making enormous, northeastern-style dumplings. Jen could have eaten three of them and called it a meal. She watched Tang from across the table, serious and quiet, and wondered what was on his mind. By the end of the meal, he was telling his stories, and Jen was listening, rapt.

That night Tang invited her out to dinner. It was not an official date—Jen thought he wanted her to teach him English—but Tang was hard not to like, ferrying her through Flushing in an ancient Subaru station wagon. He had worked in an automotive factory in China—Tang could build car parts—but had never learned to drive one until he took classes in the United States. He had found that he loved driving and drove Jen around like a teenager, fast and ebullient. He liked the freedom of driving, he told her, the ability it gave him to explore, to look at the scenery in his own, self-contained traveling space. A friend of his, knowing his enthusiasm, had given him the old car as a gift. The windows stuck, and everything rattled.

Not long after Jen and Tang met, he agreed to drive a group from New York to Princeton, New Jersey, with Jen in the front passenger seat. She noticed, while on the New Jersey Turnpike, that the hood of the car had come loose and was threatening to fly up, hit the windshield, and, she guessed, kill them all. Tang stopped the car and secured everything with a piece of rope.

Later, on a trip to visit a cousin in Tennessee, Tang was driving too fast on a highway in Virginia, singing old Chinese pop songs at the top of his lungs. The wheels began to rattle, the car swerved, and Tang spun out of control. When the police arrived at the scene, he had them call Jen to translate. That was the end of the Subaru station wagon. Jen boarded a Chinatown bus to Tennessee to see Tang and make certain he was okay. She sat too far in the back of the bus, near the bathroom, and spent hours fighting nausea and anxiety, worrying about Tang. She was in love.

She helped pull his story in the United States into focus. He would never say that she opened the country up for him completely—he was too old and too set in his ways for that—but being with her was like looking at the country through a clear window. He saw what it had to offer.

They married in 2012 but stayed in different cities. Jen had a job in Washington, D.C., that she was committed to, and Tang did not want to leave his life in Flushing. The arrangement was comfortable—they could see each other every weekend, in lives suspended somewhere between China and the United States— and during the weekdays be wholly committed to their jobs. She respected his long hours at the China Democracy Party office. He was humble about his work—he was not looking for accolades and did not kid himself about heroism. She marveled that he did not seem jaded or angry about his experiences in China. No traumas of his past popped up in his behavior; he just wanted to continue his work. He said it was because he had been through so much in prison, it was hard to get angry over trivial things. But she knew of other min yun. Not everyone came out the other side with their equilibrium intact.

On the weekends, the couple resumed their life together. Jen took Tang to museum exhibits, and they visited Mount Vernon. They sat at home together while she tried to explain the jokes in *New Yorker* cartoons. Tang gamely went along to plays and

performances—both of them still remember a particular produc-
tion of *Romeo and Juliet* because Tang made it through the whole
thing without falling asleep. He met her parents in New Jersey
and did his best to make up for the conversations they couldn't
have by cooking meals. He still felt the pull of China; politics
aside, he worried about his parents and disabled brother, who
were growing older and who had long suffered for their association with him. But the tug was not constant. Tang may not have
accepted the United States as his home, but it was the next best
option. He had built a family and a community around himself.
In the gaps between protests and political debates, they were all
finding ways to live in the United States.

• • •

Early in the summer of 2016, Yang Maosheng walked through the
heavy beige door leading to Tang Yuanjun's office. He was not a
dissident exactly. He hadn't spent time in jail or been chased by
local security. He had come to the United States out of curiosity:
he wanted to meet with activists and discuss democracy freely. He
wanted to see what a protest movement looked like in a country
that allowed protest.

At first Yang Maosheng did not, for a number of reasons, appear a likely candidate for an immigrant romance. He was in
his forties, a longtime bachelor. He had the tan, rough-handed
look of a manual laborer and spoke with a thick, slurring accent
common to his hometown of Chongqing, a sprawling municipality
in southwestern China. He was not a particularly smooth talker,
being blunt and quick to anger. "They should ask me how to solve
the Tibetan question!" he told a group gathered in Tang's office.
"I could solve it for them! You just let the Tibetans do what they
want!"

He prided himself on being perfectly capable of forming his
own opinions. He had grown up poor in a rural part of Chongqing
and, like Zhuang, had left home when he was still a teenager. He
found work as a coal miner, but after a few months on the job, he
saw a mine collapse. He did not want to spend his life breathing

in coal dust, waiting to be killed in a mining accident. He moved to Shenzhen and started working construction, building tunnels, roads, and subway stations, eventually becoming a site foreman. His life in Shenzhen wasn't terrible. But then he went online and discovered democracy.

Yang Maosheng booked his ticket to the United States in the first days of 2016, not intending to overstay his six-month visa. He had scheduled the trip to coincide with a conference on Chinese democracy that was being held in Las Vegas. He was not going to be bowled over by anyone's résumé, but he wanted to be in the same room with some of China's most famous dissidents. He wanted to hear what they had to say, breathe the same air, then decide what to do with his life. He planned to fly to New York afterward, spend a few months working off the price of the trip, then head home. Yang Maosheng had made similar trips before, traveling to Thailand to meet with a small exile community there. He had visited other parts of China to support protests that had nothing to do with his life in Shenzhen. ("He's like me," Zhuang would say, after the two became friends. "He can't ignore it when things are unfair.") He had always gone home afterward.

In New York, Yang Maosheng arrived looking for whatever work he could get. He rented a cheap bed in a hostel and spent his mornings in a park on Maple Street, waiting for foremen in need of day laborers to drive up. On his first day, he dressed too nicely, and no one offered him a job. "I didn't think about it!" he said in retrospect. "No one is going to hire you to do construction if you're wearing a clean shirt!" On his off days, he went to Tang's office. He attended meetings and got into arguments. He sat at the long folding table, drank tea, and talked to whoever else happened to be there.

The longer Yang Maosheng was in New York, the more he worried about returning home. Two things made him hesitate. The first was that while on a trip to Thailand, he had met with a bookseller famous for publishing long, salacious biographies of the Chinese elite. In early 2016 the man had reportedly been "disappeared" from his home. It later became clear that the bookseller had been kidnapped by agents from Beijing, transported to

China, and placed in criminal detention. Now Yang Maosheng, in the United States, worried that the Chinese government had been watching when he visited Thailand. If he returned to China, he might get caught up in the investigation of the bookseller.

The second thing pressing Yang Maosheng to stay was a happier one. She was a round-faced woman from Hangzhou, alone in New York and older, like Yang Maosheng. Her name was Little Li.

• • •

Despite his bullishness, Yang Maosheng had earned the respect of some of the more outspoken dissidents who came through Tang's office looking for company, tea, and some of Tang's cooking. Ma Yongtian took a sisterly interest in him. He had the right kind of temperament for activism, she thought. He was angry, but he was a good man.

Yang Maosheng met his future wife at one of Tang's Tuesday meetings. He sat close to the window as the room filled up. Tang went through the details of some recently detained dissidents quickly, then apologized—he would have to go downtown and testify in a member's asylum defense. The person in question had been denied once, and this was his appeal. "He's attended lots of actions," Tang said before he left. "Sometimes it comes down to luck." He shrugged on his suit jacket, clipped his phone in his belt, and left the group in his office to sort themselves out. A few settled in around the folding table, while others took leaflets to hand out along Main Street.

Yang Maosheng was sitting across from a woman who adjusted her glasses on her moon-shaped face firmly while she talked. In the background, a nervous man from Tianjin translated random words of their conversation into English and shouted them out. "People are scared to speak their minds," said the woman. "*Terrified!*" echoed the man from Tianjin. "It's harder and harder to get good information," said Yang Maosheng. "*Lies!*" said the man. Everyone looked at him and let it go.

Little Li had seen Yang Maosheng's name online before. She thought he was too combative. But as they sat across from each other that day, complaining about the difficulties of surviving in China, something happened. Little Li admired his passion. And Yang Maosheng liked how straightforward she was: honest, he thought. Sitting across from each other, they formed a two-person echo chamber. But they were shy. Instead of asking to see Little Li again, a few days later Yang Maosheng approached Ma Yongtian. "He asked me to help him with a 'personal matter'!" Ma Yongtian laughed later. "I said, 'You've come to the right person! Tell me all about it!'"

Ma Yongtian proposed a dinner date, and both agreed. Once romance was officially introduced, they moved quickly: within a week, Little Li and Yang Maosheng were strolling down the streets of Flushing hand in hand. She thought he was reliable and earnest. He was convinced she was one of the smartest people he knew. They were both too old to be blushing; they slipped into their roles quickly and calmly, as if they had been holding hands for years.

. . .

Around the same time Yang Maosheng arrived in New York, something happened in the city that got the attention of the min yun and almost every Chinese immigrant in Flushing. In late 2015, a New York police officer, Peter Liang, fired his gun into a stairwell in Brooklyn and killed unarmed twenty-eight-year-old Akai Gurley. It was one of a flood of high-profile instances in which police officers killed unarmed black men. It was the only case, however, to involve a Chinese policeman. In February 2016 Liang was convicted of manslaughter.

Before this episode, Zhuang had spent little time thinking about politics in his new home. (In his self-enforced isolation from other activists, he barely took note of anything happening outside Wukan.) New York was not the utopia he had imagined, and he had grown accustomed to seeing homeless people begging along Main Street. He sighed at the bureaucracy he encountered trying to apply for asylum and for his green card. But he did not worry about the leaders in Washington, D.C. For the most part, he was content to call the United States a democracy and leave it at that.

When the news hit WeChat, Zhuang discovered that Peter Liang was the only officer in a decade to be indicted for an on-duty shooting. It was a tragedy, Zhuang admitted, but why was Liang the first to be convicted? Where was the policemen's union? "It was a mistake," he told me over dumplings at the East Buffet. "Other police are killing people *on purpose*." He struggled to find the right words to explain. The United States was expected to treat everyone fairly, he said. "Maybe he should be in jail, but then, if he goes to jail, other police officers should go to jail."

In the spring of 2016, Zhuang attended a protest, organized over WeChat by a network of Chinese Americans, in support of Peter Liang. He went out of curiosity as much as solidarity. There were parallels, he felt, between Liang's case and his own experience. No one had cared about Zhuang when he first arrived in New York. No one had respected him. And many people in the United States, he worried, did not care about or respect Chinese people. It was difficult to explain this to his family and friends back in Wukan. The reality, he felt, was something that only other immigrants could understand.

• • •

For the occasion of Little Li's wedding to Yang Maosheng, held just over a month after their romance began, a small crowd gathered in Tang Yuanjun's office. They ate peanut butter candies and cracked sunflower seeds. A young China Democracy Party member arrived with a makeup kit and dabbed at the corners of Yang Maosheng's eyes with concealer. The woman, who worked at a watch store in JFK airport, selling expensive wrist-wear to Chinese tourists, was telling Little Li about a stampede she had witnessed in the terminal. There had been a false alarm about a shooter in the building—she was still feeling a little shaky. Little Li nodded in sympathy, then flashed a grin at Yang Maosheng. "You're getting almost as much makeup as me," she giggled.

At the folding table, an older man who called himself Edmond was introducing Ma Yongtian to everyone who walked in. "This is Ma Yongtian!" he said. "She introduced the two of them!" People might recognize Auntie Ma, Edmond continued, from the video of her blocking Xi Jinping's car in Washington. Ma Yongtian nodded gravely. "They are evil," she said of the Chinese government, addressing the room. "First they turn off the water and the heat. Then sometimes the developer hires thugs to come beat you up. Sometimes they just set your house on fire." Ma Yongtian was ready to die for her cause, she explained. She would happily sacrifice herself if she could wipe out the injustice in the world. The makeup artist nodded in agreement as she swiped concealer on Yang Maosheng's cheeks.

Yang Maosheng had reserved the upstairs room of a Qingdao restaurant not far from Tang's office, and the group walked over together, Tang rolling his computer and an amplifier on the kind of folding dolly that older women used to transport groceries. The couple had selected a man named Gao—a narrow, older man with long wrinkles running down his cheeks and tracing the corners of his mouth—to emcee the wedding. He was often put in charge of the China Democracy Party's more personal events: he wore red shirts for weddings and celebrations and white shirts for funerals. For Little Li and Yang Maosheng, he had put on a red-and-white-striped shirt and affixed a shiny royal blue tie to it with a golden pin. He walked ahead of the group, gleeful at the occasion, waving his long arms as he chattered.

The upstairs space at the restaurant was small and reachable by a narrow, open stairway. Gao placed his glasses low on his nose and evaluated the place, tut-tutting as he went. A handful of tables had been set out in front of a row of red pleather benches. Toward the back a split curtain did a poor job of hiding the hallway to the bathrooms, which offered a natural starting point for the procession of bride and groom. Gao posed Little Li and Yang Maosheng in a stiff marching position, rigidly holding hands. Little Li was instructed to stretch her free arm out to the side and arrange her fingers daintily, as if she were holding a cup of tea. Yang Maosheng grinned self-consciously and let his other hand dangle during their first rehearsal walk from the bathroom curtain to the center of the room.

"Your hand! Your hand!" Gao admonished him. "You must keep it behind your back!" He demanded a repeat. "First," he said, waving his hands wildly, palms flat, "you will walk this way. *Dee-ta dee-ta dee.* And then you will turn! *Dee-ta dee-ta dum.* And then walk! And turn! And face forward!"

"He's an artist," Edmond whispered about Gao. "He can play the piano."

With each practice round, Gao out in front of the couple waving his hands like a conductor, the hilarity around the tables grew. A young man—an aspiring playwright—mimed conducting his own orchestra. "Don't laugh, don't laugh," admonished a small, ancient-looking man with puffy eyes who had spent nine years in a Beijing jail in the 1980s.

"It's like they're little children!" shouted Ma Yongtian.

"I thought we were starting?" Tang wrestled with the music. "Are we starting?"

Gao declared that the wedding would start. People shifted their bags around and set up their phones and cameras. Edmond joked that an acupuncturist named Chen looked like a North Korean deputy. "Hey!" he said to me. "Did you hear about the North Korean ambassador? He defected to South Korea!"

"Stop talking about politics!" Tang called out from where he was setting up his computer. "It's a wedding!"

"Play the music!" Gao called to Tang Yuanjun, who smilingly put on a wedding march. Another China Democracy Party member pulled rose petals out of a pink plastic bag and flung them in the air as the couple processed. When they reached the front, Gao addressed the room. "Welcome to the bride and groom!" he said, mostly addressing the tiny video camera on the tripod. "Little Li is from Hangzhou," he observed, "and Yang Maosheng is from Sichuan."

"Chongqing!" called out the old man.

"Ah, yes, Chongqing. We are all far from home." Gao called

the priest up onstage, who brought out his Bible and took the pair of them through the usual vows. They swore to support each other through sickness and health, rich or poor, happy or sad. And then Yang Maosheng pulled two little red boxes out of his jacket pocket, and they held the two rings up for a picture, then shuffled them onto each other's fingers. "You can play a little music," urged Gao, and Tang turned the volume up on the computer, pumping a hit song from the late 1970s through the speaker he had lugged over, called "The Moon Represents My Heart." "You ask how deep my love is," the song begins. "My passion is steadfast, my love unchanging."

A parade of guests stood up to speak. Tang had attended a total of forty-four weddings, he said, and this was the sincerest. Ma Yongtian explained that she had tried to play matchmaker before, but this was the first time it had worked ("Start a business!" Edmond yelled from the table). Edmond said he had rarely met a young person with such an interest in Chinese traditional culture as Little Li. "If you ever have a fight, it'll be Yang Maosheng's fault!" he added.

Gao got up again and spoke to the compact camera. "We are all overseas," he said. "We don't have our families here. But look around! We have a special kind of brotherhood. We are one big family, and Little Li is our sister. We will take care of your children! And they have found some happiness!" Yang Maosheng and Little Li were already wiping their eyes.

"Yang Maosheng, would you like to leave a message for your parents?" he asked, gesturing toward a camera that had been set up on a tripod.

Yang stood forward, clutching Little Li's hand, wiping tears from his face and blurting out a stuttering, abrupt "Thank you so much for your years of support." Little Li told her father, long dead, that she was sorry he couldn't see her happiest day. She told her mother to take care of herself. Yang Maosheng draped himself over her shoulders in an awkward, supportive hug.

Gao ended things with a flourish. "Don't forget the promises you made here tonight!" he said with a wave of his hands, an odd sweeping gesture as if to include the two dinner tables in the promises. And then he pulled out a ball of chocolate wrapped in tinfoil, opened it, and stuck it into Yang's mouth. "Welcome!" he said in English, urging Little Li to bite off half of it. "To your sweet sweet sweet home!!"

15

Personal Shopping

代购 / *Dàigōu*

Little Yan and Karen, squeezed between the computer tables at LIBI, would not have considered themselves particularly entrepreneurial. They both liked to picture themselves, sometime in the future, neatly dressed and sitting behind a desk at a doctor's office. Little Yan believed she would have been perfectly happy raising children in Wukan, and Karen had felt content working in the company her college boyfriend had chosen for the both of them in Henan. But then they had come to the United States. They'd grown resourceful.

By the time Karen signed up for her second semester at LIBI, she had recovered from her breakup. She could talk about her former boyfriend magnanimously. He was a good person, she said. He just couldn't withstand the pressure of separation. She didn't blame him. She had, however, in her year of loneliness, decided on two things she would need in life to be content. She would need a family—she couldn't help looking at Little Yan with some envy, a husband to go home to, and a child coming over soon. But that was hard to control and could come later. Now Karen was determined to focus on her career. She never again wanted to feel as desperate as she had in her first year in the United States. She wanted to make enough of her own money to feel comfortable.

Karen had spent more than a year living on ramen noodles and washing her clothes at night in the bathroom sink. She had logged countless hours in the basement print shop, pressing logos onto thousands of shirts and banners. She had been terrified of losing the work. Now, however, she had fully paid off her debt. She asked her boss if she could work part time, to make studying for her LIBI classes easier. When he looked angry, she revised her request to a single day off. She walked away from the frenzied printing shop, assuring her boss that she would be back. Two days later, instead of returning, she started looking for another job. She scrolled through online ads for anything that would force her to speak English.

If Little Yan had had time to think, her aspirations might have mirrored her classmate's. But thinking about her quality of life would have been a waste of time. She was exhausted from months of night classes. On weekdays, she worked full time before her first class began at six p.m. Every cent she made was spent on their rent and essentials. When the money was not enough, she watched the numbers in their savings account go down, every dollar an extra weight on her shoulders. Every time Zhuang made money, she felt, he spent it on more frivolous things. He had recently recruited one of his admirers, a graduate student from Guangxi Province, to help him buy an expensive camera. He needed it, he told her, for a new business venture.

Little Yan had suggested that Zhuang look into driving for Uber, joining the many immigrants who had signed on with the company. Their landlord in the Tudor-style house had been driving for Uber as well as a Chinese limo company. Zhuang liked the man but admitted he could not work like that. "I want to have a life," he said. He told Little Yan she just didn't understand. "I don't speak English," he snapped at her. "How am I going to talk to people?" He listed the expenses that would go into becoming a driver—he would have to buy a new car and pay for a license.

"Your thinking is too simple!" he told his wife.

• • •

On a bright day in late April at the East Buffet, Zhuang was sitting with me at a table by the window, his nose buried in his phone, when Chen Tai rolled by in her little red apron and cap. "Little Zhuang, are you working?" she hollered, her voice gurgling. When he told her yes, she beamed. "It's so hard for us in this country. We work and work and work, and what are we? We're still poor."

Zhuang nodded, smiling across at me sheepishly. His new job, he had just explained, was getting off the ground. He had started a new venture he felt sure would work out. He just needed the patronage of a few wealthy people back in China.

He had decided to start doing *daigou*, or personal shopping, joining the thousands of Chinese immigrants in the United States buying luxury goods locally and selling them in China. The idea had come to him late in the winter, while he was working for an upscale karaoke parlor, parking Maseratis and Lamborghinis. He made a few trips to the Woodbury Outlet Mall in the New York suburbs and photographed the purses and shoes he saw there. He had been to the outlet mall before with Little Yan, to buy the North Face vest he prized and the high heels and purses Little Yan sent back to her sisters. The stuff at Woodbury Outlet Mall was part of the mythology of American living. You sent it back, and people assumed you were rich like the rest of the population. This job would feed the disconnect between his life in the United States and the story he told back home.

Daigou was an industry only a few years old, made possible by the arrival of smartphones. People would buy high-end purses and shirts at outlet malls for a fraction of their cost in China and advertise them on their social media, then ship over whatever their friends had ordered. It was, on the one hand, smuggling. They were avoiding Chinese taxes and taking advantage of disparities in global pricing. On the other hand, *daigou* existed in a legal gray area. Chinese people had long made a sport out of dodging the country's high import taxes, and as far as anyone knew, they were breaking no U.S. laws by sending back a handful of luxury items every month.

Before that day in the East Buffet, the only people who had seen Zhuang's outlet mall photos were his friends. A few days earlier, however, one of his acquaintances had added his name to a chat group full of wealthy factory bosses around Shenzhen. Just before Chen Tai rolled her cart up to the table, the first factory boss call came in. As a waiter slipped a white teapot onto the table in front of Zhuang, he hunched over his phone, listening to a message. The deep voice was slurring slightly—it was two a.m. in China. "I think I would like some polo shirts," it said, and asked what size shirts were available.

Zhuang jumped to record a response message: he would have to check the stores. He had previously photographed some large polo shirts, and now he sent them over. "Not like that, not like that," the man replied. "I want some other ones." He was looking for shirts made to resemble soccer jerseys, with white stripes down the sleeves. The pair of them went back and forth for nearly an hour. By the time Chen Tai came by, Zhuang had sold three shirts and a pair of shoes. The man was still undecided on an expensive watch.

"I am working!" Zhuang said, grinning.

• • •

Chen Tai had come to Zhuang's table to gossip. Her daughter had gotten pregnant soon after her wedding, and the older woman had stopped looking after her relative's child for a while so she could look after her grandson. She found a photo on her phone of the baby taking a bath. She zoomed in on the baby's face and held it up for everyone to see. "There he is!" she beamed at Zhuang. "He's a little fatty." She moved the photo down the baby's body with a little flourish. "And there's his little penis!" she told Zhuang, full of pride. "He's a very good baby."

Then Chen Tai asked, "How is your wife?" She knew a little about their struggles. The walls were thin in Chen Tai's apartment.

"She's fine," Zhuang said. "Studying to work in a doctor's office."

She asked after Zhuang's son. "What is his zodiac sign?" When Zhuang told her—his son had been born in the year of the

snake—she assured him that Kaizhi would be a smart, resourceful son. She rummaged in her cart and came up with two sesame
buns on a plate. They were for good luck. "If you believe it's true,
then it's true!" she said of the zodiac. "If you don't believe it, it's
not."

"The Fujianese know a lot about this stuff!" said a woman
from another cart, passing by.

"I know a guy who had two kids, a tiger and a dragon," Chen
Tai told Zhuang. "That's really bad." The sons fought so often, the
guy got sick. Chen Tai was a sheep, and her husband was a snake.
She had known another guy who was a sheep, and he had married
a tiger. "He never would have married her, had he known!"

Zhuang was a pig, a sign known for diligence, honesty, and
generosity. It would help in business, if you believed in that kind
of thing. He wasn't superstitious, but he was hopeful. The wealthy
man who had made those first orders expanded his requirements
on a nightly basis, spending upward of two thousand dollars. Little Yan could imagine what he looked like, his feet up on a desk,
bottle of *baijiu,* a Chinese liquor made of sorghum, nearby. "He's
got little feet," she declared. "But he wears really large shirts." He
was short and fat, she had decided. He had too much money and
not enough to do.

• • •

By the time Zhuang started his new business, there were hundreds of groups on WeChat discussing discounting practices and
compiling guides to outlet malls. Zhuang could use the app to
negotiate with customers and to look for discounts. He could even
use it to get paid: one feature of Zhuang's account, conspicuously
absent from the English version of WeChat, was a service called
Red Envelope, intended to facilitate the transfer of money from
friends and family members, like VenMo or PayPal. Money transferred through WeChat would show up in a Chinese account, in
yuan. Zhuang would accept a payment, and as soon as it arrived,
he would buy whatever the customer wanted. He would take a
small percentage off the top—it varied according to no specific

formula—then send it to the customer in China. Shipping centers already dotted Main Street, and they happily accepted the increased business from immigrants selling *daigou*. The system was so convenient that by 2014, one consulting company estimated that the market value of *daigou* purchases ran as high as $7.6 billion.

The money transferred to Zhuang, however, landed only in a Chinese bank account. The WeChat groups that Zhuang joined helped him get his money from China to the United States. People who were traveling back to China might offer to exchange their dollars for yuan. Zhuang would transfer money, via WeChat, into their Chinese accounts, and they would hand him cash. Other times the exchange was not so straightforward. Zhuang answered an ad placed in one of the groups, from a man looking to exchange yuan for dollars. He met the man who had placed the advertisement in the backseat of a car parked on the street. He transferred the yuan into an account via Red Envelope, the man handed him a wad of cash, and Zhuang left, the two having barely exchanged a word.

Meanwhile Zhuang was enjoying his new visibility. Friends and friends of friends might buy from him, or they might not. but they would all see a photo of him well dressed in the middle of the outlet mall, looking like he was doing well. One of Zhuang's old flames—the woman he had taken, with her friend, on a weekend-long date to the ocean, and who had never contacted him afterward—got in touch to tell him that she really regretted blowing him off.

Zhuang threw himself into *daigou* for two months straight. Little Yan looked on with skepticism but let him try. He linked up with friends in China who could spread the word about his reliability and the quality of his goods. His WeChat groups provided advice on where to look for the best deals and notices when a client was searching for a specific model of shoe or shirt. He drove to Woodbury at least once a week. Through WeChat, he arranged to fill his car with a passenger or two who could help with some of the tolls on the highway. He collected coupons and tried to charm the salespeople with his tiny arsenal of English niceties.

He also collected credit cards that would give him discounts at specific stores. Selling *daigou* had the added benefit, he explained, of improving his credit score. He was cautious about using them, though. He had heard that people in the United States frequently ran up credit card bills that they could not pay back. Zhuang knew how to spend money, but he was not quite sure how people spent money that they didn't actually have.

Polo shirts were popular, and Adidas shoes. Some of the people who sold *daigou* specialized in American vitamins and supplements. They joined cheap bulk grocers like Costco and took home huge supplies of vitamin B_1, protein powders, and supplements that were said to encourage weight loss. Zhuang stayed away from this side of the business; he preferred the panache of clothing. On a spring day, after his most reliable customer put in a new order for a different polo shirt, Zhuang stopped in on a department store off Broadway in Midtown Manhattan. He walked confidently toward the back, where the elevators were. Ornate and brass, they had an old dial mounted above their doors showing the cars moving up and down. Zhuang headed to the top floor. He rifled through the racks and then walked up to the saleswoman watching over that section.

"Today. Coupon?" he asked hopefully, holding up a shirt.

The woman, taller than Zhuang and wearing bright red lipstick, smiled in recognition. "I'll look for you, honey," she said.

Zhuang grinned back at her. "Sorry, my English is bad."

"Don't worry about it, honey," she said. "I didn't speak any when I got here, either. You gotta study, that's it."

Zhuang smiled. "Oh!" he said, halfway grasping her meaning.

"I spoke French," she said. "French and Arabic. But no English."

Zhuang nodded in sympathy. "English," he said, "is very difficult."

• • •

Zhuang told Little Yan that she had to wait just a bit while he built up his clientele. In his first month, he came out a measly few hundred dollars ahead—he had purchased the new iPhone and bought an E-ZPass for his frequent trips to the mall—and he was just figuring it all out. By the end of his second month, he had earned a full two thousand dollars. And that, he assured her, was only the beginning. "Once I'm really established, I'll be making around ten thousand dollars a month." That was what the most successful people made. And it wasn't that hard, he assured his wife. He just needed time.

"He's working hard," Little Yan said to Karen, sitting in her office chair over a class break. But she admitted it wasn't secure. Women could not live on expected future successes, she thought. They had no choice. She and Karen were grounded in the reality of their days.

Karen had found a second job at a website that connected American customers to cheap factories in China, offering discount prices on everything from iPad-like tablet computers to furniture and clothing. It was cheap and efficient and frequently befuddling for the American customers who stumbled onto the site not understanding where they had ended up. Karen would answer their calls, take their orders, and listen to their complaints. Sometimes a customer would dismiss her out of hand the moment they heard her accent. "Can I talk to someone who speaks English?" they would ask. And she would hand off the phone to someone else.

Karen quickly realized that her salary—ten dollars an hour— was just enough to cover her expenses. Before taxes, she was making four hundred dollars a week. She did not want to revisit the feeling she had had at the print shop, that she had no other options, that she could never quit. "I want to start working on the weekends," she told her roommate. "I think I want to paint nails."

"You won't make any money at it at first," her roommate warned. She told Karen to go online and pick a salon, but only stay there a month. She could get trained, and then get out. "It's not worth staying at the first place that hires you." Karen's roommate had a better nose for this kind of thing than she did, the ruthlessness of a couple of years working in salons.

Starting work at a nail salon in your third year in the United

States might seem like a step backward, but it was common for a student to use her weekends to make a little extra money. And Karen was a student now. During her university days in Henan, she had taken her classes for granted, and she had barely noticed them in Ohio, but in Flushing school had significance. Being a student meant you were not stranded in a menial job with bad pay and no other options. It meant you were moving toward something else.

The first salon that hired Karen was in northern Brooklyn. On her first day, she walked in trying to exude the kind of toughness she had seen in her roommate. She would bide her time, see how the shop was run, and decide whether to stay. It was dark in the shop, similar to the long, unlit storefront where Little Yan had spent her first summer. The boss, a woman, had been running the place for years. She could be friendly when she wanted, but for the most part she wore a dour look of world-weariness.

"You pay fifty dollars up front," she told Karen, "for training."

Karen looked the woman in the face. "Could I give you the money in the afternoon?"

The dour look washed over the woman's face. "Fine," she said. "You learn by watching. So you can watch."

The three women who had shared the van with Karen took their places behind a row of desks and set out tools. Each woman cleaned her area, set out towels, and organized the nail clippers and sponges in her plastic cart. Little sterilizing units sat behind them, with a tray on top cluttered with implements.

After about an hour and a handful of clients, the store owner walked over to Karen. "You pay the fifty dollars now," she said, "or you can find your own way home." The woman's face had hardened.

Karen barely knew where she was. She hadn't seen any buses passing by. It wasn't much of a choice. Karen handed over the fifty dollars she had brought with her. She worked there a month, learning to clip off cuticles and lay on an unblemished coat of paint.

Then her roommate recommended a job in a salon in the

suburbs north of the city, where people might tip more and the pay would be better. Karen did not get her fifty dollars back when she left the place in Brooklyn.

The new salon was more relaxed, with regular customers and a steady stream of tourists, but it was no place to make friends. The women there were assigned customers through a pen-and-paper notebook system. As soon as a salon worker finished with a customer, she was supposed to put her name in the book, getting in line. Some of the women, however, had come up with ways to cheat the system and sneak to the top of the line, writing their names down before they finished or skipping the line altogether. In slow moments, some would rush to the front of the store when they recognized the person coming in as a good tipper. Karen told herself that the other women needed the money more than she did.

• • •

In Karen's shared room off Main Street, there was more than enough heartbreak to go around in the spring of 2016. A new roommate, only a teenager, spent her days burrowed in her bedsheets, crying over the stepmother who had driven her out of the house. The girl was waiting to turn eighteen so she could start working, relying on the money her biological mother was sending from China. Karen's older roommate, the nail salon worker, had broken up with a longtime boyfriend. Families, in Karen's corner of Flushing, were fragmented things.

The older roommate had been with her boyfriend for nearly as long as she had been in the States. They had met at her first job in her first nail salon. Both of them were divorced and had left families behind in China. Then out of the blue, the man announced that he was bringing his son to the United States so he could get an American-style education. It was decided that the child couldn't live in New York without his mother. The boyfriend insisted that he couldn't split up the family. His son and ex-wife would both move in with him. And he was going to try to make a go of it with his ex-wife. They were planning on spending some time together, he said, and then, if all went well, remarrying.

Karen watched her roommate shed a few silent tears, then twist her hair back and busy herself in the kitchen. Once the woman arrived, Karen's roommate would prepare food and take it over. She would help the reunited family however she could. It was the practical, warmhearted thing to do.

Then the roommate found a new boyfriend—a masseur in a nail salon—and protected him jealously. One night Karen overheard him asking her roommate whether to invite Karen to join them at dinner. "No, she's busy," said the roommate. Karen laughed at the thought that she might steal the boyfriend. He was older! And while she didn't have anything against working in a nail salon, she couldn't imagine dating a man who worked in one. "I don't think it's *bad* to work in a nail salon," she told me thoughtfully. "But how could I be interested in a man like that?!"

Karen had chatted with a handful of men online, but most of them were working at restaurants outside the city, circling back to New York every few months. The opportunity to actually meet anyone was slim. Karen's friend Isobel, the woman she had first encountered at the immigration agency in China, met a Chinese man online and had to move to Florida just to start dating.

Little Yan watched Karen sympathetically. She remembered what it was like to be young, she told me. "If Karen was in China, she'd have no trouble! She's smart and pretty. People would be lining up to marry her." Little Yan's own frustrations were of a different kind. She was responsible for cooking, cleaning, earning, studying, and worrying about their son. She was posting articles on WeChat, arguments not only for divorce but for forgoing men altogether. "My husband thinks I'm his maid!" read one. "More divorced women are choosing to stay single!" said another. "When someone is bitten by a snake once, they'll be afraid of coiled rope for years."

• • •

In the summer after their second semester, somewhere in the fog of holding multiple jobs and doing homework, both Karen and Little Yan received letters. Karen had been waiting for months, in suspense, for her letter, and when it was delivered to her Flushing apartment, her heart jumped when she opened it. It was her green card. The card had a dull green banner across the top and featured the passport photo she had sent with her application. It wasn't much to look at, but she beamed at it. She did not celebrate in public; that would rub it in the face of all her friends who were still waiting. But she had achieved, in three short years, one of the most sought-after milestones in Flushing. With her debt paid and her status in the United States secure, she officially had no one but herself to worry about.

The letter for Little Yan and Zhuang arrived at Zhuang's father's house in Wukan in early June. Zhuang's family put it in a clear plastic sleeve, and someone took a photo of it with their phone, forwarding it to Zhuang. The couple peered at the document, which had Kaizhi's name at the top: "The U.S. Department of Homeland Security, Citizenship, and Immigration Services has approved admission into the United States for the above named alien." Little Yan carefully deciphered each line, then came to a spot in the middle of the second paragraph: "Presentation of this document will authorize a transportation line to accept the named bearer, whose photograph is attached, on board for travel to the United States on or before July 31st, 2016." She looked at it again, read it out loud, then glanced at the date in the corner. Kaizhi would have to leave for the United States within the next two months or lose his chance.

16

Strangers

陌生人 / *Mòshēngrén*

Little Yan and Zhuang had often imagined what it would be like to bring their son to the United States. They had expected it to happen after they had both been issued green cards and were free to travel. At first they had imagined going to Hong Kong together, sometime in the late fall of 2016, asking a family member to accompany Kaizhi on the ferry from Shenzhen. And then they had pushed the date back a little, to the lunar new year in 2017. Zhuang hoped his business as a personal shopper would be established by then, and he hoped to have his green card. When Little Yan had time off from her job, she went with Zhuang to the outlet mall, helping him buy shoes and bags. She laid their purchases out on the floor of their room, took short films of what they had bought, and posted them on WeChat. "We're sending this to friends in China," she wrote. "Our room isn't big enough for all the stuff. We need a bigger room!"

When the letter came giving Kaizhi official permission to travel to the United States, Little Yan worried again that Zhuang needed a real job. Trying to grow a business that was barely legal seemed insecure. Little Yan pushed Zhuang, again, to look into driving for a car service, either one based in Flushing or an online option. She left the house at eight each weekday morning and didn't get back until close to eleven at night—a punishing schedule even without a child to take care of.

Little Yan still hoped to be able to spend a week or two getting to know her son again before hopping on an airplane with him. They visited their lawyer again to ask if she could. "I think it should be safe for Little Yan to travel to China," Zhuang argued. "It's me who needed the asylum." But he again warned against it. It could affect her green card application. "What do I do?" she asked. "Between a green card and my son, can I only choose one?"

Finally, Little Yan sent messages to her acquaintances on WeChat—was anyone in China planning to come back to New York in the next two months? A woman Little Yan had known briefly from her home health aide classes answered. She had traveled back to her hometown, Wenzhou, and was planning to fly back to the United States in late July. She would bring Kaizhi. But in exchange, Zhuang and Little Yan would have to pay for her plane ticket. The woman agreed to travel to Guangdong and pick Kaizhi up.

It was the best option they had, but Zhuang worried about his son. He would be alone with a stranger in Wenzhou for a few days before getting on the plane for New York. What if the woman's house wasn't equipped for a child? What if she turned out to be unreliable? Zhuang decided to send his father and sister-in-law with Kaizhi to Wenzhou. They would ease Kaizhi's transition and could report back if the woman seemed unfit. Zhuang sent money for the train tickets.

Meanwhile Little Yan set about checking prices for two plane tickets to New York. It was going to cost them over a thousand dollars for each ticket. She worried that they were spending the last of their savings just before their son was to arrive. "If we keep going down this road," she worried, "we will not be able to pay for ourselves."

• • •

Zhuang had his own list of worries. They would need to move, he predicted. The Tudor-style house where they were living was close quarters. The landlord's two children were friendly but sometimes rambunctious. It was important to their father that they study in the evenings, and a little boy to play with might be deemed a distraction. The two tenants living in the basement were unfriendly. If Kaizhi cried all night when he arrived, if he was rowdy or played too loudly, he might keep everyone awake.

In Zhuang's ideal world, he would rent a new apartment directly. He had built up his credit score by now, adding to his selection of IDs with a carefully chosen stack of credit cards. In an apartment, he could rent out one room to another immigrant, and his family could have the run of the rest of the place to themselves. He would take care of Kaizhi while Little Yan went to work and took classes. "It's an investment," he explained. "When she graduates, she will be able to get a much better job."

When they fought, he wondered whether Little Yan really believed he was lazy. That he didn't want to go to school and study himself! But she would never support him as he supported her! She thought only about herself, he groused, while he had to think about himself and her. He still hoped he could grow his personal shopping business and make three or four thousand dollars a month—more than enough for everyone. But he needed time. And once Kaizhi arrived, he wouldn't be able to drive to the outlet malls three times a week.

Zhuang, who himself had been shuttled back and forth as a child, thought practically about space and discipline. Kaizhi was used to the village and would need space to run around. He might make messes. How would he get Kaizhi to listen to his mother and father—two people he barely knew? "In the United States," he mused, half-joking, "you can't hit your kids. I will have to think of other strategies."

Zhuang's father had been to Wenzhou and approved of the woman's apartment—her sister had children, and it was well equipped. The ticket that Little Yan purchased was for July 27, three days before Kaizhi's window to enter the United States would expire. The night before, she couldn't sleep. She had read too many new reports, lately, of airplanes falling out of the sky. "Airplanes are safer than cars!" Zhuang told her. But it didn't help. She was awake early, and went through the motions of her day, sitting in class at the hour the plane would be taking off from Wenzhou. She had the woman's WeChat contact but was letting things be. She counted the hours the plane would be in the air. And then a message came through over WeChat. Little Yan didn't see it until the class took its daily break.

"Your son was too loud, and they wouldn't let us get on the plane," the woman had written. He was too difficult to handle, she complained.

Little Yan's stomach dropped. She called Zhuang and left LIBI to head back to their room.

"She can't keep a child quiet for ten minutes to get on the plane?!" Zhuang said, when Little Yan arrived back home. He called his father to try and get the whole story. Little Yan forgot about airplanes. What if her son was about to be kidnapped? She listened as Zhuang's father's voice buzzed in the background.

"Late?" Zhuang said. As Little Yan listened, he told his father, calmly, that he would buy a ticket for the next day's flight. He would do it immediately. And that she couldn't miss the plane.

He hung up, then exploded. "Late!" he said. "She showed up at the airport late! With a child!" She had tried to blame it on their kid. "Her friends gave her too much to carry! She got stopped at security. She's traveled before, she should know what you can and can't carry on!" After the woman went through security, she had so much luggage to carry that she could not manage even to hold Kaizhi's hand. He had been forced to trot after her as she ran through the airport, crying louder and louder the farther they went, too upset to keep up.

Little Yan couldn't think about it. She chose not to. She had made so many compromises, and it had all led to this—her son getting dragged around behind a stranger. Zhuang seething with anger, started making calls, spending the last of their savings to purchase two last-minute tickets for the next day. If the woman missed that flight, Kaizhi would miss his opportunity. Little Yan would just move back to China.

She couldn't take the suspense.

• • •

The next day Zhuang and Little Yan took a handful of friends out to lunch before driving to JFK airport. She had not been so calm this time. She had sent message after message to the woman, making sure the pair of them got on the plane. In the end, the woman was contrite and arrived hours early, before the airport even opened its doors.

Zhuang dressed up that morning, wearing nice jeans and a blue Beatles T-shirt. He pulsed with energy, calling his family in China, pouring tea, laying out the schedule for the day. He didn't want to be late. He told everyone he wanted to leave for the airport an hour and a half in advance of the plane's scheduled arrival. He didn't want to be stuck in traffic and miss his son. He picked out a noodle shop a few blocks away, on Kissena Boulevard. It was good and served food quickly. They wouldn't have time, today, to linger over tea.

Little Yan ate quickly. "Young kids are really adaptable," she said to the table. "He won't even remember the trip over."

"You'll see," Zhuang said. "He won't know us when he gets here—that's natural. I think he'll feel at home, though, within three days. It won't take very much time at all."

Zhuang had prepared a handful of toys—mechanical cars that played disco music—to present to Kaizhi when they all got home. Little Yan had bought a set of new clothes. It was normal, in China, to leave a child behind with grandparents. It would be an adjustment for Kaizhi, they told themselves at lunch and piling into the car, but a quick one. Kids that age are resilient. As long as they feel safe, they don't mind where they are. Zhuang had already installed a carseat in the back of his tiny Honda. He had put it in the middle of the seat, so he would be able to see Kaizhi in the rearview mirror while he drove.

As the pair of them drove to the airport, they imagined their son into being. He had been quiet on the train ride up, happy as long as he was with his grandfather. "Of course he cried at the airport!" Zhuang said, tapping the steering wheel nervously at a red light. "You can't expect to just drag a little kid around like that!"

"He's only three," Little Yan said. "He can't be that naughty."

"He wouldn't be naughty at all if he had just stayed in Wukan!" Zhuang said, suddenly defensive, pulling into the intersection. "Your parents didn't know how to raise him!"

"And yours did?" Little Yan said.

"My father knows how to raise grandchildren!" Zhuang said. "It was too late by the time he got to Wukan!"

"I felt better when he was at my parents' house."

"You don't know anything!"

"Well, you know best."

"I do know best!"

"Well, I don't know where all this wisdom comes from."

Zhuang was yelling at the traffic in front of him. "You don't have to know!"

• • •

When Zhuang and Little Yan arrived at the airport, they lingered for a moment under a sign that read WELCOME TO JOHN F. KENNEDY INTERNATIONAL AIRPORT, WHERE AMERICA GREETS THE WORLD!

The drive had taken less than half the time that Zhuang had allotted, and the couple arrived well before Kaizhi's plane. The arrivals board listed the flight from China as *landing*, and it would continue landing for the next half hour. Zhuang pushed his way through a crowd waiting along the barrier that separated the arrivals from the people waiting to greet their loved ones. He leaned against the barrier nervously, squinting at the people flowing out into the hall. Little Yan stood farther back, her phone clutched in her hand. She had texted the woman from Wenzhou when they parked at the airport but had decided to wait for the flight's status to change before she tried again. She shifted from foot to foot, waiting.

"It has been landing for a half a day," Zhuang murmured, grinning at his nervousness. "We should text her and go find a place to sit down." Just then the flight status changed: *on the ground*. Little Yan texted madly, asking the Wenzhou woman about the flight. It had lasted fifteen hours. She hoped Kaizhi had been able to sleep. "Tell her to call us when she gets through customs," Zhuang said over her shoulder. "Tell her we're going to go sit down."

Wandering through the airport, Zhuang had met an acquaintance from Flushing. She was waiting to pick up a tour group from China and invited everyone to sit down at a table with her. She had worked at the karaoke place where Zhuang used to park cars, and they joked about it while Little Yan hugged her small Calvin Klein backpack, staring at her phone.

"They make all the valets say, 'I'll take it to the parking lot in the back!'" Zhuang said. "And there is no parking lot in the back!" He was doing a fair imitation of relaxation, laughing too loudly, stealing glances at Little Yan's phone. He told the woman he would be moving to an apartment soon.

"You could rent out your living room," she offered. "I've got someone staying in my living room right now, and they pay me four hundred fifty dollars." The supermarket with the wall of room listings had closed, she told him. He should try the other wall, near the bubble tea shop.

Little Yan's phone rang, and the whole table fell silent. "Where are you?" she asked. She grunted a few times, then hung up.

"Did you tell her to text us?" Zhuang asked.

"I did."

Zhuang clicked his tongue—a barely audible *tssk*—and said he was worried that they might miss her coming out. "You never know with this woman," he said. "And you didn't tell her."

The group sat in relative silence, Zhuang's friend talking about her job and pending asylum case.

Finally a text came through on Little Yan's phone. "They're coming out!" she said.

Zhuang pushed through the crowd to the barrier again, trying to get as close as possible to the spot where people were coming out. Little Yan again stood farther back, peering around a limo driver holding up a sign. Her eyes ran over every person who emerged, and she stretched her neck to see if there was a child hidden behind anyone's legs. Then her phone rang again, she answered, and then she was running toward the door to the outside. She looked up and down the crowded sidewalk.

There was Kaizhi, dwarfed by suitcases, his arms held stiffly down his front, one thumb gripped in the fist of his other hand. Little Yan ran to him but then slowed to a stop a few feet away, as if she were approaching a wild animal. Kaizhi stared up at her, his eyes glistening. Both his tear ducts were blocked, like Zhuang's right one, and it made him look plaintive, on the verge of tears. When Little Yan reached her hand out to him, he shook his head and backed up a step. He looked up at her as if she were a giant.

A short-haired woman appeared in the midst of the suitcases. "He was good!" she said, stepping in front of the little boy. "He slept most of the way." Kaizhi was leaning against a concrete pole.

Zhuang came threading through the crowd—"*Aiya!* Why did no one tell me!?"—and walked a direct line toward his son. He crouched down in front of him, and Kaizhi disappeared around the pole, hugging it. "Kaizhi!" said Zhuang. "Hello! I am your baba." He held out a hand, and Kaizhi retreated, working his way back toward the woman from the plane. He knew her better than anyone. She was the only person he wanted to touch.

Zhuang put a gentle hand on his son's back, crab-walking around the pole to keep up with him. "That's your mama," he said, gesturing toward Little Yan. "We're going to take you home with us." Zhuang switched to his local dialect, the language Kaizhi would have been speaking with his grandfather in Wukan. He grabbed the hem of Kaizhi's sweatshirt, keeping in contact as his son reached for the hand of the woman from Wenzhou.

"Is this all your stuff?" Zhuang asked the woman, suddenly polite. "We'll help you carry it all. You must be hungry. We will take you out to eat."

It was a half-hearted invitation, which the woman turned down. Zhuang took hold of two of her suitcases and Little Yan took a third, leaving the woman free to hold Kaizhi's hand. Little Yan opened an umbrella, protecting Kaizhi from the summer sun. They piled into an elevator in the car park, taking it up to the top level. Kaizhi slipped his hand out of the Wenzhou woman's and folded in on himself, caving in until he was almost sitting on the parking lot ground. He did not want to get into Zhuang's car.

• • •

The first noise Kaizhi made in the United States was a little *hmm* of interest when Little Yan handed him a tiny stuffed monkey after he'd settled into his carseat. He had kept up his resistance silently, trying not to allow the straps of the carseat around his arms with stiff elbows. When he finally sat down, hugging the stuffed animal, Little Yan dabbed at his eyes. It didn't matter that he was unresponsive. He had gotten on the plane, and the plane had not fallen out of the sky. She could dab at his eyes if she needed to.

Kaizhi's eyes drooped on the ride back to the Tudor-style house in Fresh Meadows, but every time it looked like he might fall asleep, he jerked himself awake. Zhuang dropped off the woman from Wenzhou and offered, again, to buy her lunch. The family drove home. The house was, for the moment, empty of everyone but Zhuang and his new family. He made tea and texted his friends in China the good news. He poured some water for Kaizhi and then made a show of drinking it, slurping it down and wiping his mouth after each sip with a long, sloppy *ahhh*. Kaizhi smiled. Zhuang pulled out the two radio-controlled cars that he had purchased and crashed one into his toe. "*Aiya!*" he yelped in mock pain.

Kaizhi sat on a child-size red chair, clutching his stuffed animal, smiling shyly at the cars. Little Yan crouched next to him and showed him how the remote control worked while Zhuang poured the tea. Kaizhi moved from the chair to the ground. He grabbed one of the cars and looked at the bottom, examining how it worked, and everyone around him grinned.

"What kind of car is this?" asked Zhuang, holding up a tiny van.

"A breadbox car!" Kaizhi said.

Zhuang beamed at him. "See!" he said. "In two days we won't seem like strangers!"

17

Services

服务 / *Fúwù*

In the foyer of the Chinese congregation at the Korean Presbyterian Church, volunteers had established a streamlined process to welcome newcomers. When Karen arrived on a Sunday in late summer, two women handed her a nametag and an information sheet to fill out. She wrote down her name, birth date, and contact information. And then they were allowed to enter the chapel, a beautiful walnut-colored space with a sweeping, curved ceiling that was covered in slats of dark wood. The women pointed Karen to a handful of rows toward the back that were reserved for first-timers. The pews were almost all full.

During her three years in Flushing, Karen had made friends. One of her closest, a woman from her English class whom Karen had taken to calling her older sister—*jiejie*—had advised her to come visit the church. It was, the woman said, a good place to meet people. Karen's friend had met her own fiancé at a church, and barely a year after she had arrived in the States, the pair were engaged to be married and were buying an apartment in Flushing. Karen took a day off from her nail salon side job and went to church.

Karen had taken stock of her new community and amassed a mental list of places that were complicated socially. The nail salon was complicated. People there were in competition for customers and guarded themselves closely. The print shop had been unfriendly, as was the office job she worked. Even the room where Karen lived was complex—her roommate was constantly measuring their successes and failures against each other. Karen believed in God but thought about church largely in terms of building a community. She could learn about the Bible, listen to the pastor's sermons, and could trust the people around her.

The Korean Presbyterian Church of Queens offered a ready-made community for immigrant believers. There were Wednesday-night socials, live music on weekends, and a big lunch on Sundays. People joined the choir or performed at evening events. People who felt lonely during the week could attend Bible studies—contemplative social events where competition and envy were actively discouraged.

On Karen's first day, as the pews filled up and the songs and the sermon got under way, some of the newcomers listened with rapt attention, muttering *amen* after everything the pastor said. Others fell asleep, exhausted from whatever work they did during the week.

The pastor was in his forties and nicely dressed. He made jokes about his young children and threw references to world affairs into his sermons. He talked critically about Uganda's crackdown on gay men. He invented parables that were both absurd and meaningful. In one, a man was harassed by a comical demon who would show up on his doorstep and bang on the door. The man gave Jesus a room in his house to help deter the demon, but to no avail. When the demon showed up, Jesus stayed in his room. Finally the man thought to offer up his whole house, and Jesus went down and answered the door. "He threw the door open, boom!" the pastor said. "And the demon said, '*Aiyaaaaa!* I didn't know this house belonged to you!'"

Every week the pastor warned his congregation to be wary of charlatans, the demons at their own doors. "Even in our own congregation, there are people who would use the name of Jesus to cheat other people," he said. They targeted immigrants. They came to churches to preach their own versions of Christianity and to rope unsuspecting congregants into their own cultlike religions.

One church, the pastor reported, had discovered that a full thirty people in its congregation were actually agents of a cult. A gasp spread through the pews. "Be vigilant!" he said. He put a photo onto a projector identifying two cult publications that had come to his attention. "If you see anyone trying to sell you these books," he told the congregation, "don't believe them. Avoid these people." One of them was titled *The Savior Has Already Returned on a White Cloud*.

• • •

During her first year in the United States, Karen had attended church services at the behest of her asylum lawyer, to help strengthen her case. Back in China, her mother and grandmother would occasionally attend a house church, a loose group of worshippers that was technically illegal in China; Karen's home province had a large population of such Christians worshipping outside state-sanctioned churches, putting themselves at risk of a crackdown. So Karen's lawyer advised her to claim religious persecution, and he prescribed regular church attendance to prove her devotion and her faith.

Flushing had a huge selection of churches to choose from, most of which offered certificates of attendance to help along their congregants' asylum cases. Some church groups met in office buildings, storefronts, and conference rooms. Older congregations met in impressive church buildings. There were Korean churches, American churches, and Chinese churches. It was difficult, for someone with little experience of organized religion, to choose. Karen had asked a colleague for a recommendation and ended up in a regular room with fluorescent lights and metal chairs. The pastor preached with a mean streak that surprised Karen. He condemned greedy people. He talked of the dangers of homosexuality and warned people against participating in Halloween. He railed against the ills of society.

When Karen switched churches, again on a recommendation, she found herself in another big conference room. The plump Chinese preacher worked himself into a lather, his face reddening, his voice growing pitchy. Then with no warning, the man leaped out of Mandarin into some other language. At the time, she guessed it was Italian. She wondered what happened. And then someone explained to her that the man had been inspired by God. He was speaking in tongues. A few weeks later the church invited another pastor, a white man, to come and talk to the congregation. He worked up to the same lather, speaking quickly in English, but instead of switching languages, he invited sick people up to the front of the room. He would heal them, he said, by putting his hands on them. To Karen, sitting in the back of the room, the performance was a relief. It wasn't just Chinese people who were afflicted by this brand of insanity.

· · ·

Karen's lawyer had advised her well. During her first year in the United States, she was granted asylum, on the basis of her first interview. She told no one about it aside from Isobel and her mother. To everyone else who struggled through court dates and defensive asylum meetings, Karen pretended she had the same complaints. It was the same muted response she would give to receiving her green card just over a year later.

A chill set in around Flushing that summer—people were waiting longer to hear about their asylum cases, waiting longer for interviews and court dates. Karen's roommate was struggling through her own asylum case. The courts were backed up, people said, because a flood of undocumented children had come up from Honduras the year before. There were more asylum applications now, people said. More competition. Longer waits. Yang Maosheng, waiting for his own interview date, spent his free afternoons at Tang Yuanjun's office, complaining about people he felt didn't deserve their asylum status. "They're making it hard for the rest of us," he complained.

Karen had been happy for Little Yan when Kaizhi arrived. She understood that pressure came with an expanded family, but she couldn't see far beyond the picture of daily companionship that came with a husband and child. She still did not have a boyfriend. What she had, in the meantime, was the security of her green card. She was growing bolder and more hopeful. The classes at LIBI were taking too long, and although she considered trying to transfer to another school, she couldn't afford it. She needed something more expedient, something that might break up the grind of her days, moving from work to school and then to work again. In a move worthy of Zhuang himself, she decided to quit her weekday job, again, and enroll in hospitality classes. She was going to become a hotel maid.

It might not have been as glamorous as managing the books in a medical office, or graduating from a four-year American college, but Karen had heard that working in a hotel paid off. Another acquaintance told her about unionization. "Work at a union hotel," she told Karen. "Not a Chinese hotel." So Karen gave notice at the online company, where she earned a steady ten dollars an hour, and enrolled in hospitality classes at a school walking distance from the narrow LIBI high-rise. She would study the hospitality industry by day and attend her LIBI classes at night. On weekends, she worked at the nail salon.

The hospitality school where Karen enrolled was run by the Chinese-American Planning Council (CPC), a nonprofit organization formed after the 1965 immigration reform, and it was cheap, for a run of six weeks. It was a risk to go six weeks without work, but the rewards were potentially enormous. Hotels in Manhattan operated outside the immigrant networks prevalent in Flushing. She wouldn't be competing with the thousands of young recent immigrants like herself. The class offered an opportunity to work outside the places where she spoke Mandarin all day to Chinese customers. It could be a window into the rest of the United States, the kind of opportunity that few new immigrants in Flushing would have or would dare to take.

Almost all the people in Karen's class at the CPC were from southern China. They spoke Cantonese when they were together, and nearly everyone spoke English with more confidence than

Karen. One petite man claimed to be adept at feng shui. He read Karen's palm and told her that her professional life would be very fulfilling. She should take care of her health, though. One of the other men told the class that his hobby (they were required to have a hobby as part of their interview prep) was watching movies. Karen recounted the conversation to me:

"What is your favorite movie?" asked the teacher.

"I don't know," he said.

"What was the most recent movie you've seen?" asked the teacher.

"I forget," he said.

"Okay," she said. "When was the last time you watched a movie?"

"Last week."

"What movie was it?"

"I can't remember."

That man, Karen predicted, was going to struggle in an interview.

Karen learned which hotels were the most desirable, how hotels operated, and the types of positions they most frequently needed filled. She dreamed of getting a job at a five-star hotel in Manhattan, then working up to a position at the front desk. She imagined simple advantages, like health insurance.

The hardest part of Karen's class, by far, was preparing for job interviews that would be conducted in English. She worried that her spoken English was not good enough—that she couldn't recall words fast enough to get them out of her mouth. She was improving, speaking English, not Mandarin, whenever she had a choice. But she was still nervous in public. She rolled her expanding vocabulary around in her mouth as if the words were sucking all the moisture off her tongue.

• • •

When Little Yan heard about Karen's new classes, she did not, for a moment, consider them an option for herself. Her schedule was so full and cleaning rooms all day would be physically exhausting. Little Yan did not think she was well suited to that kind of manual labor. Zhuang, also, would never agree to let his wife work as a maid. That kind of work had a glow of impropriety— work performed, literally, in a bedroom. It could be dangerous. Little Yan would never be able to tell her family what she did to make money. Karen was younger, she said. It didn't matter as much to her.

A month into the hospitality class, mock interviews began. The mock interviews would show the instructors how prepared the students were, which was vital to their employment chances, as the school had to maintain a reputation for sending out qualified candidates.

To help students prepare, the teachers gave them a worksheet with twenty different questions. Karen spent days agonizing over her answers. The questions ranged from broad personal statements to details about how the student would travel to work every day. "What would you do if treated unfairly by a supervisor?" read one question. "How do you feel about workplace gossip?" Karen kept her answers diplomatic.

The most important question on the worksheet, her teacher had informed them, was the first. It was a topic that confounded Karen: "Tell us about yourself." She wrote, "I am a proactive person," as her first sentence, but when she practiced it, rolling the English consonants in her mouth in front of the mirror, she kept saying, "I am a positive person." So it stuck.

"I used to work in customer service," she recited in the bathroom, "but I am looking for a different opportunity."

"I know housekeeping is a physical job, but I am young and I play tennis."

"I would someday like to work as a manager."

The tennis bit she added for color. For the interview prep, Karen had tried to invent hobbies that she might pursue. She thought about joining a dance troupe at a local community center but found herself surrounded by old ladies, so she had taken up tennis. To be honest, she was just learning to play. She had been to the court near her apartment only once or twice.

Karen wrote out all her answers on the worksheet and turned

it in to the instructor, who in turn marked it up with red pen. Then she rewrote her answers, molding them to what people might want to hear. She wanted to be seen as ambitious but not aggressive. She memorized almost all her answers.

The quality of the hotel her instructor recommended her for would be a measure of how well she had done in the mock interview. So the first hotel that they suggested to her, a small extended-stay hotel on the Upper East Side, made her feel hopeful. She waited for the hotel to schedule an interview, but the appointment was never made. Her teacher suggested another hotel. It seemed promising if only because it was also in Manhattan.

The second hotel hadn't opened yet and was looking to hire an entire staff. Seven of Karen's classmates, three other women and four men, were scheduled to interview for jobs there. They splurged on outfits. Karen purchased a white shirt and a black blazer that she wore over a skirt. She imagined a kind of audition scenario with a panel of experts staring her down. She did not sleep the night before. "I have not been this nervous," she told me, "since I took the *gaokao*." She was referring to the enormous three-day college entrance exam that, in China, students spend years preparing for—a test expected to determine the course of the rest of their lives.

• • •

Karen took the subway and showed up early. She sat across the street from the building and looked at the newly constructed facade. The hotel was in Midtown, not far from the East River, between a parking garage and a three-story stone house that looked like it was doing its best to hold back the tide of high-rises pressing around it. The exposed section of the hotel's exterior glinted in the sun, as if the whole thing had been encased in stainless steel; other parts of the building were still covered in green scaffolding. A sign instructed pedestrians to PLEASE USE THE WALKWAY. Karen decided she liked it.

She walked into the lobby and gave her name. A tall, fat American man led her into a side office, and she sat down in a hallway next to her classmates. One of the women next to her spoke perfect English. Karen felt sure she would find a job as a receptionist. Her favorite companion, however, was a second-generation immigrant who had given up a job as an accountant. It was too stressful, he said, and the expectations of his parents were too crushing, so he was going to school to be a houseman. The pay was decent, and the work was concrete and physical. You didn't take it home with you. He just wanted to work and live.

Karen watched her classmates enter and exit a door. Then a small, skinny man came out and called her name. He led her into the spare, undecorated room and indicated for her to sit at a small desk, then took a seat next to another, larger man across from her. The room was not what Karen had expected. Like everything in New York, it was gritty and transitional, not staid and formal as she had imagined.

The small, skinny man cleared his throat and started the interview. "So," he said, adjusting his position in his chair, "tell me about yourself."

Karen launched into her best paragraph. "I am a positive person!" she said. She recited her sentences, her interest in tennis, and her hope to someday become a manager. She did not smile or pause for breath. "I know that this job is physically demanding," she said. She attacked the multisyllabic words with determination. "I am excited about this opportunity." After she finished reciting her lines, she looked up across the desk at the skinny man, his expression one of mild surprise. Karen smiled, then nodded just a bit. She had finished.

"Well, okay!" said the man. "Let me tell you about the hotel." She nodded again, barely hearing what he said. The hotel maids would use carts to move from room to room, he explained. They carried phones with intercoms, in case anything dangerous happened.

She asked her prepared questions, then ran out of them, and the interview ended. She had talked too quickly. The whole thing had taken all of five minutes. The large man told Karen she would hear about the job by Friday, and the small, skinny man gave her his card.

She wandered back out through the lobby and texted the classmates who had gone in before her. The former accountant had been in for the same five minutes and answered the same question. Everyone was shocked by the brevity.

Karen stopped at a Starbucks to meet her classmates, giddy with worry. They took photographs to commemorate the day, all in their best professional clothes. And then she walked to the subway and took the train back to Flushing—a forty-five-minute trip—for her LIBI class. Before it started, she sat down at the Paris Baguette across the street, eating nothing and turning the man's card over in her hands. A group of teenagers, dressed nicely in brand-name clothing and Nike shoes, were leaning over a tray of pastries. "Maybe I should e-mail him?" she asked no one, rhetorically. Her instructors had mentioned that at some point after the interview, she could send an e-mail. She tapped out a message on her iPhone: she was eager, she said, to "join your team." She smiled as she sent it off. It was a good e-mail. Not everyone would think to e-mail. And then she leaned back into her chair at the Paris Baguette, took a deep breath, and pushed her old glasses up her nose. "If I don't get this job, it will be okay," she said, and grinned. "I am a very positive person!"

• • •

Karen had made her first trip to the Korean Presbyterian Church of Queens on a Sunday in late summer, near the end of her hospitality class. She had developed a two-pronged approach to improving her situation in Flushing. The classes were for her career. The church was for the rest of her life.

The Korean Presbyterian Church of Queens had real pews rather than plastic chairs, with little wooden tables attached to the back of each row that could be flipped down and used to support a Bible. Its services opened with a group of well-dressed girls singing into microphones, a portly younger man behind them strumming on a guitar. They sang songs about God's love with their eyes closed, one hand on their chest, the other uplifted.

Toward the end of her first service, the pastor asked all the new attendees to rise when he called out their names. The chapel launched into an enthusiastic welcome song, and afterward they gathered Karen and the rest of them in an adjacent room to offer party favors and to take their pictures. As a newcomer, she received a set of food vouchers for the lunch served downstairs. Everyone encouraged her to join.

The moment she walked out of the little room across from the chapel, Karen's friend grabbed her. She had joined the congregation months before, and then the church choir, along with her fiancé. She was planning a wedding in the chapel. She led Karen down to the church basement, into a mint-green, windowless room, where a crowd had gathered for a brief Bible study and then lunch.

The friend introduced Karen to a young man sporting a ponytail, who showed Karen around. He was solicitous and kind. "He's not the one I want you to meet," Karen's friend whispered. "He has a girlfriend already, I think." Karen's friend had someone else in mind for her.

Some people at the church weren't interested in meeting Karen—they just wanted to listen to the sermons and go home. Others came only for the money and their asylum cases. But some were friendly and eager, and many of them were single men just the right age. In the mint-green basement, with her food vouchers in hand, Karen felt hopeful.

• • •

The Friday after Karen's interview at the hotel, she got a phone call telling her they were making her an offer. She would be paid eighteen dollars an hour to clean rooms—a salary beyond Karen's wildest dreams. The offer e-mail came the next Monday, and Karen was so happy it gave her a stomachache. When she told her old roommate, she lied about how much money she would be making, cutting it down to fourteen. "Oh, well then," said the roommate. "That's a very good salary, but I don't see what the big deal is all about."

There was a catch to the job, however. Karen would have to

wait a month before the hotel opened. She would have to extend her period of unemployment. She could do it if she was careful, she thought. She would keep working weekends at the nail salon and look for any other temporary work. She decided to redouble her effort in her classes at LIBI. She would teach herself to use Adobe Premiere, a video editing program. She would play tennis. When her classes ended in early September, she kept herself busy in the cheapest ways possible.

After a week or two, however, Karen found herself sitting on her bed, watching movies, feeling depressed. She took a weekend off at the nail salon and went to church. She tried to go to whatever functions she could, but her evening classes frequently interfered. One night she went to a music concert, where a man named Jack was playing guitar. He was the one her friend had had in mind for her. A stocky, boisterous young man, he worked as an accountant but would have liked to be a musician. Karen's friend, however, was not there to introduce the two, and Jack barely said two words to her. He was busy and surrounded by friends.

By the end of the month, Karen was going stir-crazy. And then the hotel e-mailed to tell her that her start date had been delayed. The next week it was delayed again. Finally, Karen got an e-mail assuring her that she would be starting her job on October 31. She would have to stretch her savings as far as they would go. By the time she at last started training—cleaning empty rooms, tucking in bedsheets, and folding towels just right—she was completely broke.

18

Wukan! Wukan!
Rule of Law

法治 / *Fǎzhì*

MARCH 2014

After Zhuang retired from the village committee, it had taken him more than a year to perfect his escape plan and go to New York. During that time, things in the village deteriorated. Old Lin, Zhuang complained, was too weak. The old man had been slow to stand up to the corrupt officials in Lufeng City. In 2012, when the council started negotiations for the return of the pig farm land, Old Lin had accepted the two small parcels as a gesture of goodwill, then stopped informing the villagers on how talks with Lufeng were proceeding. He had brought the pig farm protest on himself.

In the spring of 2013, shortly after the city security forces broke up the blockade at the pig farm, I was drinking tea with Zhuang unaware that a corruption scandal had erupted behind the scenes. "There are things I cannot talk about," Old Lin had told me, a few weeks after accepting the written confessions of two council members, Yang Semao and Hong Ruichao.

The scandal that ensnared Yang Semao and Hong could be traced back to the rubble-filled doorstep of Zhang Jianxing, the young member of the Hot Blooded Youth who had helped Zhuang early on. Jianxing had become, through the years of protest, interviews, and online activism, a media darling. He had gotten over his acne and had adopted a rakish, brooding persona, wearing a black peacoat for interviews and carefully managing his hair, long on the top and shaved on the sides. He perfected the art of stylish cigarette lighting

After the protests, Jianxing began running a photography and camera equipment shop across from the village vegetable market. A wealthy villager had approached him and offered to help bankroll the project. Jianxing didn't know him well, but he accepted the funds. The man seemed genuinely interested in the business. A few months later the wealthy villager asked for an introduction to Hong Ruichao.

A few months after that, about a year after the 2012 election, a water project came up for bidding, and the wealthy villager asked Hong Ruichao to deliver bribes to the council. "The plan is to start with Hong Ruichao," the wealthy man told an associate on a 2013 phone call that was, mysteriously, recorded and then leaked to villagers a year later, in 2014. "He's the window into the other council members."

When Zhuang heard about the scandal, he thought the scheme was obvious—the wealthy villager was creating a scandal for the benefit of the corrupt officials in Lufeng. If Hong and the other council members accepted the bribes, Lufeng could use the scandal to discredit the people involved. They could threaten criminal charges if any council member decided to oppose them.

As bribery schemes go, the one that took down Hong Ruichao and Yang Semao was haphazard and poorly executed. Hong took the wads of cash he had been given to a handful of council members and discussed what to do. Old Lin turned down the offer on the spot, but Hong and Yang took the money into their possession and conferred, then both decided to return it. Whether the Lufeng government had orchestrated it or not, the officials overseeing Wukan soon found out about the exchange of cash and used it to their advantage.

Lufeng gave everyone in Wukan's village council who was involved in the bribery scheme the opportunity to submit a written confession. "In order to model the behavior that village chief Lin advocates—I made an appointment . . . in March and gave back the 30,000 yuan," Hong Ruichao wrote in his. He had offered Yang and Old Lin each ten thousand. "The other reason I did this was because I couldn't help Zhu Dakui [the wealthy villager] with what he was asking me to do." It was early summer 2013, and all three of the men admitted what they had done and wrote down confessions, and everyone kept the affair quiet. It stayed that way until a few weeks after Zhuang had landed in New York, when Yang Semao was led out of the village committee office in handcuffs.

• • •

The crackdown that Zhuang foresaw after the pig farm protest was slow to arrive. Right before he fled, after nearly nine months of planning, the people he shared his plans with scoffed at his paranoia. He was abandoning the village, they scolded, and taking the cowardly way out. Things in the village would not get so bad as he predicted, they said. Yang Semao and Hong Ruichao plowed ahead with a plan to hold another meeting of the larger village representative assembly. They wanted to discuss the next election, set for some time in March, and to hold the Lufeng officials to account for blocking the return of stolen village land. "Land is the farmer's life, and elections are the farmer's soul," Yang told me.

It was the threat of making the officials accountable, Zhuang thinks, that got the pair detained. Yang had known Lufeng was holding the corruption scandal over his head, but after nearly a year, he had been hopeful that it had passed. He was still the same elfin, energetic man who insisted on jogging every morning along Wukan's dusty roads.

They came for Yang Semao during the workday. They entered his first-floor office, where the door was nearly always open to allow in the breeze, placed him in handcuffs, and led him away. "I thought that was a little theatrical," Yang said, later. "Leading me out of there in front of everyone—they could have just asked me to go to Lufeng myself."

They released Yang, temporarily, after twenty-four hours.

Then a summons arrived for Hong Ruichao. Hong, still young and bold at twenty-nine, turned himself in. His family waited for him to come out. His wife tended to his infant son in his father's little concrete house. His sister spent impatient days at the village salon that she had opened. But Hong never came out.

• • •

In March 2014, soon after Zhuang's arrival in New York, I made my way back to Wukan Village without him. It was a week after the detention of Yang and Hong. The second election they had anticipated had been scheduled for early March. Whoever was elected to the village committee would serve an extended term—a full five years. But with Yang preoccupied and Hong gone, I went instead to Jianxing's photography shop.

The day I arrived, I had heard rumors that foreigners were being detained and kicked out of the village, so I waited until it was dark and made my way into the village. Jianxing's shop had a row of floor-to-ceiling windows facing out toward the vegetable market. He had pulled the tan shades down, the lights of a television flashing out around the corners. When I knocked, he peered around a shade and then ushered me inside and into a back room, shaken enough that he had forgotten to be stylish. There were rumors that more arrests would be made. Jianxing had not been directly involved, but he had been privy to the details of the corruption scandal and witnessed Hong's deliberations over the thirty thousand yuan. Hong's disappearance had made him jittery. Every time someone walked into the shop, Jianxing paused to listen before opening the door. "Stay back here," he said. "Someone is looking for me."

He left me in the room to contemplate the jumble of electronics equipment, the bookcases, the fake machine gun, and the decals he had pasted on the wall—a treble clef and two inspirational quotes about having a simple lifestyle. "We have a simple lifestyle and only one passion," said one. "Simple lifestyle changes are all that you need to feel better," said the other.

When Jianxing came back in, he told me he had made a mistake when he decided not to run in the first election. "I think I was a very important factor," he said, leaning forward on a little bed, his elbows on his knees and his combat boots planted firmly on the floor. "I think, had I been on the village committee, we would not have ended up with this terrible result."

The night before Wukan's second election, it poured rain. The village turned the dark gray color of wet concrete. Pools formed in empty lots, rivers coursed down alleyways, and the rolling croak of bullfrogs grew so loud that they competed with the thunder.

Old Lin, after two years of pointing out his advanced age and fantasizing about retirement, was at home, preparing to run again for village chief. "There are some things that I have left unfinished!" he told a group of journalists who had stumbled in out of the rain.

His house was a new tile construction sitting in a freshly paved alleyway that ran toward the local school where elections were being held. To gain entrance to his home, visitors were required to stand outside two gigantic metal doors and look up into a security camera aimed at the stoop. There was no doorbell, and the rain made it impossible to hear anyone knocking. Old Lin's wife was in charge of opening the doors, scurrying through a small uncovered courtyard that was being pelted with rain. She ferried people back inside to where Old Lin was sitting.

Erect in his chair, wearing a soft brown leather jacket, he emphasized his thoughts with pursed lips and raised eyebrows. He leaned forward, opening his eyes wide, when he felt his point was particularly important. While he talked, his wife poured tea. "I haven't even eaten dinner yet!" he announced, smiling wildly. "Make us some food!!" His wife looked shocked, and everyone declined politely.

"The law doesn't always work quickly," Lin said regarding the yearlong lead-up to Hong Ruichao's arrest. "Isn't that true? But we have to obey the law, even if it doesn't seem to make sense. Isn't that true?" He had been tempted by bribes, he said, but had withstood it. Money had entered into Hong Ruichao's hands illegally, so Hong Ruichao had broken a law. "It doesn't matter if they gave it back or not, the money was in their hands. It's illegal, and we must let the law decide."

The old village committee had never been jailed for stealing Wukan's land. Officials in Lufeng, the same officials who had jailed Hong, had never been censured for their role in the land sales. But Old Lin was content to make his argument absent of that part of the story. He was adhering to the party line.

"We are making progress on the land problem," he said. "The villagers just have to be patient." He paused to pour out a cup of tea, yellow flowers floating up to the top of the glass teapot. "My skin is much thicker this time around," he said. "I'm really fine whatever the outcome of the election. I'm just worried about this rain—hopefully people will still show up."

• • •

Before the polls opened the next morning, between bursts of rain, a line of buses (some counted ten, others eight) headed down the road from Lufeng City and turned onto the narrow street leading to the school where Wukan's second election would be held. They created a small, temporary traffic jam as they dropped off their passengers and then attempted to turn around. They left a small force of soldiers from the People's Liberation Army and a fleet of men wearing plain clothes with the world's must unhelpful ID badges, identifying them only as *gongzuo renyuan*, workers. The soldiers took up posts by the gates of the school, six standing guard at a time, while the mysterious workers helped election volunteers set up umbrellas against the rain. The workers set up a media table to offer visiting journalists official press passes, informational packets on Wukan, and a hardback book on Lufeng culture. There had been a handful of police at the first election, but nothing like this. The men wandered the alleyways of the village and took photos of people with their phones, making sure they were seen.

Still more journalists were arriving in the village, and many of them gathered at Jianxing's shop. Reporters who had been in Wukan for the uprising, and for the first election, were returning to follow up on a captivating story. Journalists from Japan, Singapore, Australia, France, and the UK arrived, along with multiple Chinese filmmakers. Reporters from Hong Kong greeted Jianxing like an old friend. A group of filmmakers from Al Jazeera occupied his couches. Everyone waited for Jianxing, as the noise of his blow-dryer echoed out of a back room. They gossiped about Zhuang's recent escape to New York and told jokes about the two gigantic Serbian photographers who had arrived for Reuters. When Jianxing finally emerged, his hair perfectly coiffed and his black peacoat already on, he betrayed none of the nerves of the previous night. He led the group through the village toward the school, smoking a cigarette as he went.

Villagers went in and out of the schoolyard all day, running through the downpours and passing through the phalanx of anonymous, camera-wielding workers. This time the election had no official ballot—voters could write in any name for any position. A few hours into the voting, Jianxing ran out of the school entrance, a slip of paper in his hand. "Look at this!" he called out as he ran. "One of the villagers just passed it to me."

The flyer suggested people for different roles on the village committee. It named Yang Semao for council chief, Hong Ruichao and one other person for deputy chief, and then, under the heading for the four regular council members, was Jianxing's name. "I had given up running for council!" he said. "Someone is pulling me in! Well, pull away! I'm ready for it!"

Jianxing let another villager hold the paper for a few seconds while it got slightly wet. "Be careful!" he said. "You're ripping it!" He took it gingerly back and slipped it into a pocket. "If I get enough votes, I will move on to the runoffs!" he said.

Later, in his shop, waiting for the voting to end, he sat talking with a friend about the election. All those buses of strangers were intimidating people, his friend complained. "I voted for Old Lin," he said. "And Hong Ruichao and Zhuang Liehong."

"Did you vote for me?" asked Jianxing.

"No! Of course not, you're too young," said the friend.

"But what's the point of voting for Zhuang Liehong?" asked Jianxing. "He's not in China!"

"His body may not be in Wukan," the friend shot back, "but his heart is still here."

. . .

The election results were announced after dark, by a man who had arrived with the soldiers. Old Lin had been elected chief, with more than 5,000 votes (out of 8,000 eligible voters in the village). Yang Semao had received only about 2,500 votes. Jianxing had gotten 500, not quite enough to get him into the runoff.

Old Lin was a few doors down at his cousin's house when he got the news of his victory. He came walking down the alley, under an umbrella, accepting accolades as he went. He opened up his house, poured some tea, and beamed. He was very happy to have the support of the villagers, he said. He knew he had years of hard work ahead of him. It didn't feel like a victory to celebrate—it was a call to do more.

When a French journalist arrived and asked about the corruption case, Old Lin mentioned that he was in possession of some "evidence." And here Old Lin paused and looked around. When nobody took him up on his offer of evidence, he mentioned it again. Finally, when it came up a third time, someone took the hint. Old Lin went over to a chest of drawers in the living room and pulled out a pack of papers. He crouched on the floor with them, spreading them out and naming them as he went. "This is Yang Semao's confession," he said. "This has to do with Zhang Jianxing's role in the corruption. This is Hong Ruichao. And this one has to do with my own situation." He spread them out in a semicircle around himself. "Hong Ruichao's family called the village committee office earlier today," he added. "They wanted to withdraw him from the election, but since he's in jail and didn't make the request himself, we're not sure if it's legal." Hong Ruichao's name, he said, would go ahead to the runoff.

Later that night someone would show me a photo of Hong Ruichao that his lawyer had posted on the Internet. His head was shaved and he looked out forlornly from behind bars. Hong's father spent the evening of the election in the living room of his drafty concrete house. He soberly smoked cigarettes, covering the entire bottom half of his face with his hand every time he took a drag while Hong Ruichao's wife mixed up milk powder in a bowl. "I was very happy when Hong Ruichao decided to run for election the first time," he said, taking a long drag. "I encouraged him to do it." He had felt heartened by the prospect of democracy. He thought his son would be a fair member of the council. Now Hong Ruichao was in jail, and the lawyer they had hired to represent him hadn't been to see the family in over a week. No one on the outside knew what was happening. "The only thing I care about is my son. I never thought we would end up here. But I don't care about the election. I don't care if it was fair or not. I don't care about the village government. The only thing I can think about now is my son."

The runoff election was held the following day, with Hong Ruichao's name on the list. Yang Semao came in second only to Old Lin and could easily have been voted in as deputy chief again. Late on the night of the first election, however, he had withdrawn, complaining that he could not work again under Old Lin. The older man was too slow-moving and too quick to agree with demands coming from Lufeng. And Yang Semao was a natural upstart. He couldn't help himself.

That night a group gathered at Yang Semao's house, talking over the din from the television as Yang's youngest son watched cartoons. His wife declared that she was glad it was over. Working on the council was dangerous, she said, and useless.

The group paused when the sound of Yang Semao's scooter cut off outside. He came walking in slowly, shuffling in plastic slippers. He smiled and nodded sadly. He sat briefly on a polished wooden couch, poured some tea, and answered some questions. "This has been hanging over my head for the past year," he said. "When I decided to oppose the Lufeng government, I did so knowing that this might happen. I knew they had the confession, and they made it clear they could use it against me. I just hoped they wouldn't."

Yang Semao paused to pour out more tea. "It is my fault, anyway," he said. "I took the money. I wanted to donate it to the local school. But I did it knowing what I was doing was wrong. I knew very clearly it was not legal. And I did it anyway. I knew it was wrong." He had dreamed of bringing democracy to the village he loved. He had worked tirelessly, a familiar sight riding his scooter around the alleyways in flip-flops and his triangular fisherman's hat. He had been hopeful right up until the last moment, even after the police handcuffed him and led him out of the council offices. It had taken the election to shake Yang's resolve.

As he talked, more and more people showed up. They took all the seats on the wooden furniture, and some pulled plastic chairs out of a corner to accommodate the newcomers. "I think the elections were as fair as possible," Yang said. His wife, settling down next to him, let out an audible snort. Everyone in the plastic chairs chuckled. Yang managed another weak smile and retired to the kitchen as the conversation picked up. He was visible through a glass partition, leaning against the kitchen counter and eating in silence, his shoulders collapsed over a small bowl of rice while everyone in the living room continued carrying on. A few weeks later Yang would be detained again. He would receive a two-year prison sentence, and Hong Ruichao would be handed four. And even when Yang's time was up, when his two years turned into three, he would never return to live in Wukan Village.

19

A Man of Wukan

乌坎人 / *Wūkǎn Rén*

Something else happened in that summer of Kaizhi's arrival: Old Lin was arrested. Ever since he took over as village chief, officials had been obstructing him—the same officials who had tried to steal land with a fake map of Wukan. Finally the old man, after years of trying to do things legally and slowly, had gotten fed up. Lin had posted an open letter online calling on the village to stage a mass protest. "During the last four years, the sky of Wukan has lingered in the darkness before dawn," he had written. The time had come to fight back.

Zhuang found out about the arrest at lunch, sitting next to a window in the East Buffet, in the middle of a meal of shrimp dumplings and congee. He had had a feeling that something might happen. He had heard there was a buildup of security forces in the area the day before. And then his phone, on the table next to him, buzzed. "Oh," Zhuang said, thumbing through photos. "They've come to take Lin Zulian."

People in the village were sending him updates. It was around two in the morning in Wukan, and the village looked like it was being invaded. In one photo, a wall of policeman in helmets, holding shields, blocked a narrow lane, while the light from another camera—one belonging to the police—flashed in the background.

In a video, a group of people offscreen watched footage coming from the security camera Lin Zulian had mounted outside the enormous blank door leading to his home. The tassels from a red lantern were blowing in and out of a lower corner of the camera when the outline of a person came into view, made visible in the dark by what looked like a yellow security vest. The light above the door glinted off the man's helmet. A swarm of police followed him, fighting to squeeze in the door three or four at a time, all in vests and helmets. They streamed in and then out again without pause—a handful of police popping out the door, followed by an unidentified man in a white shirt, and then Old Lin, skinny and frail in a white undershirt, his hands tied behind his back, pushed along by the policeman. "There he is," a voice murmured, and then another repeated, in disbelief, "There he is." In an instant, Old Lin left the range of the camera. The old man was gone.

"He was going to hold a protest," Zhuang told me, across the table. "But it was too late. He waited too long." It was Old Lin's own fault that it had come to this, he thought. The outcome wasn't predetermined from the start. But it didn't matter who was to blame—no matter what, Old Lin didn't deserve this treatment—and it didn't change what Zhuang would have to do. He was a man from Wukan, and he was being called back into action. He had to spread the word.

Zhuang sent out texts over WeChat, told friends in Wukan to stay safe, but the app was based in China, under the control of the country's censors. If he tried to use it to broadcast what was happening in his village, his posts would be blocked and his account taken down. He turned to Facebook, where he had opened an account a few years before. He had rarely used it; he had a total of two friends. Nevertheless he posted swaths of photos.

He went about contacting every reporter he still knew in Hong Kong, China, and the United States. "The gongs are ringing again in Wukan!" he wrote online. "Villagers are confronting more than 200 SWAT police." By the end of the day, Zhuang had more than seven hundred friends on Facebook, and the number was growing. It was as if he were Patriot Number One again, adding friends over QQ.

• • •

A day after the arrest, the Lufeng Public Security Bureau released a statement about Lin Zulian.

> To the people of Wukan Village, Donghai Township, June 17th, 2016. On suspicion of using the power of his position to solicit bribes, the Lufeng People's Procuratorate has already investigated Wukan Village Party Chief and Village Committee Chairman Lin Zulian, and has taken the appropriate action. We call upon Wukan's villagers to actively support and cooperate as the judicial authorities carry out their work, and defend our hard-earned, shared, stable environment. Don't allow a small number of lawbreakers to take advantage of you and lead you into extreme actions.

The protests started right away. Villagers called on their relatives in Guangzhou and Shenzhen and told them to come back and stand up again. Zhuang watched videos clips showing a crowd forming in front of the local temple, waving Chinese flags and holding up umbrellas against the sun. Journalists perched on the stage in the old temple, where traveling opera troupes used to perform, so they could photograph the crowd chanting. Lin Zulian's wife appeared with a bandage wrapped around her right forearm. Once the crowd had amassed, it moved out of the village, past the police station, where squads of armed police, marching in formation or standing still, watched the villagers pass. Zhuang knew all the streets and landmarks as well as he knew anything.

Every day a group of protesters gathered. They signed their names to a banner calling for the return of Wukan's land. When the Lufeng government tried to install a new village chief, the villagers followed the man through the streets, yelling. The government released a statement announcing the formation of a group to help "stabilize the situation." It urged the villagers to support the group and warned them to stop demonstrating, "or else you will be held responsible!"

A few days after Lin was taken, another two a.m. raid took place, and a handful of the more visible protesters, including Hong Ruichao's sister, disappeared. The local school was instructed not to allow students to leave the building until six or seven at night, to keep them from participating in the protests. A mob of confused parents formed in front of the school until the students were released. The village was in an uproar. And then a video was released online—this time by the Lufeng government.

The summer of 2016, in China, was the season of videotaped confessions. Back in February, a bookseller who had been kidnapped from his home in Hong Kong had appeared in a video, broadcast on China's Central Television, claiming that he had sneaked into China of his own accord. He leaned back awkwardly in his chair in a wood-paneled room, two oversize wineglasses full of flowers behind his right shoulder. The bookseller told the camera that he wanted to give up his residence rights in the UK.

Then in July, China's police force launched a crackdown on human rights lawyers, and a string of televised confessions followed, the lawyers in orange jumpsuits, the words CRIMINAL SUSPECT splashed across the bottom of the screen. By the end of the summer, a TV show would launch on CCTV, the Chinese state-run television service, comprised almost entirely of confessions made by officials who had been arrested as part of a nationwide anticorruption campaign. One disgraced party secretary from Sichuan broke down in front of the camera, choking out the words, "Life is like a live broadcast, there is no going back."

Old Lin's confessional video, compared to these, was low-rent. The picture was blurred, and a light somewhere in the room seemed to be flashing on and off. Lin sat slumped sideways in a blue plastic chair with a shelf over his lap that made it impossible for him to stand. He was dressed in an oversize short-sleeved shirt, its collar open. His face shining in the TV light, he spoke haltingly, listing the crimes he was guilty of. "I took kickbacks in livelihood projects," he said, his fingers twitching on the plastic restraint in front of him. "I also took kickbacks from collective purchases from the village. These are my serious crimes." He blamed the problems on his ignorance. He didn't understand the law.

As soon as the video was shown, Old Lin's wife was out in the village denouncing it. No one believed what Old Lin had said from the blue plastic chair. Hundreds of villagers staged a march every day, no matter what the weather. They marched that summer through heat, rain, and at least one typhoon. Zhuang, meanwhile, did what he could. He posted the photos on Facebook, his captions thick with pride in his fellow villagers and tinged with envy. "Rudderless with no leader!" he wrote on the sixty-fourth day of marching in Wukan, using a Chinese proverb to reference Lin Zulian's absence. "But every day they persist; even typhoons do not stop them. This is the spirit of Wukan. I am proud to be a Wukan villager! I regret that I'm not there to march with them."

Zhuang shied away from protesting in the streets of New York. At the time Lin was arrested, Kaizhi was still more than a month away from arriving in the United States. Zhuang's finances were dwindling, and he was still trying to run the personal shopping business. Posting online about the marches was, he felt, his best use. It was a daily reminder, in his isolating, quotidian life, of who he really was.

• • •

Kaizhi spent his first four days in New York in the warm bustle of his parents' welcome. They took Kleenexes and wiped his eyes clear over and over. They took him shopping for new clothes and bought him another toy car. On his first night, Kaizhi had proved unable to stay in his chair at a celebratory dinner. He danced, arms dangling at his side, on the sticky floor of the East Buffet's downstairs restaurant, wild-eyed with sensory overload.

Zhuang scolded Little Yan for feeding him a patty of shrimp all at once. "It's too much!" he said, while Kaizhi looked up at him, one cheek puffed out with half-chewed fish. "*Aiya!* What are you doing? Don't you know you should cut it up first?" As if to prove his point, a few pieces of shrimp erupted out of Kaizhi's mouth, sticking to his chin for a moment and then falling to the floor.

Little Yan looked at her husband impassively. "Why don't you cut it up, then?"

Kaizhi slept on the hard mattress with his parents. Every

night, for the first few days, after settling in under the covers, he would roll toward the wall and make tiny gasping noises, like an injured animal. Kaizhi was trying his best to be brave, Little Yan said. He didn't want them to know that he was terrified. He would finally fall asleep on the verge of tears.

Zhuang had many early thoughts on what Kaizhi should eat and which parks he should play in. He would joke his way into his son's heart, pretending the cars that crashed into his toes had injured him gravely. He would speak about himself in the third person. "Eat this food that your baba has gotten you!" or "If Kaizhi doesn't behave, Baba and Mama will go to the store without him!"

Little Yan was quieter. She played with Kaizhi, letting him take photos of her with her cell phone, watching him roll around on the bed until he dissolved into a fit of giggles. At the start, she couldn't understand everything Kaizhi said. He spoke a mix of Mandarin and the local dialect from Zhuang's village. On his second morning, she made him rice congee, and Kaizhi, who had barely touched his food after the shrimp patty exploded from his mouth, slurped it up. He was starting to trust her. He grew louder and more opinionated. In the bath one morning, not a week after he arrived, he looked up at Little Yan and told her he liked her. But he didn't call them Baba and Mama yet.

Little Yan's schedule started off forgiving. She had four days to help Kaizhi adjust, then had her nights free for the next two weeks—her school was on a break between semesters. Kaizhi would fall asleep in his carseat while Zhuang drove to pick her up from her job at five. At home, Little Yan would cook and keep an eye on her son, while Zhuang glued himself to his phone, trying to keep his *daigou* business afloat and follow what was happening in Wukan. Little Yan kept tabs on local restaurants that offered discounts on certain nights of the week, planning for when Zhuang would have to take over. "He's not going to cook," she said. It didn't matter whether her husband was ready to take Kaizhi on from seven to ten every evening. He didn't have a choice.

• • •

Zhuang wanted to be a doting father, but a son was more disrupting than he could have imagined. Kaizhi still did not like to eat much, and Zhuang bargained and wheedled and threatened to little effect. "Yum!" he said at lunch one day, stuffing a dumpling into his mouth at the East Buffet. "Look, Kaizhi! Baba has ordered some really tasty dumplings! Oh, so fresh!" Kaizhi eyed him suspiciously, standing up next to his chair and staring toward some of the other people in the restaurant. Zhuang had just purchased a new toy train on the street. Kaizhi couldn't stop peering at it through its plastic packaging. Zhuang called the server over and asked him to take the train to the front desk so Kaizhi wouldn't be so distracted. "I have to do it," he told Kaizhi. "You have to eat." His son's eyes welled up with real tears.

"He's sometimes very naughty," Zhuang said to me. "But you can't always give him what he wants. You have to teach him. But even now, looking at him, it's really hard to watch him cry."

At home in the Tudor-style cottage in Fresh Meadows, Zhuang and Little Yan's bedroom door faced that of their landlord's two children, who soon discovered Kaizhi and wanted to play with him—a new roommate who had arrived complete with remote control cars. The girl, a gangly twelve-year-old, would slip into Zhuang's room in the afternoons, after her summer classes let out. She spoke to Zhuang in rapid English and called him John. She renamed his son, calling him Kai. Zhuang had become an exhausted wrangler of two, sometimes three, children.

"Oh my god!" the landlord's daughter shouted one afternoon in August, driving one of the remote control cars. "I'm stuck! John my car is stuck! John!" Kaizhi was half-lying on the floor, examining another car that lit up and played club music while it drove itself in circles.

"He's too smart for me!" she hollered. "Kai doesn't want to let me play with his car so he turns it off."

"John! John!" she said. "I think the car is broken." She tried to drive the car into his closet. "I'm going to park it!"

"Please don't drive it into the closet," Zhuang said in Chinese. "Just keep it in the room."

"But I'm parking it!" the girl said in English.

Zhuang looked blank. "You are going to have to teach me English," he said. "How do you say 'turn everything off' in English?" he asked. "Can we please turn everything off?"

"Okay, okay," said the girl.

In addition to stealing the toy cars, the landlord's daughter had an altruistic reason for coming into Zhuang's room: she wanted to help Kaizhi learn English. She had been born in the United States but spent her early childhood with her grandmother in China. English was the biggest gift she could think to offer. She had noticed a number of new kids in her summer school classes who had just been brought over from their grandparents' houses in China. Their English was bad. "I think they are just going to school so their mothers can work," she said derisively. "I don't want to say anything bad about anyone, but I think they got brought over now so they can go to school here." Whatever the case, it was an embarrassment to show up to summer school at twelve unable to speak English. The girl was heading into seventh grade now and was observant of the social hierarchy. The kids in her classes whose families had come over decades or generations ago would ask her where she had been born, and she suspected it was meant to embarrass her.

"Hey, John!" she said after switching off the toy cars. "Can we watch the cartoon? The one with two beavers and a bald guy?"

Zhuang sighed. He pulled up the Chinese cartoon that Kaizhi liked, an updated Elmer Fudd rip-off in which a bald hunter tries to outsmart two bears.

"I think they're otters," said the girl.

Zhuang wasn't sure the program offered much in the way of education. In fact, he worried it might teach Kaizhi undesirable behavior, as the hunter and the two bears were constantly yelling and hitting each other. But it was the one thing Kaizhi liked to watch; he had been a fan in Wukan. The only quiet moments Zhuang got were thanks to that bald hunter and his bears.

• • •

For all its drawbacks—the distance from town, the impromptu child care—Zhuang and Little Yan liked the Tudor-style house. Staying there, however, would be difficult. The people who rented the basement apartment were already complaining about the noise—the little thumps of Kaizhi's feet racing back and forth and the rumble of his two miniature construction trucks, the yellow front-end loader and the dump truck. At night, when he was always full of energy, Kaizhi's parents followed him around shushing him: *No jumping, no rolling your cars on the floor, no gymnastics on the bed.* Even Zhuang's landlord, the tolerant man from Fujian, looked nervous when Kaizhi tumbled out of Zhuang's single room, all loose arms and legs, to check on his mom in the kitchen.

Zhuang was already counting the days before Kaizhi could attend preschool. He had to be four for the free public option, and Kaizhi had just turned three in May. So Zhuang had nearly ten months in which to tend him. The for-profit day care services around the neighborhood charged about eight hundred dollars a month. If Zhuang could guarantee making that much money with his *daigou* business, he would certainly put Kaizhi in day care. But he would have to wait until Kaizhi got his Social Security card. He wanted to get Kaizhi's eyes seen to by an American doctor. Until then it would be hard to run his business. He still went to Woodbury on the weekends, but the summer made it increasingly difficult to turn a profit. Some of the wealthy bosses he knew were taking vacations in Europe or the United States, where they planned on picking up their own branded jeans and handbags. And following the crackdown in Wukan, friends there who were once happy to place orders with Zhuang were now otherwise occupied or nervous about keeping in contact with an old activist.

By the time August turned into September, Zhuang admitted to himself that his business was not going to be the success he had once hoped. He and his family were eligible, a year after receiving asylum, to apply for their green cards—for which, Zhuang found out, they would have to pay a fee of more than a thousand dollars each. They could not live on Little Yan's fourteen hundred dollars a month. They had finally run through the money Zhuang had brought from China in 2014. For once, Zhuang gave in to Little Yan's vision of the future: he would buy a new car and get his taxi and limo license. In the meantime, Zhuang and Little Yan, two and a half years after they arrived debt-free, needed to borrow money from their families in China.

It was only a matter of a few thousand dollars, but it let the pressure out of their lives almost instantaneously. Zhuang started looking for a new apartment, a large place with two or three rooms. With the extra money, he could afford to put down a larger deposit, and then he could sublease the additional rooms and take the bite out of his own monthly rent. In the end, it would save him money.

Zhuang found a basement apartment in a generic brick house a few minutes' drive from the heart of Flushing. It would make Little Yan's commute easier, and Kaizhi would have free rein over the shared spaces. The apartment was chilly and covered in white tile, but it didn't matter. It was Zhuang's domain. He put his tea table out in the common space—with a proper tea tray on it. Kaizhi drove his trucks in and out of the bedroom, down a little hall, and into the kitchen. He nursed a budding obsession with trains, watching a video of different locomotive engines roll, fast and slow, over tracks. He could watch the train video for half an hour and not get bored.

Zhuang put an advertisement online for the two extra rooms in his basement, then used a lesson he had learned from Chen Tai: he surveilled the wall of advertisements near Main Street, looking for upstanding tenants. The smaller room he rented out to a Chinese woman who worked in Florida but wanted a place to stay and keep her stuff when she came to New York. The other he let to a young woman, not much younger than Karen, who had just arrived in New York and was looking for a job. Eventually this younger tenant would invite another woman to share her room. They were polite and spent most of their time working, so nothing bothered Zhuang. Even with Kaizhi running back and forth and Zhuang's inviting tea setup, everyone kept to themselves.

The only drawback to the new apartment was that in the move, Kaizhi had lost his only two friends. Zhuang tried to get his son to play with other children in Flushing playgrounds, but he stayed close to Zhuang's feet, driving his toys in a tight circle. Zhuang sighed.

• • •

Throughout all this, the villagers in Wukan kept marching. And every few days Zhuang would post their photos on Facebook, noting the number of days they had been marching. In August they hit seventy and kept going. They sent Zhuang photos of themselves, their numbers reduced, but still impressive. He applauded their efforts from afar. If it was harder to find time to post now that Kaizhi was here, he had also grown bolder with his son out of harm's way. He used both of his phones (his collection of devices had proliferated when he started selling *daigou*), moving from We-Chat to WhatsApp (another chat service) to Facebook, tailoring his use to each application. He used a third application, a South Korean messaging service, to chat with me and a handful of other people. He would incorporate a fourth by the end of the year—a program called Signal that was becoming more popular with activists wanting to protect their data.

Those evenings of posting photos and swapping phones were all it took for Zhuang to suddenly, after two years, make activist friends in Flushing. Yao Cheng, the man Zhuang had first met in the East Buffet—the bespectacled, outspoken friend of the German journalist, who had done jail time for drawing attention to the problem of child abductions in China—got back in touch and offered his support. Another man, Sun, appeared on Facebook early on in the protests of 2016 and commented on one of Zhuang's posts. "I support Wukan," he wrote. "I'm in Flushing." He left his phone number. At first, Zhuang ignored it. He had other things on his mind.

Zhuang had not been back to Tang Yuanjun's office. The Peter Liang protest was the only time he had dipped his toe into the waters of activism in the United States. He knew nothing about the min yun who threw themselves at the cars of visiting Chinese leaders. Nor did he know that talk of Wukan had slipped back into Tang's meetings. He was still just a man of Wukan, following its events with concern and excitement. And then a second wave of crackdowns hit the village.

The daily marches had continued for eighty-three days before the Lufeng authorities got fed up. On September 5, village protesters received a letter from the Lufeng authorities warning them to stop their participation in illegal protests within five days. If they stopped, the letter informed them, no further investigation or action would be taken against them. On the seventh, pink notices were pasted up on the walls of the village, offering to distribute residential land. ("To this day, the lawbreakers who stole Wukan's land haven't returned an inch, how can they distribute any land?" Zhuang asked on Facebook. "Hong Ruichao, Yang Semao, and Lin Zulian didn't fall into this bribery trap for residential land. . . . They did it to reclaim communal land and to establish an autonomous village democracy.") Protesters kept marching but hid their faces in the photographs they sent Zhuang.

And then, on the night of September 12, two days after the deadline, the police invaded the village again. They went house to house, breaking down doors, throwing people onto the ground and detaining them. On the morning of the thirteenth, riot police moved in small units through the village, shuffling pods protected by their shields. They shot rubber bullets and tear gas at the villagers who came out to protest. The villagers ran into the street throwing chunks of concrete and tossed bricks out their windows. They picked up canisters of tear gas and threw them back. Old ladies put on scooter helmets and got down on their knees to try to block the police on their way through the alleyways.

The photos they sent Zhuang were bloody and frightening. He tried to post them on Facebook when, suddenly, his account was suspended. Twenty-four hours later Facebook asked him to verify his account and reopened it. Zhuang blamed it on hackers from China. The police and the villagers kept fighting, and the arrests continued. People were arrested just for walking the street.

Zhuang started posting photos of his WeChat conversations with the names blocked out. "They're not letting us go," one reads. "I don't know why."

"Has everyone been beaten up?"

"Most people."

In the first two days, the police came for Zhuang's father. They burst into Zhuang Songkun's house at night and threw him onto the ground. When Zhuang's mother tried to hand her husband some clothes to take with him, the police pushed her back into a metal bedframe. They dragged the old man out, leaving Zhuang's mother and his older, disabled brother in the house. They left her with a piece of paper that said NOTICE OF DETENTION across the top.

Overnight, Zhuang's role in the Wukan protests transformed. He did not talk about his father in those first few days. He did not dwell on his family's situation. He didn't give himself time. Later he would explain that this was not the first time he had suffered hardship. It was not the first time his family had splintered. And he knew he was not the only one suffering. For all his dreaming, Zhuang was firm during a crisis.

Instead, Zhuang returned to what he knew. He set Kaizhi down in front of his favorite video and called the handful of journalists he still knew in Hong Kong. He told them what was happening in the village. He gave directions to the Al Jazeera filmmakers, who hoped to sneak around the police blockades and report from the village. The police, however, had done a thorough job of blocking the roads. The Lufeng government offered a three-thousand-dollar reward to anyone who could lead them to the journalists hiding out in the village. Security forces raided more houses and beat up a group of journalists from Hong Kong. After four years of relying on the media to publicize their struggle and pressure the government, the old Wukan tactics failed. Lufeng had grown bolder. And Zhuang was the only person from Wukan who still felt able to speak out. His son was here—Kaizhi was his responsibility now. The family needed money. But Zhuang had already let the United States diminish him. If he didn't do something now, he would not be able to call himself a man.

20

Dissent

异议 / *Yìyì*

Zhuang was not sure how to protest in the United States. He was proud of the media connections he had kept up, but he did not have a village to try to galvanize. New York was enormous and indifferent. Zhuang might write a pamphlet, but he wasn't sure who would read it. He could go stand outside the Chinese consulate and talk to the people who were standing in line for visas, but he wanted to have an impact. For the first time in the United States, Patriot Number One did not want to go it alone. He was brimming with too much information and too many questions. His father had been arrested, the situation in the village had grown worse than he could ever have imagined, and he wanted to do something active to help. He made a plan to visit the only person he knew with experience protesting China's government from New York.

Tang Yuanjun, over the years, had grown careful about taking on the cause of every new immigrant who arrived in Flushing. Every time a Chinese leader made his way into the United States, he traveled to Washington, and he attended all the democracy conferences. He did what he could, but the need was bottomless. "I can't support everyone's protest," he explained. But Tang was connected to the new dissidents coming in. His meetings attracted a regular crowd. He also knew how to make a protest poster. So Zhuang called him and arranged to meet him the next day.

Zhuang arrived with Kaizhi in tow, ready to play a train video on one of his two cell phones. Kaizhi's obsession with trains was full-blown after a month and a half in New York. He walked down the street imitating the blast of a train's horn, the *ding ding* of a crossing. His favorite video, a half-hour montage of different trains blowing past stations and crossings, kept him quiet when Zhuang needed to talk to adults. Zhuang and Little Yan had no one they could leave Kaizhi with when they needed to go to the bank or meet with the agent who could get Kaizhi's health insurance in order, so it was business as usual that Zhuang had brought him.

In Tang's office, Kaizhi wiggled in his seat, complaining whenever the Internet stalled and the trains stopped moving. Zhuang showed Tang Yuanjun some of the videos he had put up on YouTube after arriving in the United States. Tang was impressed. "The opening of this one is really well done," he said, pointing to the credits of a film titled *Wukan! Wukan! III*, the final installment of a trilogy that Zhuang had finished in 2014. Tang himself had considered working as a video editor to make money on the side.

"I thought I would make some signs," said Zhuang. "I want to say 'Wukan Village blames the party secretary Hu Chunhua!' I want to point the finger at him." Hu Chunhua had taken over the leadership of Guangdong Province after Wang Yang, the man responsible for resolving the 2011 crisis in the village. The security forces in the village were too numerous, Zhuang argued, for them to have been sent without approval from the provincial party secretary himself.

Tang told Zhuang that he was in luck—China's premier, Li Keqiang, would be arriving in New York to attend the UN General Assembly the next week. Zhuang could go protest at the United Nations, and if that wasn't enough, he could go over to the Chinese consulate and stand outside.

"You are only one person," Tang said, leaning toward a stack of small protest signs that he had amassed over the years. "So you might just want to take two or three small signs and hold them up." He pulled out two small posters, each one showing a China Democracy Party member who was still in jail in China. "You could hold them up like this." He put an arm around the two small posters and balanced them at his sides. Zhuang looked pensively at the posters. He was imagining something bigger.

"Do you have any banners?"

"I do," said Tang. "But they might be difficult to hold up." The wind along the sidewalk near the Chinese consulate could be particularly blustery, he explained. "It is right on the water." Tang didn't think he could lend Zhuang any protesters. Most people at the China Democracy Party took off work only on Tuesdays so they could attend the regularly scheduled meetings. "*Aiya*," said Zhuang, "I had so many Facebook followers, I'm sure some of them would have come. But my Facebook account has been closed down.

"Maybe I could tie one end of the banner to something. I would like a banner anyway."

Tang's banners were stored, rolled up, next to an office window, behind a whiteboard he sometimes pulled out for meetings. "We just use old ones and put paper signs on top of them," he explained, rolling a banner along the surface of the office floor.

"Who wrote these characters?" Zhuang asked. "Did you write them?"

Tang nodded.

"*Aiya*, they are too good-looking. Would you help me write the characters for my banner?"

Tang nodded again, pleased. "Of course, of course! You will need something like ten characters. If there are too few, they will be too big and people can't read them. If there are too many, people won't bother to read."

Zhuang nodded and shuffled through Tang's stack of cardboard squares, wondering what to put on them. "I will need some photos of the police in the village," he said.

"And some photos that show the extent of the violence," Tang piped in. Those typically got more attention.

"My father was also taken." Zhuang dropped the information as if it were a detail he had almost forgotten. "Should I also include a photo of him?"

"I don't think so. You don't want people to think you're protesting just because it's a personal matter." Tang thought it would be better if Zhuang seemed like he was protesting for all of Wukan.

Zhuang nodded.

"What kind of detention is your father being held under?" asked Tang.

"*Xingshi*," said Zhuang. Criminal detention.

"Oh," said Tang. "They won't let him out anytime soon. That usually takes at least thirty days before sentencing."

Kai climbed into his father's lap and complained that the train video on the phone was stalled. "It's not there anymore!" he said. "It's gone!"

Zhuang shushed him.

• • •

Now more than two thousand people were following Zhuang on Facebook. People were supporting him in the comments, clicking "like" and leaving behind emojis of crying faces. But he knew that comments on his posts would not translate directly into bodies at a protest. Tang had helped Zhuang prepare the materials he would need, but it was Yao Cheng who accompanied him to the United Nations Headquarters during the UN General Assembly. It would tie Zhuang to an event that was already newsworthy and put him on the street where China's premier, Li Keqiang, would be passing on the way to and from his meetings. A man on the street with a sign on a random day might seem desperate. A man outside the UN General Assembly was a man with a purpose.

When Zhuang first met Yao Cheng, during that early lunch at the East Buffet, the older activist had talked a big game about raising an army to resist the Communist Party of China. Zhuang had not been sure what to make of him, with his glasses balanced moodily on the tip of his nose, his tales of a past in China's military and of the multiple jail sentences he had served in before escaping to the United States. It hadn't been Zhuang's practice then to accept advice from other immigrants, much less other dissidents. But now that he had resigned himself to needing help, he was keeping a more open mind.

Yao Cheng, for his part, saw himself in Zhuang. He treated the younger man as an equal, but Yao also felt he had things to teach. He could help Zhuang see how Wukan was connected to the rest of China—how various protests were interconnected. He could help Zhuang with public speaking. He could serve as a bridge between Zhuang and other Chinese dissidents in New York. Yao Cheng credited his own education to Chai Ling, the Tiananmen Square protest leader who had recruited him to help rescue kidnapped girls. Chai Ling's associates in Hong Kong had given him history lessons, and they had taught him how to present himself. Yao Cheng decided to offer the same kind of support to Zhuang. And Zhuang, although he did not believe every word Yao Cheng said, was moved by the older man's support for Wukan. "He doesn't have another, hidden motive," Zhuang told me. "He just wants to help Wukan." Yao Cheng became a near permanent presence by Zhuang's side.

On Zhuang's first day of open protest in the United States, September 19, he and Yao Cheng left Flushing early on the 7 train. The two dissidents had met outside the Main Street station, in the rain, clutching the plastic handles of their cheap bodega umbrellas. They were worried that it might take them some time to find a good spot outside UN Headquarters. Neither of them spent much time in Manhattan, and they knew very little about the UN building itself. They just needed a place to unfurl the banner that Tang had helped Zhuang create.

It was actually an old banner, repurposed with printer paper taped to its surface. Tang had painted a single character on each square of paper with a thick brush. "Protesting the Guangdong Party Secretary Hu Chunhua's Oppression of Wukan People!" it read. "Release Wukan's Arrested Villagers!" Zhuang had blown up bloody photos of the villagers who had been beaten or hit with rubber bullets, along with a photo of the party secretary he was blaming for the crackdown. Zhuang and Yao Cheng had decided to hold Hu Chunhua's picture upside down. "It doesn't have any particular meaning," Zhuang explained. "We're just doing it to be disrespectful."

The pair arrived at the United Nations so early that the police barricades had yet to be erected. They wandered around the corner from 42nd Street and photographed themselves in front of the main building. They walked over to the designated media area and handed out some flyers telling the story of the Wukan Village crackdown. Zhuang had written the account himself. He had asked me to do a quick translation of what he had written and printed out two versions—one in Mandarin, the other in English.

Most of the journalists behind the metal barricades took the pamphlet, gave it a glance, and stuffed it into a pocket. One or two reporters offered Zhuang their cards. Then a news anchor from China's CCTV saw what they were doing and walked over, her hair perfect, her makeup camera-ready, her eyes narrowed. The woman shouted at them in rapid Mandarin. "What are you doing? You can't come in here!" she said. "Get out!" She threatened to call security and have them removed.

Zhuang told her she couldn't treat them like that. "This isn't China!" he said. But the pair headed off anyway. They needed a place to set up their banner.

• • •

The designated protest area for the UN General Assembly had been set up to the north of the building itself. A long park along the last block of 47th Street had been cordoned off with metal traffic barriers, leaving rows of wet benches and trees. The area gave protesters access to a short half-block of street where official cars might pass. For the most part, however, whoever gathered faced an empty road, the media area just visible to the south of them.

When Zhuang and Yao Cheng got there, a group of Falun Gong protesters—a Chinese spiritual movement that had faced a crackdown in the late 1990s, its practitioners imprisoned and tortured—had already clustered under the awning of Dag's Restaurant, a free-standing food kiosk named after the UN's second secretary general. Just past Dag's, where East 47th Street dead-ends into UN Plaza, the police had set out additional barriers, dingy blue wooden fences that would serve to separate protesters into groups. Later, on the second day of the General Assembly, supporters of the Egyptian president Abdel Fattah el-Sisi would yell at Sisi protesters through loudspeakers, and vice versa, jeering at each other over the heads of a confused, quiet group of Falun Gong.

Zhuang and Yao Cheng marched up holding their plastic bags and umbrellas and picked a row just behind the Falun Gong, who were taking a meditation break to pray. Almost all wore matching yellow rain jackets. They had strung up professional-looking banners across the barriers for anyone to see. FALUN GONG IS GOOD! one read. The group was silent, the rain pattering on their umbrellas and signs. Some were holding a hand up to their lips. Zhuang and Yao Cheng settled in quietly, unsure how to approach their neighbors.

As they unfurled their banner and looked for a place to hang it, two Falun Gong members walked over hesitantly. Zhuang and Yao Cheng were gracious, but Zhuang fended off their offers to help. He was opening himself up to other democracy activists, but his mistrust of other movements was hard to shake. He gave off an air of slightly superior benevolence. When an old woman told Zhuang that he should contact them ("We have our own newspaper," she told him) to promote his cause, he smiled. "I'm not going to go to them," he said. "If they're interested, they can write about it."

The success of this protest, Zhuang had decided, was as much about the photos he would post to social media as it was about getting Li Keqiang's attention. Even if they did attract his notice, he was under no delusion that China's premier, second only to the president, Xi Jinping, would care about one man holding up a banner by the side of the road. Zhuang rolled out his banner, held up his photos, and Yao Cheng photographed him looking determined. They tried different angles to get the text of the banner into one photo. They held up Hu Chunhua's headshot, turning him upside down and staring straight at the camera. They did their best to include a view of the UN building. And then the pair took a break and stood for a few minutes, cell phones in hand, both of them posting the photos to Facebook.

"I just got a message from my friend," Yao Cheng informed Zhuang, talking about Ma Yongtian. "Li Keqiang is at the Waldorf Astoria. We should go over there and take a photo." Zhuang agreed. They packed up their materials and headed out of the protest area, politely thanking the NYPD as they went. Yao Cheng pulled his phone out of his fanny pack and consulted a map. "This way," he said, and started walking.

Zhuang offered him a cigarette. The pair moved slowly, smoking and recounting their successes. People dressed for a day at the office, some with UN lanyards hanging off their necks, found their way around them. "No one else got inside!" Zhuang said, referring to their time in the media tent. "And that CCTV anchor! What does she think the security guards are going to do?"

"You're exactly right!" said Yao Cheng. "Those TV anchors are too corrupt. They think everywhere is like China. Everyone else there was very happy to take your pamphlet." He consulted his phone again. "I don't have her phone number," he said, of Ma Yongtian. She was in Manhattan, stalking the Chinese premier, hoping to block his car. "I can only send her messages over Facebook." They walked a few blocks too far, then circled back toward the Waldorf Astoria. "It's where all the Chinese leaders stay," Yao Cheng said. "It's excessive."

The rain was letting up when Zhuang and Yao Cheng passed a group of Chinese men in matching blue rain ponchos. They had clustered on a street corner, some older with glasses, others young and severe-looking. They looked off into the middle distance and sipped coffee.

"Did you see that?" asked Zhuang after he had passed them. "They looked at me, and I just looked right back at them!"

Together the pair walked to the next corner and found that New York police had cordoned off the block leading to the hotel entrance. As they considered their next move, seven of the men they had just passed came to a halt a few feet behind them, doing their best to look as casual as possible for seven men occupying the sidewalk in matching blue rain ponchos. Zhuang glanced back and tapped Yao Cheng. Most of the men were holding umbrellas. One had a visible earpiece. An older one, in glasses, looked on impassively, still sipping at his cup of coffee.

"Uh-oh!" said Yao Cheng, then waved a hand. "Ignore them."

But Zhuang could not. He turned and addressed them. "I am Zhuang Liehong!" he said to them. "I am from Wukan! You can follow me if you want! All I have ever done is spoken the truth!"

"Don't bother with them." Yao sucked on a cigarette and took a few steps away. "They're not worth talking to."

Zhuang looked as if he were going to follow his friend's advice, then thought better of it. "I am a Wukan villager! Why is the government oppressing Wukan people? They are too corrupt, too terrible!"

One of the men in glasses sneered at him. Another group member stepped forward. "You can talk if you want, but you don't have to make a scene," he said calmly.

"Okay, I will talk to you!" said Zhuang. "I am from Wukan Village. Do you know what is happening there?"

The man pulled back the hood of his poncho and ran his hand over his mostly shaved head. A small patch of long hair sprayed up at the top of his forehead, clumped together by the rain. He didn't mean to answer.

"Here!" Zhuang Liehong said, rifling through one of his plastic bags. He pulled out his open letter and tried to hand it over. The man didn't move. "Here!" Zhuang said again. "You said you would listen, so take this. I'm not afraid of you!"

At this point Yao Cheng seemed to forget his earlier dismissal and walked back over. "The Communist Party is a bunch of criminals!" he said. "It killed its own people at Tiananmen Square!"

One of the blue ponchos laughed. "How do you know what happened at Tiananmen Square?" he asked. "Were you there?"

Yao Cheng spluttered. "It's worthless even talking to them!" he said to Zhuang.

Another man joined in. "You people, you've betrayed your father."

"You've betrayed your own people!" Zhuang shot back. ("What is he trying to say?" Zhuang asked later. "That the Communist Party is my father?")

Yao Cheng waved Zhuang away from the blue raincoats, who trailed after them down the sidewalk, continuing to feign nonchalance. "Do they think they can intimidate us?" Zhuang asked. "This is the United States, it's not like they can beat you up here."

"You should be very careful," Yao Cheng said in a low voice, sticking out his lower lip and raising his eyebrows. "Even in the United States, the Chinese government can make people disappear!"

"*Aiya,*" said Zhuang.

• • •

Zhuang returned to the protest area outside the UN every day he could while the General Assembly was still meeting. The days that he dedicated to protests were days that Little Yan had to stay home from work. The family she was working for was, for the most part, flexible about it. If he was gone for just a few hours, sometimes they would let her take Kaizhi with her. It was one more instance in which she employed the video of trains, endless trains. "I'm worried that we are showing him too many videos," she said to me. "But I don't know what we can do about it." She felt she was being run ragged, and yet she didn't begrudge Zhuang the days of protest. She understood it was something he had to do. One of the good things about her husband, she said, was that his heart was big. He couldn't stand by when his friends were suffering.

Even with the loan from family in China, Little Yan was struggling to keep her head above water financially. They did their best to keep their expenses down, but Kaizhi needed winter clothing, and the pair were too proud to accept donations or buy secondhand. Little Yan was still bringing home fourteen hundred dollars in a good month, when the family she worked for asked her to come every working day. When they took vacation, she didn't work, and she didn't get paid.

On weekends, she tried to take Kai out on walks. When she

could, she picked him up after work and took him for a ride on the subway. He sat on his knees on the plastic seat next to her, face pressed against the window, pointing out the lights and cars. "School bus!" he said, pointing. "Another school bus!" There was no playground near their house, no community of mothers and kids. A subway ride was the best she could do.

Zhuang, on the other hand, spent the month both crushed and elated. He felt responsible for his whole village and thrilled by his return to activism. He had, in his first two years, collected a small number of people he could rely on. His former landlord, the one in the Tudor-style house, was happy to help him in small matters that required a better grasp of English. A few of his former classmates at the Flushing Library still kept in touch. And his reputation was growing with a small group of activists—the regulars at Tang's office all knew him, and his name was spreading outside the city to groups of dissidents in Washington, Los Angeles, and Seattle. He was beginning to sound like Tang—he did not have to agree with every opinion his friends had. It was pointless to hold everyone he met to an impossible moral standard. People could be more than one thing at once. Yao Cheng could exaggerate when he talked about his life and, at the same time, be a loyal friend.

The acquaintance who put Zhuang's newfound openness to the test was surnamed Sun—the same Sun who had contacted Zhuang with his phone number over Facebook. Sun was a sensitive man in his forties, with thin wire-rimmed glasses that matched his narrow frame. He said he had joined the New Citizens Movement—a group founded by the legal scholar and activist Xu Zhiyong to promote civic engagement and government accountability—in China and fled when the group's leaders had been caught up in a political crackdown. In China, Sun had also run what he called an "immigration agency" that helped Chinese citizens acquire U.S. visas. He advised them on passing interviews and helped them understand what kind of evidence they needed. Sometimes, he told Zhuang, people would have to organize a trip to Korea or Thailand first, just to show that they had traveled as tourists in the past.

Sun was struggling with his new life in New York. His wife

would not work, and Sun was too sensitive for the stress of working in a kitchen or on a construction team. He was interested in
renewing his immigration business and was on the lookout for
families who might host Chinese middle-school students coming to study in the United States, or people with citizenship who
might be willing to participate in a green card marriage. Sun
brought up his schemes guilelessly, in front of people he had just
met. ("You could make lots of money if you were willing to divorce
your husband," he told me, proposing to broker a green card marriage.) Zhuang didn't agree with his business ideas, but Sun came
to his protests and was a dedicated supporter of Wukan. "He's
complicated," Zhuang said. Everyone was.

Sun helped Zhuang try to find lawyers in China who were willing to take on the criminal charges that were being levied against
Wukan villagers. It didn't do much good. The lawyers they did
find weren't allowed to meet with their prospective clients. Some
were openly intimidated. "Right now, law in China is purely theo-
retical," one lawyer told Sun. But Sun was full of alternative ideas
and eager to help. Sun, Zhuang, and Yao Cheng would gather in
Zhuang's basement apartment, Sun refusing to drink tea because
his constitution couldn't handle the caffeine, coming up with
plans for future protests and discussing the potential fall of the
Chinese government. They debated whether it would happen in
five years, ten, or twenty. And then Sun or Yao Cheng would lean
back in his chair and sigh. *"Aiya,"* they would say. "The Communist Party is too awful."

• • •

The morning after Zhuang's first protest at the UN, he got a call
from the Lufeng government. "Is this Zhuang Liehong?" a voice
asked. When he said yes, he heard a few muffled noises, and then
his father got on the phone. "Zhuang Liehong," his father said. "If
you act this way, you will hurt your family. While you're outside
China, be careful not to be influenced by certain people. Don't
engage in certain activities. Don't let anyone use you."

Zhuang paused, then asked his father if he was being treated well. "These comrades are good to me," said Zhuang Songkun. He had a bed and enough to eat.

"How can you say they're treating you well?" Zhuang responded. "If they were treating you well, they wouldn't have arrested you for no reason!" Then the call ended.

Zhuang went back to the UN on the second day of the General Assembly meeting. Yao Cheng came with him. In public at least, Zhuang was not going to dwell on the difficulties his family was facing. His mother was left at home with his disabled older brother. People were afraid to even visit their ramshackle house. But it was good, Zhuang told Yao Cheng, that the authorities had called him and put his father on the phone. It meant his own protests were having an impact. "They're scared of you!" Yao Cheng said approvingly.

"I told them not to call me again," Zhuang said. "It won't make a difference!" The more they tried to bully him, the more determined he was. He wrote about the phone call on his Facebook page and invited journalists to interview him about it. "I have been low key for a long time, and now I regret it!" he wrote. "Before my son came to the United States, I refused to be interviewed by some members of the media—I apologize for it!"

He spent the rest of the week protesting at the UN. Every time he went in, he thanked the NYPD monitoring the area and offered them bottles of water. On one day, while he was stringing up his banner, two dueling groups of Senegalese protesters filed in on either side of him, each in its own barricaded section. He stood for photographs while the Senegalese beat drums, played music, and shouted over his head with a megaphone. "I'm not sure," he said, "whether this kind of protest is really appropriate."

For the most part, all the interviews that Zhuang gave during that week in September were conducted in Mandarin and printed in Chinese. On the fourth day, a reporter from Voice of America asked him questions about his village. Yao Cheng had tried to coach him in advance. He told Zhuang not to get nervous and to try to speak slowly. Zhuang had a habit of stuttering when he had something important to say. They planned what he might say about his father. He tried to take Yao Cheng's advice, speaking slowly and carefully. He tried to appear calm. When the reporter asked if he had spoken to his father since the arrest, Zhuang faltered. "No," he said, then corrected himself. "I mean, not until a few days ago."

It did not matter if Americans knew about his protests specifically. Reports published in Mandarin were just as effective at getting the attention of the local officials in Guangdong Province. Reporters from Hong Kong and Taiwan were more likely to know about Wukan and to care about the dwindling prospects of a single Chinese village. When a reporter from Radio Free Asia asked if the phone call from Zhuang's father would change his thinking about protest, Zhuang responded with typical bravado. "Of course not! Am I stupid? Look what they've done to Wukan!"

Even in private, Zhuang rarely let his guard down when talking about his father. He would shake his head and lament the situation in simple terms, then move on to more practical matters. "I worry about my mother and my brother," he would say. "*Meibanfa*." There was nothing he could do about it.

21

Politics

政治 / *Zhèngzhì*

There were days when Little Yan attributed her arguments with Zhuang to a condition of all masculinity. Men could live on protest alone and not worry about how they would eat. Now that Zhuang had befriended Flushing's democracy activists, her theory was bolstered: many of the male activists in Flushing were financially dependent on the women in their lives. There wasn't much money in protest. Tang put funds from China Democracy Party membership back into running the office and sent money to help the wives and children of jailed activists. He took odd jobs when he needed extra cash to support himself, and was thankful that he had an understanding wife and daughter. The leader of another China Democracy Party, a prominent dissident named Wang Juntao, spent much of his time in Flushing while his wife supported the family in New Jersey. He might have been an academic, but he had chosen a life of protest. "We have to be honest about it," laughed Yang Maosheng, whose wife had been absent from Tang's office since the wedding—the hours she worked were too onerous. "Most of us are being supported by our wives."

Other days Little Yan was more critical of Zhuang's shortcomings. After he had given up on selling *daigou* and warmed to Little

Yan's suggestion that he look into driving for Uber, it became clear that the new job would require training and money. He had to attend a course and pass a test to get a TLC (Taxi and Limousine Commission) license. And then they would have to take some of the money they had borrowed from relatives and put it toward a car.

Zhuang dutifully attended classes in Brooklyn when he wasn't protesting. He needed to finish twenty-four hours of class time covering map reading, customer relations, and local geography. He would have to pass an exam testing his knowledge of the city, and then he would have to take a short defensive driving class. For his final application, he would need to have a car already. He went to a Chinese-run car dealership and, with some of their borrowed money as a down payment, purchased a silver Nissan SUV. He came equipped with the good credit score he had spent the last year building up. When the man on the car lot tried to demand a 20 percent down payment, Zhuang threatened to walk off the lot. He knew now how these things worked.

Zhuang estimated the ongoing costs—the insurance, the car payments, gas, and the percentage that Uber would take off every transaction. He expected to be able to drive every night. Little Yan worried that he would not work the hours it would take to cover all their growing expenses. She tried, however, to be generous. They were mismatched in so many ways, she said to me, but Zhuang had a big heart—he could not ignore his village. And besides, politics were starting to infiltrate all their lives.

• • •

In the lead-up to the 2016 U.S. presidential election, an outpouring of Chinese-language articles circulated over WeChat, posted by Web-savvy Chinese-American Trump supporters. One popular source called itself the Chinese Voice of America, or CVA, and offered alarmist, typically false takes on the issues and candidates. Stories warned of terrorism and unchecked immigration. One of the waiters at the East Buffet, himself an immigrant and asylee, posted an article entitled "Why Is This American Election

So Important?" Largely, it concluded, because Hillary Clinton was likely to open the floodgates of immigration, allowing dangers outside U.S. borders to enter. CVA posted original pieces and articles translated from similar-minded American websites. One article circulating over WeChat urged people to vote for Clinton if they wanted their taxes to go up and the country to be taken over by ISIS. Another warned that progressives were banning the consumption of pork, out of deference to the eating preferences of Muslim Americans.

It was a strange sensation, for Zhuang and Little Yan, to open their social media accounts and read political rants. In China, political conversation on WeChat is tracked and censored. If a WeChat post in China gets more than five thousand views, its originator can be charged with defamation and sentenced to seven years in prison. But when it came to the 2016 election in the United States, political rants and misinformation spread quickly. People like Zhuang didn't have the ability to read English or listen to the presidential debates, so they often took the WeChat stories at face value. In China, censors used the phenomenon of "fake news" as proof of their value. The owner of WeChat, the CEO of an umbrella company called Tencent Media, made comments following the November 8 election, lauding WeChat's valuable efforts to curb fake news in China—implying that online censorship and monitoring carried out by the Chinese government was warranted and necessary.

For the most part, the immigrants whom Zhuang and Little Yan met in Flushing were not yet citizens. If they were, their English was often bad and their schedules were as packed as those of their newer immigrant counterparts. Few voted. Across the United States, Asian Americans have a long record of avoiding political participation. In 2012 less than half of the Asian Americans eligible to vote went to the polls.

There had been signs, however, that the Chinese community in Flushing was starting to take more interest in American politics. In 2012 Flushing had helped elect Grace Meng to the House of Representatives—one of twelve Asian American congresspeople in the 435-person body. Thousands had participated in the protests after Peter Liang was convicted of manslaughter. And in 2016 people in Flushing were paying attention.

In Tang Yuanjun's office, U.S. politics filtered regularly into the conversations around his folding table. People voiced concern about Clinton's unsecured e-mail server. They wondered if it was bad to have a second Clinton take over the White House. No one knew what, exactly, to make of Donald Trump.

Even Little Yan was forming an opinion. "Look, I have only been in the United States for a short time," she explained to me. "My opinions have all been influenced by the people around me." Everyone in Flushing, she assured me, supported Clinton. The people who didn't were just afraid of new immigration. "There aren't many of them," she said. They were just particularly noisy on WeChat. At one of her nail salon jobs, she had befriended two longtime immigrants, women who had lived in the United States for ten years or more, "and they support Hillary Clinton." Political conversations also happened in her classes at LIBI. One of her professors complained about the Affordable Care Act ("Obamacare," Little Yan translated) but still did not support Trump. Another professor joked that any Trump supporters might as well get up and leave his class now, because he was about to disparage the presidential candidate. "Everybody thinks he's a little too crazy," Little Yan explained. "For me, I think Obama has been a very good president, and Hillary is part of Obama's group. She'll do things like Obama has done. So I support her."

There was no question in Little Yan's mind that a woman could do the job required. Hillary Clinton had worked in government before, and her husband had been president. "Maybe some leaders won't want to listen to what she's saying," Little Yan said. But if she won, Hillary Clinton would be the president of the United States, and everyone would have to listen.

• • •

While Donald Trump was preparing to take office, Zhuang, Sun, and Yao Cheng were coming up with new campaigns to bring attention to Wukan. They brought their protest banners and pictures to Fifth Avenue, outside Trump Tower, with a new message: DEAR MR. TRUMP, PLEASE PAY ATTENTION TO HUMAN RIGHTS IN CHINA. They took up part of the sidewalk just past a man who was selling comic books that incorporated Donald Trump's victory with well-known books like *The Wizard of Oz*, with Hillary Clinton repurposed as the Wicked Witch. "They're great Christmas presents!" said the man selling them.

Zhuang and Sun and a handful of others sat on the sidewalk for half an hour before the police came and politely herded them to a designated protest area. People walked by and looked at their posters. Some inquired politely about the human rights situation in China. An older man in what looked like a tan fishing vest asked sincerely about the situation with foot binding. "Why don't you go protest in China?" someone yelled at them. "Why do we have to pay attention to your problems?" A woman in a floor-length fur coat walked up and posed for a photograph raising two middle fingers at the Trump building. Another woman, holding a tourist map of the subway system, threw her hands up and shouted, "We love you, Donald!"

Zhuang's political world was expanding one step at a time. The more time he spent with Yao Cheng, the more he paid attention to other villages and cities in China—the crackdown on human rights lawyers, the kidnapping of the booksellers. Tang invited Zhuang to speak at democracy meetings in Flushing, and Zhuang spent time in Tang's office, discussing politics in China and sometimes the United States.

Zhuang came to respect Tang Yuanjun. They had different approaches to protest and life. Zhuang was younger and quick to anger, while Tang was more likely to move slowly. Tang, however, had supported Zhuang's protests with advice and supplies, and sometimes his own party members had attended protests. Tang had modeled a way to accept immigrants from all walks of life, with different aims and ways of expressing themselves, all the while maintaining his own ideas and integrity. Now whenever Zhuang planned a protest or launched an online campaign, he would talk it over with Ma Yongtian, Yang Maosheng, and other dissidents who gathered at Tang's headquarters.

For the most part, Flushing's democracy activists decided to oppose Trump. They made jokes about him and in general took the new president in stride. He might still be helpful to their core purpose. They were encouraged when Trump took a phone call with Taiwan's president Tsai Ing-wen—the first call between a sitting president in Taiwan and an American president or president-elect since 1979. Trump, some thought, would stand up to China. He wouldn't be bullied.

"Don't worry about it," Zhuang told everyone. "In the United States, there are checks and balances."

Tang Yuanjun tended to agree. Nothing the United States could throw at him would be as bad as what he had experienced in China. People in the United States could protest if they disagreed. Someone leaning back in his chair on the far end of the folding table cracked a sunflower seed, then pointed out that Trump was a businessman. "He has millions of dollars," the man said. "He's not dumb."

Sun, while not a supporter, was fascinated by the new president. He liked Trump's brash, outlandish style. "With Trump, you know he is not very refined or educated," he observed unprompted. "Xi Jinping is worse because he pretends to be very educated but really isn't." At least with Trump, you knew. And Sun admired the man's wealth.

"Most people don't drive into Manhattan, right?" Sun asked Zhuang one day, walking from Zhuang's parked car toward Tang's office.

"That's right," Zhuang said. "Not if you want to park and stay there. It's easier to take the subway than to find a parking space."

"I bet Trump drives in Manhattan," Sun mused. "I bet he has all the parking spaces he needs, since he owns that whole building."

"Well," Zhuang answered, "he's president. I don't think they let him take the subway."

• • •

In January, a few days before Trump's inauguration, Sun, Zhuang, and Yao Cheng gathered around one of the circular tables at the East Buffet. Kaizhi was crouched in a chair beside them, gazing intently at the most recent train video. Yao Cheng was looking down at his phone over the rims of his glasses. Sun had, for once, agreed to drink some tea.

The latest events in Wukan, all three agreed, were grim. A handful of new arrests had been made. Zhuang's mother had been forced to sign documents that she could not read. "Wukan is like a big prison," Zhuang wrote in his latest piece for a website called China Change. On the positive side, they said, the local government seemed to be feeling pressured by all the interviews and social media. "They wouldn't be harassing people in the village if they didn't feel nervous," Yao Cheng said. The trio had plans to meet, the next day, with the Dalai Lama's representative in D.C. "He's very powerful," Yao Cheng, who had arranged the meetup, assured everyone. "He can get us a meeting with the U.S. Congress. He can even talk to the president."

Today the three men had come together to help Zhuang author a petition calling for the release of arrested Wukan villagers. They had posted it, hopefully, on WeChat and amassed four hundred signatures in a week or so. It wasn't many, Zhuang said. The government kept taking their posts off WeChat. "I put it up one night, then woke up and it had been deleted," said Sun, pushing up his glasses. "Zhuang put it up, and it was gone by the next morning. As long as we don't post anything about Wukan, it's no problem. But as soon as something goes up with Wukan in it, they erase it."

"We probably have a dedicated WeChat censor," said Sun.

Zhuang laughed. "More like a team! The Wukan censorship team!"

Sun focused on the shrimp roll in front of him and sipped tea. Then he brought up an idea. "Almost everyone in the United States . . . goes to see a psychiatrist, right?" He looked around the table for a friendly indication. "I can't sleep. I wake up and start thinking. I think about work. I think about Wukan. I think about money. And I can't go back to sleep. What do you think a psychiatrist does?"

Zhuang answered quickly and kindly. "It's not a big deal in the United States!" he said. "In China they think something's wrong with you. But here people go if they're feeling bad."

"Do you think it would help me?" Sun asked.

"It might," said Zhuang.

"What?" Yao Cheng piped in, peering at the younger man over his glasses. "If you feel pressure, you're making yourself feel pressure!" Yao Cheng didn't feel pressure, he huffed at Sun. "I don't have a job right now, I don't have money, but I have enough to eat."

Sun smiled at the older man. Yao Cheng didn't have a family to take care of. Sun slipped a piece of pork into his mouth. "You already have asylum," he said to Yao Cheng. "Everything is so expensive."

Zhuang explained that his asylum had taken nearly a year.

"It's not expensive!" Yao Cheng shot back. "You don't have to have a lawyer! We have a group that supports people applying for asylum, and everyone has gotten through!" Chai Ling, he said, had helped a number of people.

Sun grimaced. He did not have the luxury of a connection with Chai Ling.

Just then Little Yan arrived at the restaurant. She slipped up behind her son and ran a finger across his cheek. She had started a new job, working at an adult day care center. It was not as exhausting as her previous job, and the days started early so she could leave around one or two in the afternoon. That allowed her to come and take care of Kaizhi before her classes.

"Oh, hello!" said Sun. "Have you eaten?"

"Yes, you should eat!" Zhuang pushed food toward her. He was planning on paying for lunch.

Little Yan told everyone she had eaten at work and was there to pick up Kaizhi and take him home.

Kaizhi was set to start going to day care the next week. He had been opposed to the idea until they went to see the place, a

school not far from their apartment. He saw children playing in
the yard of a small house, speaking Mandarin, and disappeared
into the melee. He didn't want to leave. Kaizhi, Little Yan felt,
was ready to be with other children. He was getting bored being
cooped up all day and asked to be quiet while Zhuang and his
friends debated the best way to pressure the Lufeng government.
She would take him outside to play when she could, but she was
not a three-year-old. All she could do was take videos of him, help
him build a snowman, and admonish him to not throw snow at
passing cars.

Kaizhi was getting more confident by the day. When he first
arrived in New York, he had barely been able to speak, but now
he sounded like a small adult. "If I tell you I'm full, it means I'm
full!" he told his father at lunch. As everyone left, Kaizhi stopped
at the restaurant doors, ready to let everyone else go ahead of
him. "Go ahead, go ahead," he said. "You are walking slowly,
and I am going to wait and run really fast." He waited, then put
his arms back and his head forward, charging down the crowded
sidewalk. Little Yan trotted after him unsteadily on her platform
heels—the nice ones that she was wearing to work at her new job.

"Can you get off work at one tomorrow?" Zhuang asked her.

"No," she said. "The insurance company is coming to do an
inspection. The boss wants everyone there all day."

She hoped Zhuang would start working in earnest once he
didn't have to deal with Kaizhi all day. "Who knows?" she said
to me. "He's so busy with other things right now." The two bargained and decided that Zhuang could drop Kaizhi off at Little
Yan's work before heading out to meet the Tibetan dignitary.

• • •

Zhuang had more to juggle now than ever before, but he threw
himself into it all. He gave interviews and wrote articles for
Mandarin-language websites run by democracy advocates.
Zhuang and Yao Cheng traveled to Washington to talk to re-
searchers at the Congressional Executive Committee on China.

They protested in front of the White House, Kaizhi rolling a yellow plastic dump truck around the sidewalk in front of them. They wrote open letters to China's government and to the media.

In December, Zhuang's father, along with nine other villagers, was convicted of crimes that included, according to the Haifeng People's Court website, "unlawful assembly," "disseminating false information," and "disturbing public transport." Zhuang Songkun was sentenced to three years in prison, and his son filmed his own reaction. "I think it is obvious that the government is trying to suppress any dissent," he said. After all, his father had been sentenced to more jail time than Yang Semao, who had been convicted of corruption. Zhuang intended to have family members file an appeal, but Zhuang Songkun was moved to a different prison without notice. The appeal was never accepted.

In conversations with Yao Cheng and Sun, the trio kept returning to what was legal and what was not. It was clearly illegal for the Chinese government to prevent Zhuang Songkun from meeting with his lawyer. It was illegal to coerce people into signing documents they couldn't read. Recently people Zhuang had contacted in the village had been called in for a chat with the local security bureau. One person, Zhuang had heard, had been hit in the head and the stomach with the butt of a machine gun when the police came to detain him. "*That's* illegal," Yao Cheng pointed out. It was all illegal. Talking about the right and wrong of it, however, didn't matter much. Conversations, if Zhuang wasn't careful, could turn into long recitations of abuses of government power. Yao Cheng could spend half an hour just listing the beatings he had suffered in prison. When that happened, one of them would rein the conversation back in. Zhuang would nod, looking more and more like Tang Yuanjun. It was no use dwelling on the heartbreak.

Sun, for his part, had come up with the latest protest slogan: "Go to Wukan!" It would encourage activists to visit the village and publicize the ongoing police crackdown. In Tang's office, he explained his thinking. "It is simple," he said. "People will remember it." A political slogan had to be catchy.

"You can learn something from Trump," Sun said. Say what

you would about the president-elect, but he knew how to write a slogan. Sun pumped his fist into the air and shouted his rhetorical inspiration in Zhuang's direction, in English: "Make America Great Again!!"

Zhuang looked up from his phone. "Make America what again?"

· · ·

In late January, with the inauguration past and Chinese New Year approaching, Zhuang started driving for Uber. It was their first New Year in the United States with Kaizhi, and the first one since Zhuang had returned to activism. Every year since Zhuang and Little Yan came to the United States, the pair had celebrated with a new group of people. They had spent their very first Spring Festival in the United States with their tour group. Their second, they had eaten alone. For their third, in the Tudor-style house, Little Yan had set up a hotpot in the middle of their bedroom. A small group of graduate students from China—who had contacted Zhuang out of interest in his role in the Wukan protests—had come to visit and eat.

Two thousand seventeen was the first year the holiday felt like a family event. Kaizhi drove his toy trains in circles around everyone's feet. Little Yan cooked, and friends brought red envelopes full of money to give to Kaizhi, per Chinese tradition. Although she hadn't been working at the adult day care center for long, Little Yan's new boss gave her a hundred-dollar bonus. Yao Cheng and Sun came over for dinner and opened an expensive bottle of Chinese liquor, a brand of *baijiu* called Mao Tai. They toasted each other and talked politics, their faces turning red in the steam of the hotpot. It was a New Year with a purpose. Zhuang had many faults, and he admitted them—he was not particularly well educated or clever. But he was stubborn. He would keep protesting—and planning, and scheming, and doing his best to make ends meet—until there was no need to protest anymore.

22

Labors

劳动 / *Láodong*

Karen began working as a maid just before the 2016 election. She heard about it from friends, who had different opinions, but was too tired to take note. The hotel was understaffed, so she worked overtime at least three nights a week. The wheels of her cart hummed in the empty hallways while she raced to finish her tasks for the day. Her supervisor was constantly on edge, losing her temper over the pace of her cleaners and ending a long day with an angry tirade. For the maids and housemen, it was bad enough to be working so frantically with little time off. But no matter how hard they worked, only so many days a week could pass before a mishap left them running behind schedule.

On average, Karen was required to clean sixteen hotel rooms in an eight-hour shift: to clean the bathroom, vacuum the floors, change the sheets and pillowcases, empty the trash, and disinfect all the surfaces. But to do it all in half an hour was nearly impossible. Even if she did manage, she had no time to organize her trolley at the start of her shift and to clean up at the end. In her second month on the job, she slammed her thumb into a piece of furniture. Her thumb swelled up, and she spent days worrying that it was broken, that she would be unable to do her job and, as a consequence, would be fired.

The hardest shifts, however, were made just tolerable by the fact that Jack, the guitar-playing immigrant whom Karen's friend had liked for her, had started talking. Jack was from Shanghai. He had come over to the United States with his parents when he was a teenager, and his English was nearly perfect. He was stocky and fun-loving, organizing outings with friends and playing the guitar on weekends. "I never expected to be with someone like him," Karen said. Her boyfriend in China had been quiet, reserved and studious.

After their first meeting, when Jack ignored Karen, she had stood there for a few moments, then walked away. Karen brushed off the moment—she had learned to sail past awkward social interactions—and didn't think much more about him. It was her friend who reconnected the pair. She had been aiming to introduce Karen to Jack for over a month. The man with the ponytail, the one that had gone out of his way to be nice to Karen when she showed up and sat in the first-timers section of the Korean Presbyterian Church, had not actually had a girlfriend. He had inquired about Karen. And Karen's friend had deflected him. Jack, she thought, was a better match.

The second time Karen met Jack, it was a formal setup. She met his parents and shook their hands, under the watchful eye of her surrogate sister. Jack had not been aloof, and Karen had been more herself. She told him about her life in Flushing and laughed at his jokes. He was more at home in New York than she was. He drove a car and knew the city outside Flushing. He took Karen out to a restaurant along Main Street serving hearty food from northern China and then arranged a date at the top of the Empire State Building. Karen liked his family. And Jack's whole family loved her.

On Karen's long days—the ones that required hours of overtime, sometimes spilling out until two in the morning—Jack would drive into Manhattan to pick her up. He would take her back to her apartment in Flushing or, if it was early enough, back to his parents' apartment for a meal. In a matter of weeks, Karen started feeling like she had a family again. They celebrated Christmas together. In advance of Spring Festival, Jack and

Karen made an electronic card that they sent to friends—photos of the two of them doctored with a Spring Festival filter that gave them red lips and huge eyes, bordered by a red paper cutout. On Chinese New Year, Karen would have to work during the day, but after her shift she had a family meal to attend.

Karen would have liked to travel back to Henan and introduce her boyfriend to her family, but she was worried about traveling on a green card. Just over a month earlier, the first executive order banning immigrants from seven Muslim-majority countries had gone into effect, ensnaring even green card holders. "It's not like Trump loves China," Karen said. "Even if you have a green card, it doesn't seem safe." She finally had gained the earliest outlines of a life in the United States, and she didn't want to risk it on an ill-timed trip back home. Karen's boyfriend had supported Trump in the election, having kept up with the same barrage of WeChat articles as everyone else, but he had lately changed his mind. And Karen, all of a sudden, started paying attention to politics. Trump, she said, seemed like bad news for immigrants and for hotel workers. "He seems a little . . . unpredictable," she said.

The simple fact that she was no longer working in Flushing or Manhattan's Chinatown made her life more expansive, as she had hoped. Working as a hotel maid was educational. There were only eight other Chinese immigrants working at her hotel—every person from her class in Flushing who had interviewed at the hotel had been hired. The majority of Karen's co-workers, however, were from South America. They communicated with Karen in their only shared language: English.

Karen talked to new people every day. "I'm a little bolder now," she told me. Before coming to work in the hotel, she had been afraid to talk to people who were not Chinese. When speaking Mandarin, she still called Americans "foreigners." Now she used her English more and cared less when she made mistakes.

A few months after she started work, the Hotel Trades Council—New York's hotel workers' union—came to her hotel. Late in the winter of 2017, Karen joined and, almost immediately, noticed a difference. She and her co-workers paid their dues, got their ID cards, and learned about their rights. Her supervisor no longer dared to yell at them as she had at first. When she did, Karen and her co-workers felt free to complain. The management promised to hire more staff to cover the two hundred open rooms. And although Karen was still expected to clean sixteen rooms in a shift, only a few of them were checkouts; before, the majority of the rooms had required extensive cleaning in preparation for the next guest. It was exhausting, but most weeks it was possible. A few months after joining the union, Karen attended a meeting to announce the Hotel Trades Council's endorsement of New York's mayor Bill de Blasio in his run for reelection. She was one of the only Asian faces there. She forwarded me a photo over WeChat. Bill de Blasio, she commented, was very tall.

• • •

Little Yan saw less of Karen after she left the medical office program and switched to classes focusing on the hospitality industry, then started at the hotel. Then after Christmas, Karen decided to take a semester off, to make room for her new job and personal life. She turned into one of the statistics that drive down LIBI's graduation rates.

Little Yan, however, was as determined as ever to finish her classes. Zhuang didn't want her to quit. It was important to keep thinking about the future, he said. He had just got his license to drive for Uber. He had stocked his car with sticks of gum to offer his passengers. He would drive when he could. "He likes to remind me that he supported me going to school," Little Yan said to me. "Okay, fine. But he didn't support me *financially*."

"Little Yan," Zhuang reflected to me one day, at another East Buffet lunch, "is easy to please." She wanted a simple life. She didn't want to go to the beach. She didn't want to fight for freedom. She wanted to be comfortable. She didn't want to worry too much or work too hard. "It's a good thing, and it's a bad thing," he said. "She likes quiet. She never wants to go out. And I am some of both—I want to go out sometimes. I want to enjoy myself." They were, he admitted, opposites.

Little Yan still sighed when she discussed her relationship with Zhuang. They didn't sleep enough. They worried about money. All their energy and patience were spent by the time they got home. The silver lining was that for the first time Little Yan felt that they were both working toward something. Zhuang's agreement to start driving for Uber placated her. It was the first of his schemes that she really believed in. When they filed their 2017 tax return, Zhuang found that they were getting nearly five thousand dollars in refunds from Little Yan's last year of work. It wasn't much, but it was enough to ease the pressure Little Yan had been feeling. Little Yan agreed with Zhuang's assessment—she didn't need much. She didn't want flowers or luxury. She just wanted to sleep well.

In his first week of driving for Uber, Zhuang tested the limits of his English and found he could muddle through. "I'm sorry!" he told his passengers. "My English is no good!" Then he offered them gum. He drove people from Queens to Brooklyn, from Brooklyn to Manhattan, and back. He jumped out of the car and opened doors. He grinned his best grin. And his reviews were, largely, glowing. "We love Liehong!" one passenger wrote, even spelling his name right. "Great driver! He even opened my door!" wrote someone else. In another review, a passenger who had clearly been drunk praised Zhuang for being tolerant.

But making money as a driver was almost as difficult as making money as a local Chinese cook. As he was a new driver, Uber took 25 percent off the top of all his fares. If Zhuang worked a ten- or twelve-hour day, after the fees taken out by Uber, he could come home with two hundred dollars. Taking gas and the cost of maintaining his car into account, he made less. He joined other car services with slightly better driving rates—Lyft, Juno, and Gett—but Uber did the most business.

Zhuang blamed his difficulties, in part, on the fact that he had made a mistake in purchasing his car: it did not qualify for Uber Black. He had selected his car carefully for its luxury and price point, but he had not realized the specificity of what Uber considered a black car. Zhuang was forced to drive for UberX, a service that commanded significantly lower fares. Almost as soon as he started driving, much to Little Yan's annoyance, he started wondering how he might manage to upgrade his car.

Relying on driving for his living, Zhuang realized, could also be precarious. He was a careful driver. He pulled into intersections slowly, judged distances with caution, and rarely drove over the speed limit. A ticket could lower the rating of an Uber driver. Too many, and a driver risked being removed from the service entirely. For that reason, drivers in Flushing went to great lengths to get their tickets dismissed. They hired lawyers and lost more money. Zhuang smiled at his passengers, opened doors, handed out gum—worried that his investment would not pay off.

Zhuang had poured too much money into his new car to see this venture, too, fail. And like Little Yan, he was ready to feel stable. He wanted to provide for Kaizhi. He was planning to arrange surgeries for both himself and his son to fix their blocked tear ducts. He needed to send money home to help his mother and brother, who were struggling without Zhuang's father. Zhuang had found himself again among the dissidents of Flushing. He felt like a man again. And a man needed to work.

• • •

Barely a week into driving his new car, Zhuang received a letter from Geico informing him that the insurance on his first car, the little two-door he had bought secondhand, had lapsed. Zhuang was mystified—he had set up an automatic payment when he opened the account. It turned out that Geico had erroneously disconnected Zhuang's bank account from his insurance payments, and when they notified Zhuang, he hadn't been able to read the letters they sent. When he called Geico to remedy the problem, the company told him that because his insurance had lapsed, the cheapest rate they could give him was double what he had been paying before.

Zhuang lived in a flood of letters that he could barely make out. He signed up for health insurance, car insurance, bank accounts, and credit cards with assistance from local offices. He paid his taxes with the help of local accountants. Sometimes he sent me photographs of letters that looked urgent, asking me for a translation. But after that, Zhuang was on his own, attempting to decipher the letters he thought were important and letting others slide. He was doing his best.

In Tang's office, the problem with letters was common. A little mistake could cascade into a huge problem, a fine, and impenetrable layers of bureaucracy. One member went in for a medical checkup, and when his insurance made a mistake, he received a bill for six hundred dollars that he couldn't read. Another filed his taxes incorrectly and received a letter telling him his fines ran up to 50 percent of his original tax bill. People would show up in Tang's office and spread their mail out on his folding table, asking for help translating or advice on how to respond. It was like making your way through a fog: obstacles would appear without warning, outlined but not complete.

The confusion of negotiating life in the United States was easier to bear with company. In the world of min yun, Zhuang and Yao Cheng had become a unit. Yao Cheng accompanied Zhuang on almost all his trips, and the pair puzzled their way through train stations and traffic signs in tandem. They went to Washington together. They attended democracy conferences and frequented Tang's office together.

Since the New Year, Sun had become controversial. Other exiles from the New Citizens Movement had questioned the extent of his activism while in China. And though Zhuang had been content to consider his friend's half-baked business ideas an area separated from his activism, the two had recently started to overlap. Sun had proposed that Zhuang join him in opening their own democracy office, this one directly connected to immigration lawyers, sharing in the fees that the lawyers charged. Zhuang had refused. Sun had then proposed that Zhuang accept money from a Chinese person hoping to apply for asylum, in exchange for falsely testifying that the person was an activist from Wukan. Zhuang refused.

Sun presented almost all his schemes as innocent business propositions. He spoke in a tone that suggested that he hadn't for a moment considered his plans' ethical or legal implications. But as time went on, Sun used Wukan's name more often as if the cause were his own. He started a WhatsApp group, called American Visa Sharing Group, and put a photo of a man holding up a GO TO WUKAN! poster in the profile—a poster from the awareness campaign Zhuang, Yao Cheng, and Sun had conceived together.

"I'm not going to do anything dramatic," Zhuang said. "But I don't think I can be associated with him anymore." The more Sun leaned on Wukan, the more Zhuang's reputation was at stake.

• • •

One afternoon in late March, the folding table in Tang's office was filled with activists, and Tang put a video up on the television screen at the front of the room. "Have I told you about the last time she blocked Xi Jinping's car?" Tang asked. Half the people in the room nodded, including Ma Yongtian. "There's a video on YouTube!"

As the video ran, people in the office continued chatting, sipping the tea that Tang had brewed. Someone had filmed Ma and a group of protesters from across the street, standing on a corner somewhere in Washington, when a string of black cars pulled out of a drive, turning right. There was a scuffle, and then suddenly she was being dragged belly down across the road. "Aiya, there she is!" someone exclaimed. Sitting now in Tang's office, Ma smiled at the memory. She was hoping she might soon repeat the performance.

In the same month that Zhuang was negotiating his new insurance rate and trying to rein in Sun, the min yun community in New York got some electrifying news. Xi Jinping, China's president, would be making a short trip to the United States. He would not stop in Washington, D.C., but would go directly to Palm Beach, Florida, to meet Donald Trump in his geographically named private club, Mar-a-Lago. None of the reports confirmed an exact date, but anyone who had been paying attention could guess that the trip would be made toward the end of the first week of April.

The news reached the community in early March, when

Zhuang was in Las Vegas at a democracy conference. He had been invited to make a speech, and the organizers had paid his way—the farthest Zhuang had traveled since his arrival in New York. As soon as they heard, all the activists at the conference began planning their trips to Florida. Some protesters bought plane tickets in bulk. People would fly in from California and Seattle. They would drive from New York. Everyone in New York with a car had their seats filled quickly. No one in Flushing had much money, but most were willing to do whatever they could to make it to Mar-a-Lago.

The schedule for the official visit was announced not quite two weeks in advance. Xi Jinping would arrive on April 6 and stay overnight. Zhuang reserved a place in a car with Yao Cheng and Ma Yongtian. He would bring his posters and his loudspeaker. He planned to make a Chinese flag out of red cloth and burn it.

Then, sitting in Tang's office, Yang Maosheng asked a question that threw this plan into disarray. "How long does it take to get to Florida?" he asked.

Zhuang said, "I heard it takes about fifteen hours."

"What?" said Ma. "It takes at least twenty-four, and that's if you don't stop and eat!"

Ma told them she had to leave on the weekend. "I need to be there early to take a look at the area." There was, she said, an art to her vocation. When Li Keqiang came to New York, they had planted spies around the outside of the hotel, and one in the lobby, to monitor when he might be coming and going. This time Ma needed to know the streets where Xi Jinping and his convoy would be traveling. She wanted to be sure, when she picked her moment, that she had a good chance of success. She was taking her son and a handful of accomplices. One couldn't just throw oneself in front of a head of state without doing some prior reconnaissance.

Zhuang realized that his ride to Florida had just fallen through—he couldn't leave as early as Ma was planning. The surgery to unblock Kaizhi's two tear ducts would take place in New York the day before Xi Jinping's visit. He had to attend—he was not going to abandon his son. And he was not going to reschedule the surgery: he was concerned that Trump would pass a law that canceled his Medicaid. If he and Kaizhi did not get surgery soon, they would never be able to afford it.

"*Aiya*," he said. "If I have to buy a plane ticket, I guess I will buy a plane ticket." He booked his flight later that day.

• • •

The dedication that Zhuang and the other activists felt in Tang's office had been hardened by the fruitlessness of protest in China. In Florida, the protesters would get only seconds, barely a flash of wheels and tinted windows, but it was the closest anyone in the world could get to Xi Jinping. It was Zhuang's responsibility to take his village's grievances and put them in the Chinese president's path. Flushing's democracy activists would not let Xi Jinping forget that there was simmering anger in China, that he could not limit people's freedoms and escape unscathed. "He doesn't want to be bothered with us for even a second," Yang Maosheng explained. "So the best we can do is make him see us just for a second."

In the weeks leading up to Xi Jinping's visit, Zhuang did his best to keep his sanity. He could have handled the daily pressures of driving for Uber, dealing with insurance bills, and worrying about Kaizhi's surgery. It was Wukan that threatened to crush him under its weight. His father had been sentenced to three years in jail, and his mother had signed the mysterious paper presented to her by the police. The village itself was quiet, with no journalists getting in or out. No friends were willing to contact Zhuang. But that didn't mean the phone calls had stopped.

The call Zhuang had gotten from his father in September— the first one made from jail, following Zhuang's first rainy day of protest in New York—had not been the last. He had been receiving regular warnings from his father and then his mother, in calls that were almost always overseen by some police officer or prison official in China. They ebbed and flowed, following a script that accused Zhuang of being overly influenced by foreigners, of betraying his family by his actions. And then in early 2017, as the Year of the Rooster got under way, the threats became more pointed. Zhuang, his mother said, was risking his own safety. Just because he was in the United States didn't make him unreachable. Someone might hurt him. She even used, in one conversation, the word *assassinate*.

Zhuang stopped answering phone calls coming from China. It was better for him to place a call to his mother at an unexpected time, hopeful that no security officer or official—whoever was getting her to place the threatening calls—would be there to overhear the conversation. The Lufeng government was mistaken if it thought it could stop Zhuang from protesting.

The number of calls increased in March, when Zhuang was on his way to Las Vegas. They reached a peak when Xi Jinping's Palm Beach plans became clear, unidentified calls coming in on both his phones. Zhuang ignored them.

23

Blocking Traffic

拦车 / *Lánchē*

APRIL 2017

The day Xi Jinping flew into Palm Beach International Airport was clear and hot. He arrived a few hours after Donald Trump, who had recently been given the go-ahead to use a heliport at Mar-a-Lago and who generally helicoptered over from the airport, not risking the drive. Usually when the president visited, he arrived on a Friday, and everyone at the airport was prepared. This time, however, it was a Thursday and in the middle of spring break season, when college students and families flood airports all over Florida. The cavalcade of motorcycles and police cars came and went as quickly as possible, blocking streets and shutting down traffic, but airport personnel still sighed and threw up their hands while they explained to travelers that everyone was going to have to wait.

To save money, Zhuang had gotten a connecting flight through Atlanta, where he touched down and found his gate without incident. Then he watched the board as his plane was delayed later and later. Then it was canceled altogether. There might have been an announcement helping stranded passengers find hotel rooms, but Zhuang didn't understand. He was too nervous about missing his flight to stray far. He spent most of Wednesday night trying to sleep on a row of airport seats, shoving his feet under an armrest as best he could, praying that his morning flight would not be delayed.

Zhuang caught an early morning flight and arrived in Florida with time to spare. But by the time he got to Palm Beach, he had barely slept at all. Yao Cheng came to pick him up—he had hitched a ride with another activist driving down from New York, and the pair moved through Palm Beach together, picking people up and depositing them at protest sites. The activists were all nervous about staking their territory outside Xi Jinping's hotel. Protesting a visiting head of state was a waiting game that began with arriving before the streets were shut down.

The democracy activists were only a small part of the crowd that arrived to greet Xi Jinping. The Falun Gong had started setting up before Zhuang got there, stringing up their banners and organizing group meditation by the side of the road. The hotel, called the Eau Palm Beach Resort and Spa, had blocked off its parking lots a few days earlier, stacking one concrete traffic barrier on top of another so that the protesters couldn't even see inside. Everyone had staked out their space hours in advance. They started shouting long before Xi Jinping's convoy was scheduled to arrive.

Zhuang carved out a spot for himself in the grass along the road, in front of a row of palm trees not so different from the ones you might find in Wukan, their leaves splayed out behind him. Behind him he strung up the new sign he had made: a professional-looking banner featuring the faces of Wukan's arrested villagers across from the looming black and white face of the party secretary of Guangdong. He hung his homemade Chinese flag beside it, with a picture of a gun taped across its front. He spread the rest of the posters and banners he had made over the last seven months on the grass. In his hand he held one of the early posters, the one that simply said, in handwritten black letters, FREE WUKAN.

Yao Cheng stayed with Zhuang for a time, then wandered off. The other activists had scattered to street corners along the road that Xi Jinping's convoy would be taking. Yang Maosheng had paired off with an activist from Henan Province, helping him write democracy slogans on his arms and chest. The man was a hopeful convoy blocker and planned to tear off his shirt as he ran into traffic. No one knew where Ma Yongtian was. Zhuang was alone.

Then a line of tour buses drove up and disgorged crowds of Chinese people in matching red T-shirts and baseball caps. They swelled onto the sides of the roads, blocking Zhuang's carefully prepared display. Across the street, a group rolled out a banner that said WELCOME. A handful of people waved Chinese flags in front of Zhuang's face. When asked, most of the supporters would claim they were U.S. citizens living in Florida.

For the most part, they were lackadaisical. Most had thrown on the red T-shirts over their street clothes. Half of the men near Zhuang were smoking cigarettes and looking bored.

A few of them, however, were there to argue. An older woman in sunglasses, with a black scarf around her head, told Zhuang he should get a job. She asked him where he was born, reminding him that he wasn't really American. He had forgotten, she was suggesting, that he was Chinese.

Zhuang lost his temper. "How much money are you getting to come here?" he yelled at her. "Do you dare say it?! You don't dare! I am Zhuang Liehong! I am from Wukan Village! No one paid me to be here!"

With his phone, he started filming the crowd of people around him. Some hid their faces behind red binders that they were carrying or put on sunglasses. Some tried to knock the phone out of his hands. He, in turn, spewed a string of harsh words into his amplifier, yelling at the woman, yelling at the apathetic smoking men and the WELCOME sign across the street.

These people had blithely sold their souls. They were fakes, he yelled. And even if someone hadn't paid them to be there, they were unthinkingly destroying the lives of people like him. Zhuang had not asked to be born in Wukan; he had not asked for his land to be stolen and his friends thrown in jail. He could have been in Shunde, still driving his motorcycle, still drinking tea in the warm, open air. Instead he had ended up in Florida, holding a sign.

It didn't matter that Yao Cheng had disappeared and the other min yun had scattered: Zhuang had years of humiliation and injustice to fuel him. He would keep yelling until his voice gave out.

• • •

The town of Palm Beach is clustered along the northern half of a sixteen-mile barrier island occupied almost entirely by hotels and luxurious estates. The rest of Palm Beach, West Palm Beach, sits on the mainland, across Lake Worth Lagoon, where real estate is cheaper and hotels less ostentatious. In West Palm Beach, the roads are wider and the city is crisscrossed by highways. The beachfront gives way to a hot, low-slung stretch of urban sprawl.

Palm Beach is connected to West Palm Beach by a few scattered bridges. The length of the island is traversed by Florida State Road A1A, a thoroughfare that stretches all the way down to Miami. In Palm Beach, A1A shrinks to two lanes and is marked by signs for South Ocean Boulevard. The road takes on a meandering, tropical feel, moving from one side of the island to the other. And on the weekend of Xi Jinping's visit, drivers came to a dead halt as they neared Mar-a-Lago, turned back by a sheriff's deputy who advised everyone to go to the nearest bridge and cross into West Palm Beach.

The setup of the bridges, the long barrier island, and the town made it easier to predict the roads that Xi Jinping would be using. There was the bridge closest to Mar-a-Lago, and a bridge that deposited cars directly outside the Eau Palm Beach Resort and Spa.

Finally Xi Jinping's convoy sped by in a swirl of motorcycles and flashing lights. Stern-looking Palm Beach police standing along the roadsides told everyone to stay back. In a flash, barely fifteen seconds, the line of black suburbans moved past the concrete barriers. A ripple of noise moved through the crowd—chants and screams—then died down again.

Yang Maosheng and his friend had waited on opposing corners of the road for the cars to arrive. Yang was there to film the action, if there was any. The dissident from Henan unbuttoned his shirt and walked toward the road, but a policeman blocked him.

Another two policemen walked toward him from different directions. "*Aiya*," he said later, debriefing at his motel. "There was no way for me to run into the street. It was really a loss of face."

• • •

The protesters who had scattered and separated throughout the day reconvened in the lounge of the Rodeway Inn, sunburnt and exhausted. The motel was conveniently located only a few blocks away from Palm Beach International Airport, next to an IHOP, its roadside sign wrapped in a plastic tarp suggesting the motel had recently changed franchises. A handful of warty Muscovy ducks wandered the parking lot, looking for scraps.

The lounge at the Rodeway Inn was surrounded by windows and, on the afternoon of April 7, entirely filled with chattering dissidents, charging their phones, eating out of Styrofoam boxes, and resting their heads on tabletops. Two fake leather couches sat on the side of the room closest to the hotel carport, and Zhuang collapsed on one of them, leaning his head back and falling asleep. He had spent the night before in the airport and the night before that worrying about Kaizhi's surgery, which had not succeeded in completely unblocking the three-year-old's tear ducts.

Yang Maosheng settled in next to him and gave him a poke. "Hey, do you want to go sleep in my room?"

Zhuang shook his head no. "I have a room," he said. Yao Cheng and another friend were already napping in it for the afternoon.

At the other end of the lounge, the leader of Flushing's other prominent China Democracy Party, Wang Juntao, occupied a chair near a little round table, and the rest of the protesters had formed a semicircle around him. Wang Juntao had gone to the protest in basketball shorts and a Nike baseball cap. His forearms were burned red. "If the Communist Party falls," whispered the man with the writing on his chest, "Wang Juntao might be the one to take over."

Wang Juntao was recounting the events of the day to the people around him. "There were four or five people arrested," he said. Two had already been released. "We should thank them.

They've helped us have a good outcome to our protest." He was going to go, with one of his party members, to try to find the remaining activists.

On the fake leather couches toward the back, an argument broke out about who the Xi Jinping supporters really were. "The Chinese consulate was paying their way!" one activist claimed. It was difficult to believe that regular Chinese Americans, with unblocked access to the Internet at their fingertips, would go out of their way to welcome the Chinese president. Some members of the welcome party had stood directly in front of the dissidents, intentionally preventing Xi Jinping from seeing them. Those people, someone argued, must have acted on instructions from the Chinese government.

"Xi Jinping doesn't want to see us! He doesn't even want to look at us for five seconds from the car," someone said.

On the adjacent couch, Zhuang had woken up and was talking about the possibility of burning the flag he had made the next day.

"Do you think Xi Jinping is looking at you?" someone asked him. "He has a lot of things to do—there are so many people protesting. Do you think he's in the car saying, 'Hmmm, let me look and see who's here protesting'?"

Zhuang shook his head, without an answer.

While they argued, someone in the hotel turned the overhead television to MSNBC, where *Hardball* host Chris Matthews was opining that the summit between Xi Jinping and President Trump almost seemed like a sideshow, particularly compared to the recent crisis in Syria. The show broadcast a clip of Trump and his family sitting with the Chinese president at a long, narrow table in a room filled with candelabras and draperies. Xi and his wife were sandwiched between Donald Trump and his son-in-law, Jared Kushner. "It looks like Versailles in that room!" Matthews guffawed. "It's all mirrors and gold gilded."

Zhuang was leaning forward off the brown coach in midargument, and Matthews wondering what Trump would do when he needed someone to pass the salt, when the group of activists who had gone to the local jail walked back in to the lounge area, an older protester in their midst. Everyone in the room jumped up from their seats, shouting questions. "Where is Ma Yongtian?" someone yelled.

"We don't know!" came the answer. "They're holding her somewhere else."

The older man they had retrieved from jail sat down at a table, and everyone clustered around him, eager to find out what had happened. He pulled out his phone to show a video. "Ma Yongtian was successful," he said. "She blocked the convoy."

He turned his phone sideways, and the image of an empty four-lane road filled the screen, a few policemen standing beside their motorcycles by the side of the road. A bank of motorcycles passes through, followed by a group of black suburbans. Then from out of nowhere, a portly Chinese man—Ma's son—sprints out over the sidewalk, past the waiting cop, through two empty lanes, and into the center of the speeding vehicles. The drivers jerk the cars around him, never slowing down. And then the camera shifts to Ma, a little farther down the road, running with less speed than her son but making the same beeline toward the middle of the road. A policeman chases her, and Ma swerves, the man nearly falling in his attempt to change course. He catches up to her and hits her twice, pulling out a white baton, slamming her head to the ground with it and holding her there for a few moments. Then another policeman runs over and grabs her, carrying her inelegantly by her elbow, her hands already in handcuffs, to the side of the road. Whatever happens next is lost in the blur of the phone getting knocked to the ground.

The crowd around the older man took in the video and let out a brief sigh of awe before grabbing the phone and sending the video around. "*Wah*, Ma Yongtian," somebody said. "She's not afraid of anything!"

"Did they knock you down?" someone asked the old dissident.

"It was nothing," he said, calmly leaning back in his chair. He'd been in prison for years in China. He wasn't bothered by a few hours in a Florida police station.

• • •

That night the protesters all went out to a Chinese restaurant and occupied a back room. Zhuang took responsibility for ordering and serving the tea. There was little alcohol in the room, but the success of Ma Yongtian buoyed everyone's spirits. People chattered about the day and wondered where she was being held. And then Zhuang put music on his phone and led everyone in a rendition of a famous 1980s protest song, "Nothing to My Name," by the Chinese rock legend Cui Jian. He stood and started belting out the lyrics with gusto, in his gravelly smoker's voice: "I want to give you my dreams / and my freedom / But you always laugh at me / for having nothing." Everyone joined in, tapping their plates with their chopsticks, laughing with Zhuang as he pushed through all the lyrics, waving a toothpick in the air.

The next morning, when Zhuang woke up, Donald Trump had bombed Syria, and there was one last protest to stage before everyone would head home. Zhuang climbed into a car with Yao Cheng, who was discussing the types of missiles the United States had launched.

The group gathered at the base of the bridge that led to the barrier island and Mar-a-Lago. They waited for hours for Xi Jinping's convoys, joined by Free Tibet protesters and a handful of flag-waving pro-China counterprotesters. Yang Maosheng got into a screaming match with an older pro-China woman who told him to "roll out of here." The police came with dogs and tipped over traffic barrels, letting them sniff for bombs.

In the background, a group of plainclothes police had gathered. "We usually blend in a little better," said one, a tall Caucasian man in jeans. "But there's no chance of that today." Another pair of men in Harley-Davidson shirts soon arrived, hanging back and observing. "They're not with our department," said the tall policeman. Not long after that a tiny Chinese man with a backpack walked through the crowd, tailed closely by a tall, thickly muscled man in a shiny purple shirt with a white wire curling out from an earpiece. "Who's *that* guy, do you think?" the undercover police officer asked his partner.

The protesters lingered for hours, watching the police check traffic barrels with the bomb-sniffing dog. They walked up and down the sidewalk, addressing most of their protests to the officers. Things dragged on until Zhuang decided to burn his Chinese flag. The police watched suspiciously as Yang Maosheng poured lighter fluid from a water bottle. "Wait, what is that?" said a policeman. "Look, I don't care what you do to that flag, but you can't set it on fire!"

A group of police gathered to douse the flag in water, and a woman with a braid sprouting from the top of her head took the microphone that Zhuang had brought. "Look, the police are helping us destroy the flag of the Communist Party of China!" she announced. "They are getting it wet!"

Zhuang quickly switched strategies, thanked the police, and invited everyone to come over and stomp on the wet flag.

The collection of plainclothes officers increased as the hours went by. A group of plainclothes Chinese men arrived in the parking lot, taking photos of the protesters. When one protester, in turn, walked up to take a photo of the men, they emptied their water bottle onto his shirt, feigning a punch and laughing when the man shrank back. One of the men, the most dapper, started up a conversation with a reporter from Radio Free Asia. "I don't understand your organization. Every country has problems," he said. "But all you report is bad news. There were Tibetans here to welcome Xi Jinping. They love Xi Jinping, but the media just hides it. They don't report it.

"This," he said, his face serious, "is fake news!"

• • •

Xi Jinping drove by again, and a shout rippled through the crowd on the side of the road. The pressure of the undercover officers of all types was too great—no one managed to run into the road. Afterward everyone dispersed. They rolled up their banners and tossed their posters into the backs of cars. "Maybe it's better when they have official meetings in small towns," someone observed. "They're not used to it, so it's a bigger story in the news."

The group retreated to the Rodeway Inn lounge, lingering after the noon checkout. The television news was dominated by the bombing in Syria. People ordered food from IHOP, plugged in their phones, and tried to determine how they would get to the airport.

As people milled around the lounge, a car pulled into the parking lot. Its door slid open, and out popped Ma Yongtian, looking fresh and triumphant, her wrist in a brace. Her son trailed close behind, a little more disheveled, a cast on his wrist suggesting a more serious injury. She strode into the check-in area, paused at the top of the stairs for a moment of adoration, then descended into the sunken lounge.

Zhuang jumped up with everyone else to shake her good hand. "*Xinku le*," he said. "So much hardship."

Ma smiled in acknowledgment, then brushed it off.

"Are you hurt?" someone asked.

"This? This is nothing!" Ma said. "They took us to the hospital. It isn't broken."

Someone pointed to a scrape that ran down one of Ma's cheeks. "It looked like they beat you," they said, referring to policeman in the video.

"Oh, it wasn't bad," she said. "Every time he hit me, he hit me in the butt. Luckily, my butt is very well padded!!" Ma pulled down the edge of her pants a little to show off the bruises. The worst part was when they carried her, their arms hooked under her elbows, her weight hanging on the place where her wrists were bound together. Everything else had gone as expected. They had been treated well by the police.

Ma listened to a few more questions, then announced that she had to start the drive back to New York. It was a brief victory lap before returning to reality.

She left, and a handful of protesters piled into another car to try to catch Xi Jinping as he left Mar-a-Lago and headed to the airport. Zhuang, Yang Maosheng, and a handful of other activists were still in the lounge when someone walked in to tell them that police had blocked off the road outside. "Do you think Xi Jinping is going to drive by the hotel?" someone asked. The handful of stragglers gathered together whatever posters they had left and walked out into the sun, down past the IHOP, and clustered in the shadow of the Rodeway Inn sign. The six-lane road was empty, and the group squinted in one direction—toward the highway where the police were lined up—and then in the other, where a stoplight was running through its lights without purpose. Overhead, a handful of helicopters buzzed.

"He must be coming this way," said Yang Maosheng. Somewhere far off, there was a siren.

They stood by the road, shading their eyes, when the first in a pack of police motorcycles appeared, about two hundred yards away, turning at the empty stoplight. "Wait!" said someone. "Is he going that way?!" Someone ran toward the intersection, waving a sign. Yang Maosheng waved his arms above his head, shouting as if he were stranded on an island and Xi Jinping were a rescue vessel about to pass him by. The rest of the protesters ran out into the road, yelling into the empty street, their voices lost in the rumble of the black suburbans as they rolled through, still far off.

"Oh, whatever," said Yang Maosheng, already walking back toward the motel. "He's gone. Chinese people are the world's most pitiable." They had waited in the sun, again, just for a chance to yell into the wind.

24

Simplicity

单纯 / *Dānchún*

On an overcast Saturday in June, Little Yan and Karen wandered around the sea lion enclosure at the Central Park Zoo, Kaizhi leaning on the glass, watching the animals swim back and forth.

"Kaizhi, do you still think the zoo is scary?" Little Yan asked, laughing. On the subway ride into the city, which had taken forty-five minutes longer than it should have because of a train mixup, Kaizhi had complained that he didn't like zoos. He both wanted, and did not at all want, to see a lion. Little Yan smiled. These were the only lions at the Central Park Zoo.

In the weeks since Zhuang returned from Florida in April, Little Yan had discovered she was pregnant. By now her belly was already showing, a barely noticeable swell under her black dress. She was past the worst of it, she told Karen. For the first three months, she had struggled with morning sickness that lasted most of the day. Her appetite had been off, and she had struggled to find food that didn't make her nauseated. But she was happier than she had been in over a year.

Zhuang had asked her to stop working. "I have taken all the pressure of our life," she said. "And I have handed it over to him."

Zhuang had been thrilled by the news. He hoped for a girl, so his family would be complete and balanced. He was determined to overcome the prejudices he had grown up with—girls could be just as successful as boys. "I am not going to tell them what they should do with their lives," Zhuang said. He expected that Kaizhi and his new baby would go to a university somewhere in the United States. He didn't care if they made money or picked high-powered careers. He would not push Kaizhi to become an accountant or a lawyer. "I just want him to be happy," he said.

Zhuang did not expect his children to move back to China. "As long as they go back once a year," he said, "for Tomb Sweeping Festival." He didn't want to ask anything of his children except that they tend to the graves of their ancestors.

Zhuang took on all the pressure that Little Yan had handed him with energy that, until recently, he had reserved for his activism. Driving was respectable, and he could set his own hours. And his life in Flushing had grown branches. He met Yao Cheng for lunch, organized protests, and gave interviews. The more people he met, the more invitations he received to tell his story. He worked on improving his stutter and kept his speeches simple—he wasn't an educated man, but he knew every detail of Wukan's story. He had practiced telling it over and over, minimizing his own role, telling the story of the village as a whole.

Zhuang had changed since his days as Patriot Number One. He wasn't speaking to his fellow villagers anymore; he was speaking for them. He could drive a car all night if he had to—he was still Zhuang Liehong.

To maintain all these different parts of his life, Zhuang kept a packed schedule. In his first weeks as a driver, he would frequently recount, over lunch, his latest day of driving. He had driven down to Long Island, up to Brooklyn, out to LaGuardia. He learned all the bridges and the highways, the rhythms of traffic and driving fares. On weekends he would drive all night, always offering his passengers gum. During the week, he did his best to drive every day, disrupting his schedule for protests and meetings with his activist friends, getting back behind the wheel afterward.

Zhuang complained that he couldn't make real money until he somehow managed to buy a more expensive vehicle, one that fulfilled all the qualifications for Uber's black car service, but he had buckled down. As he became more familiar with the work, he stopped telling stories about his daily routes. The fares from Long Island were reduced. The work became more of a grind, and he accepted it. "The only people who take Uber are Americans," he told Yao Cheng one day over lunch. "Chinese people all take Chinese car services."

"That's fine," said Yao Cheng. "Chinese people never tip. Americans are more generous." Yao Cheng had developed a theory. Westerners in general were always saying whatever came into their head. They had no filter. They were too trusting. He called them *danchun*, a word that lands somewhere in between "unsophisticated" and "simple."

Zhuang gave some thought to Yao Cheng's assessment. Chinese people, he said, were always thinking about status. They would think carefully about consequences before speaking their mind. They were suspicious of other people's motives.

Zhuang decided he would like his children to be more American—able to speak their mind whenever they wanted. "I don't think this is innocence," Zhuang said. "I think it's freedom."

• • •

As Zhuang's community in Flushing grew, Wukan was increasingly closed off to him. He could not call anyone in the village for fear that their phones were tapped. No one wanted to talk to him anyway. Old Lin received a jail sentence of three years, the same length that his father had received. Lin's twenty-one-year-old grandson had been detained right after the old man, then released. The villagers suspected the charges levied against the younger man were invented in order to pressure Old Lin's confession. Whatever the reason for the detention, Old Lin's grandson confessed that he felt responsible. Zhuang followed him on social media, where Lin's grandson posted updates on his two suicide attempts. The 2012 Wukan election, so triumphant and hopeful, had swept Old Lin up. No matter how hard the old man had tried to compromise—to do things legally, slowly, and systematically—he was in conflict with the officials above him. His term as village chief had destroyed his life and scattered his family.

Zhuang, from the outside, felt helpless. "I'm worried that there is not much I can do," he said of the grandson. "I can't call him without causing trouble." Even if he could get in contact with the boy, Zhuang couldn't offer much hope. He could not give anyone in Wukan a way out. He could barely help his own mother and brother, who continued to get regular visits from security forces. His father was still serving out his three-year sentence. The road that he and Little Yan had taken to New York—the passport and the tourist visa—had been closed after them. Officials in Lufeng had started monitoring the villagers, making it difficult for them to get passports.

In the September 2016 crackdown, Zhang Jianxing, the rakish young man in the peacoat, had been detained by a police unit that his older brother had recently joined. From rumors that Zhuang heard, Jianxiang hadn't been put in jail. He had been taken for show, for his own protection, and was living somewhere outside the village.

One family from Wukan—people Zhuang had been acquainted with—managed to escape to Thailand and contacted Zhuang as soon as they could. They were hiding out from the Thai government, worried the local police would send them back to China. They wanted Zhuang to help them get a visa to the United States. It wouldn't change the situation in Wukan, but the family's predicament gave Zhuang an opportunity to do more than just protest on the street. He threw himself into trying to contact the U.S. embassy in Thailand. He recruited other activists in New York to help. "He's so optimistic," one young woman commented. "You meet other dissidents who are so depressed. They can't take themselves out of all the bad things that have happened." Zhuang, she said, managed to smile through everything.

Zhuang's status among the New York dissidents was another source of relief for Little Yan. He did not lean on her so heavily. The pair were still convinced that they were mismatched as a couple—they did not spend much time together, even now—but they were settling into roles that made them both comfortable. Zhuang left Little Yan to cook, clean, and take care of Kaizhi. He had found friends, and respect outside their tiny home.

A year had passed since Little Yan first suggested that Zhuang drive for Uber, and his disdain had melted away. Finally he had embraced the idea as if it were his own. He did not always drive as many hours as she hoped he would, but his new work was secure enough that she could relax, at least temporarily. She was happy to be pregnant with a second child. She had enjoying tending to Kaizhi when he was an infant. The break from work meant that she was sleeping again. She had time to make her hair look nice before she left the house. She had, happily, rearranged her classes at LIBI so that she went three days a week, all during the day, while Kaizhi was in day care.

There were still some things to worry about—the pregnancy had come faster than she had expected, and the baby might arrive before she had finished her courses at LIBI. Kaizhi had been born early, and she expected her second child would follow the same pattern. "It seems like a waste that I've gone all this way and still won't finish," she said. Eventually she might go back to class and find the office job she had envisioned, but for now Little Yan had carved out her corner of New York. It was isolated—she rarely saw people outside her classes at LIBI and hardly ever left Flushing—but it was comfortable.

Little Yan's life was not, she felt, particularly exceptional. She had gone from her village in Guangxi to Guangzhou on her own. She had married a dissident and fled to New York. She had jumped into unfamiliar vans, worked long hours at unforgiving jobs, and kept her family afloat. She insisted that she was a regular person who had come to the United States. And finally, after three years of work and uncertainty, her days were quiet but full. She felt at home.

• • •

As Little Yan grew more comfortable in her basement apartment, and Zhuang continued rediscovering himself as an activist, Tang

Yuanjun was still struggling with his life in the United States. His landlord had raised the rent in his office. It was too expensive for Tang to keep on his own, so he reached a compromise. One of his party members offered to help him split the space with a temporary wall to create an extra office. Tang would rent it out and squeeze the folding table into what was left. He had to find other places to store some of his posters and banners, but he kept the poster of Abe Lincoln just behind his little metal-framed desk, the quote "When I do good, I feel good" hanging above his head when he turned to greet people. The party member with the drywall helped create a common area that he could use for his Tuesday meetings. And then Tang put out an ad in the local papers for a reasonable-size office in a good location.

A few months before he learned that his rent would be increased, his teeth had started causing him more pain than usual. "When I was growing up, we didn't really brush our teeth," he explained. And during China's Cultural Revolution, Tang had joined the "sent-down youth"—millions of young people who had followed Mao's injunction to travel to the countryside and learn from rural farmers—and suffered from malnourishment. His time in prison probably hadn't helped, either. Whatever the cause of the holes in his smile, Tang felt self-conscious about them. He had a set of false teeth made but wasn't comfortable with them. He was far from his family, experiencing pain that was rooted in his past life in China, and still struggling to keep his movement afloat. It was discouraging.

A year earlier Tang had been quick to tell people that he thought it unlikely he would see China again in his lifetime. Now he modified his answer. "Change can happen fast," he said. "That's why the voice of dissidents living outside China should continue to be loud." Sometimes he let himself think that things in China were improving. They were better, certainly, than during the 1970s. "During Mao's time, you didn't even have sham trials. People just had their throats cut." Maybe, he thought, China would change just enough that he could go home. "Sometimes we can't see the real situation," he said hopefully. "If there's a change in China, perhaps it's not a complete change, but if the struggle has hope . . ." He trailed off, then sighed. "This is an individual question. I just don't know what the next step should be." He worried about his elderly parents and his parapalegic brother who had recently fallen ill again. Thoughts of his family in China kept him up at night.

Tang had built a life in the United States. His daughter was here. He loved his wife. But he had spent all his time—over fifteen years—living in a Chinese neighborhood. He had not learned any English, despite some early aspirations. Nothing seemed to be getting any easier.

Tang was considering the decades that he had left and wondering where his home was. His daughter, the lawyer, was happy in New York. "She's not shedding any tears for China," he said. But she was younger; she spoke English. Her boyfriend had recently arrived from China and had upset the comfort Tang had established at home, living with his daughter during the week when he was in Flushing. The boyfriend was more conservative, much like Tang's ex-wife. When Tang's daughter considered a career as a prosecutor or legal aid lawyer, her boyfriend discouraged it.

"How is the world like this?" Tang wondered out loud, in his newly compact office. "I have always been focused on changing China. It's a place where they use violence to suppress their own people. How has a country like this gotten so powerful?"

All this was weighing on Tang's mind the day a compact immigrant wandered into his office, inquiring about the office rental. He hoped to set up a practice in Chinese medicine. Tang poured the man tea and asked him how long he had been in New York. It didn't take long before Tang was telling the man his own escape story, pausing at the same punch lines, recounting his face-down with the fisherman who had transported him toward Taiwan. "I said, 'Stand back! I have a gun!'" Tang recounted, shoving his hand in his pocket to show how he had playacted.

When the man admitted he didn't know what happened in 1989 at Tiananmen Square, Tang groaned. "They don't teach people the truth about our history," he said.

The pair shook hands on the deal, and Tang smiled. He invited the man to a China Democracy Party meeting. "There are lots of people coming in and out—they might be potential clients," Tang told him. "And maybe you could learn something about China's real history."

· · ·

A few weeks before she met Little Yan at the Central Park Zoo, Karen had come to the conclusion that she needed more space for her things, so she moved to a new apartment. It was two minutes from Tang's office, not far from the Flushing Library, and she had one roommate rather than two. Her life in New York was still expanding. Her English was getting better. Her mother, in Henan, told her things would only get better from here. Karen was careful not to advertise her good fortune to Little Yan; she did not talk much about her job or mention her boyfriend, although Little Yan knew she had met someone. She asked, instead, about the classes at LIBI. Little Yan was one of the only students she knew who hadn't dropped out.

The classes were getting more difficult, Little Yan told her. One of the teachers had left and tried to start her own ESL program. "I am studying more now, and it's still hard to understand," Little Yan said. A few teachers, Karen knew, would meander through their lessons in English, leaving half the class behind at the first new vocabulary word they encountered. Zhuang had been adamant that Little Yan should complain, but she had quietly ignored him.

Two weekends before Karen met Little Yan at the zoo, Jack had taken her to the Bronx Zoo, where she worried that the polar bears were suffering from the heat. The month before that, she had gone hiking with Jack and his school friends on a mountain in Upstate New York. "He takes me somewhere every month," she said quietly, trying not to show off. She grinned despite herself. She pulled up a photo on her phone from April, when Jack had taken her to Washington, D.C., to see the cherry blossoms. "We've gone so many places!" she said.

Jack was, as far as she could tell, a perfect companion in the United States. He spoke fluent English but was Chinese. He loved to travel, but his home was in Flushing. His job was comfortable. He was a model of success—at home in both worlds at once. And Karen was learning, she said, that people are people, no matter where they come from. Some were good, and some were bad. The better her English got, and the bolder she became, the easier it was for her to see a future in which she was at home in the world like her boyfriend. She still worked hard as a maid. Joining the union had not eliminated her overtime hours, but her abusive supervisor had been fired, along with the person overseeing the supervisor. The union had come in, done interviews, and made it happen. Karen was busy, but she was happy.

At the zoo, Little Yan chattered about the animals and her son. Karen didn't have to worry about sparing her feelings—Little Yan was not envious. Now that she slept more and worried less, she had become talkative. She was more patient with her son. She laughed when he finally found a tiger to look at, but Kaizhi was disappointed. "It's asleep!" he said. She smiled when he was too shy to answer any of Karen's questions.

The three of them completed the circuit through the zoo, then wandered over to the petting zoo. In one enclosure, a large black and white pig was standing just close enough to a showerhead spraying water that it was catching a mist. Karen said the pig looked comfortable. "Kaizhi, do you remember the pigs at your grandmother's house?" Little Yan asked. Kaizhi shook his head and wandered over to the goats.

"He doesn't remember anything about my mother's house," Little Yan said. "He remembers his grandfather's house still." She wondered if he would eventually forget the months he had spent in Wukan as well. She smiled at the pig. "We used to give our pigs showers, too!" she told Karen, who had never kept pigs. "A happy pig gets fatter faster!" Little Yan laughed. "I don't think we raised pigs like this one. Maybe once we had one that was black and white." Every Lunar New Year, she said, they would slaughter one of their pigs. "For a week or two, the whole house would be covered in pork and grease!" The pigs at the zoo were lucky. They would stay fat and comfortable.

Little Yan watched Kaizhi climb onto a web of rope set out for the children, a giant plastic spider hanging overhead. He was still shy, she said, but he was getting better.

Karen thought it was cute. She and Jack had talked about having children, but she didn't think it would happen soon. "I really worry about it," she said.

"Worry about what?" asked Little Yan.

"Jack says that sometimes kids grow up here, and they're confused. They don't know whether they're Chinese or American. He says you have to tell them from the very beginning that they're American. As soon as they're born, you have to tell them. And then you tell them over and over again."

Little Yan considered the question. "Well, if your child is born in the United States, are they American? Or do they have the same immigration status as you do?" she asked.

"They're already citizens," said Karen.

"Are you sure?"

"I'm pretty sure."

Little Yan didn't see what the worry was. "Then it's simple," she said. "They're Americans."

This book is a work of nonfiction, reported over five years in China and New York City. I began reporting in 2012, intending to write a magazine story about Wukan Village in the aftermath of the protests. As events unfolded in the village, and I continued to push back my deadline, it became clear that I was working on something much bigger than a magazine piece. And then in 2014, Zhuang and Little Yan arrived in New York, and the story I was working on split in two—it was impossible to tell one without the other.

Although I had lived in New York City for almost two years by the time Zhuang and Little Yan arrived, I had visited Flushing only once before—to eat at a Chinese restaurant. I discovered the neighborhood alongside them, documenting the process with notes, recorded interviews, photographs, and video.

Zhuang is a complicated figure, heroic and sometimes frustrating. When he agreed to participate in this book project, he generously allowed me to write both about his accomplishments as a dissident in Wukan and about his struggles as an immigrant. Little Yan was, at first, bewildered by my desire to include her, but she gamely agreed to my presence and interviews and became a valuable guide to the nuances of life in Flushing.

I owe a great debt to all the men and women in Flushing and Wukan Village who took time out from their overloaded days to welcome me into their homes. All the events described in the book were either witnessed by me or reconstructed through interviews. While I spent hundreds of hours in Flushing, in people's homes, on the street, and in Tang Yuanjun's office, some spaces were off-limits to me. Little Yan and Karen both asked that I not visit them at their workplaces, worried that their association with a non-Chinese person would raise suspicion. I relied on their own accounts of their workplace experiences, visits to other Chinese-run salons, shops, and offices in the city, and interviews with other nail salon, restaurant, and home care workers.

Where possible, I corroborated the stories Zhuang and Little Yan told me about Wukan through repeated interviews of their fellow villagers. I spent many hours interviewing Zhuang's fellow village committee members, including Old Lin, Yang Semao, Hong Ruichao, and Xue Jianwan. When it became impossible for me, much like Zhuang, to travel back to Wukan, I relied on the accounts being sent over WeChat. Zhuang is an expert collector of documentation, and particularly when Wukan erupted in protests again in 2016, he was an invaluable co-investigator, collecting photos, documents, and films from the village.

I used no hard and fast rule for transliterating Chinese names. Where full names are present, I use the pinyin system of Romanization and follow the traditional Chinese practice of putting surnames first, given names second. In the case of Zhang Jianxing, I chose to refer to him by his first name to avoid confusion between *Zhang* and *Zhuang*. The majority of the names used in the book are real, save for a few notable exceptions. *Karen* is an alias, and she asked that I change the names of her friends and acquaintances as well. She also requested that I use English names to reflect the fact that, even among her Chinese friends in Flushing, she goes by her chosen English name.

I use the words "arrest" and "detention" interchangeably throughout the book. Although, in China, someone can be detained by security forces for up to thirty days before they are formally arrested, I have chosen to use the conventional English definition of "arrest" to indicate the moment when a person is taken into custody.

So much of immigrant life in the United States is based on myth and legend: a country drives people to move across oceans, and they then send rose-tinted stories back home. But almost no one I spoke to in Flushing was prepared for the challenge of upending their lives and building new ones in a strange country. The people who participated in this book were eager to discuss the disconnection they felt between the perception of life in the United States and the reality. Karen, Tang, Little Yan, and Zhuang all bent themselves to fit the responsibilities, sacrifices, and opportunities that Flushing presented. They grappled daily with what it meant to be rebuilding their lives in the United States and imagining their adopted country anew. And all of them met the challenges of their new lives with ingenuity, generosity, and an enormous capacity for hope.

ACKNOWLEDGMENTS

My deepest gratitude is for the patience and bravery of Little Yan, Zhuang, Karen, Tang Yuanjun, and all the men and women featured in this book. In addition, I am indebted to the following people and organizations:

In China: Natasa Huliev, Sean O'Rourke, Aritz Parra, Maxim Duncan, Yang Xifan, Zhang Jieqian, Barbara Demick, Deb and James Fallows, Ian Hanks, Micah Lewis-Kraus, Sydnie Reed, Rachel Sussman, Kerin Lanyi, and Sanushka Mudaliar. In the U.S.: Riley Lipschitz, Jess Benko, Katia Bachko, Lisa Weir, Alexandra Goncalves-Pena, Jason Ng, Alexa Olesen, Jen Salen, Ran Wei, Nathan Thornburgh, Adam Higginbothom, Samir Patel, Chris Cox, Sophie Xiong, Yan Cong, Michael Chu, and Meredith Jacks.

Rebecca Whitehurst, for making that first trip to Beijing with me. Christopher Colvin and Behice Kutay, who encouraged me to write and let me look after their eight cats. Gary Hendrickson, who gave seventeen-year-old me more confidence than I probably deserved.

Rafil Kroll-Zaidi, who first sent me on my way to Wukan and whose insight and counsel over the years have made me an immeasurably better writer and person.

Lynn Lee, James Leong, and Zhu Rikun, for their company in Wukan. Gideon Lewis-Kraus, for his extreme generosity and encouragement. Jennifer Jones, for her diligent and thoughtful reading. The MacDowell Colony, for a blissful few weeks in the woods.

My agent, Elyse Cheney, who pushed me to make this book a reality and who unexpectedly talked me through hours of contractions on the day my daughter was born. Rachel Klayman and Meghan Houser at Crown Publishing, who have been watching over the project ever since.

My parents, Joan and David Hilgers, to whom I owe nearly everything. All of the women in Austin who took my ambition seriously even when it was not yet fully formed, particularly Dinah Chenven, Frances Schenkkan, and Cynthia Levinson.

Diao Lumin, whose calm, practical shepherding of my daughter has made it possible for me to live a double life and write this book.

Kelly Winship, my phenomenal sister, who has been providing helpful editorial suggestions since birth.

Taylor Price, for his lack of pretension, his deadpan jokes, and his talent for making all newcomers feel welcome.

Chapter 2: A Fisherman's Son

18 **on the edge of Hong Kong:** Xiangming Chen and Tomas de' Medici, "The 'Instant City' Coming of Age: China's Shenzhen Special Economic Zone in Thirty Years," *Urban Geography* 31, no. 8 (2010): 1141–47.

18 **the freedom to move:** Mary Ann O'Donnell, Winnie Wong, and Jonathan Bach, *Learning from Shenzhen: China's Post-Mao Experiment from Special Zone to Model City* (Chicago: University of Chicago Press, 2017), 25–27.

18 **"the floating population":** Ibid., 5–6.

20 **better healthcare, and higher incomes:** John Knight and Lina Song, *The Rural-Urban Divide: Economic Disparities and Interactions in China* (Oxford: Oxford University Press, 1999), chaps. 4–6.

20 **booming real-estate sector:** George Lin and Samuel P. S. Ho, "The State, Land System, and Land Development Processes in Contemporary China," *Annals of the Association of American Geographers* 95 (2005): 411–36.

20 **earlier than his urban counterpart:** Yuhui Li and Linda Dorsten, "Regional and Urban: Rural Differences of Public Health in China," *Global Journal of Health Sciences* 2, no. 1 (April 2010): 20–30.

20 **by the time he was sixteen:** O'Donnell, Wong, and Bach, *Learning from Shenzhen*, 5–6.

Chapter 3: Wukan! Wukan! Revolution

28 **left up to interpretation:** Vince Wong, "Land Policy Reform in China: Dealing with Forced Expropriation and the Dual Land Tenure System," Centre for Comparative and Public Law Occasional Paper no. 25 (Hong Kong: Faculty of Law, University of Hong Kong, 2014).

29 **three tons of methamphetamines:** Dan Levin, "Synthetic Drug Manufacturing Is an Open Secret in China," *New York Times,* June 23, 2013.

29 **20 to 25 different government departments:** Yang Zhong, "Dissecting Chinese County Governmental Authorities," China Policy Institute Discussion Paper no. 11 (Nottingham, U.K.: University of Nottingham, September 2006).

29 **gap has to be made up somehow:** Donald C. Clarke, "The Law of China's Local Government Debt Crisis: Local Government Financing Vehicles and Their Bonds," George Washington University Law School Public Law Research Paper no. 2016–31 (Washington, D.C.: George Washington University, June 2016).

29 **illegal taxes on villages and towns:** T. P. Bernstein and Xiaobo Lu, "Taxation Without Representation: Peasants, the Central and the Local States in Reform China," *China Quarterly* 163 (2000): 742–63.

30 **Wukan Port Industrial Development Company:** Yanbing Zhang and Zhimin Zheng, "The End of Government-Business Relations, Solidification and Collapse: Local Government Autonomy and Social Power in Wukan," School of Public Policy and Management Working Paper no. 2015-001 (Beijing: Tsinghua University, January 2015) (Chinese); Tianyu Peng, "The Revelations of the Wukan Incident," in *Grassroots Democracy in China—2012* (Beijing: World and China Institute, 2012): 300–10 (Chinese).

30 **sold to developers:** "Summary of 2011 17-Province Survey's Findings: Insecure Land Rights, The Single Greatest Challenge Facing China's Sustainable Development and Continued Stability," Landesa Rural Development Institute, 2012, https://www.landesa .org/china-survey-6/.

Chapter 4: In Queens

39   **West Egg to New York City:** Jason D. Antos, *Then and Now: Flushing* (Mount Pleasant, S.C.: Arcadia, 2010), 75.

39   **"man's achievement":** Lawrence R. Samuel, *The End of the Innocence: The 1964–1965 New York World's Fair* (Syracuse, N.Y.: Syracuse University Press, 2010), 18; Bruce W. Dearstyne, *The Spirit of New York: Defining Moments in the Empire State's History* (Albany: SUNY Press, 2015), 259.

39   **Quakers circled back:** Tyler Anbinder, *City of Dreams: The 400-Year Epic History of Immigrant New York* (New York: Houghton Mifflin Harcourt, 2016), 30–31.

40   **"Jews, Turks and Egyptians":** Giles Henry Mandeville, *Flushing, Past and Present* (Flushing: Home Lecture Committee of 1857–58, 1860), https://archive.org/details/flushingpastpres00mand.

40   **ash heap on the edge:** James Driscoll, *Flushing: 1880–1935* (Mount Pleasant, S.C.: Arcadia, 2005), 17.

40   **invested in real estate and opened restaurants:** Weishan Huang, "Immigration and Gentrification: A Case Study of Cultural Restructuring in Flushing, Queens," *Diversities* 12, no. 1 (2010): 56–69, www.unesco.org/shs/diversities/vol12/issue1/art4.

40   **more than two hundred thousand Chinese:** U.S. Census Bureau, *American Community Survey* (2015), https://factfinder.census .gov/faces/tableservices/jsf/pages/productview.xhtml?src=bkmk.

44   **largest Chinese population of any city:** Kate Hooper and Jeanne Batalova, "Chinese Immigrants in the United States," Migration Policy Institute, January 28, 2015, http://www.migrationpolicy.org /article/chinese-immigrants-united-states.

44   **fastest-growing immigrant group:** *The Newest New Yorkers: Characteristics of the City's Foreign-born Population* (New York: Department of City Planning and Office of Immigrant Affairs, December 2013), https://www1.nyc.gov/assets/planning/download/pdf/data-maps/nyc -population/nny2013/nny_2013.pdf.

45   **immigrants from southern China:** Kenneth J. Guest, "From Mott Street to East Broadway: Fuzhounese Immigrants and the Revitalization of New York's Chinatown," *Journal of Chinese Overseas* 7 (2011): 24–44, esp. 40.

45   **people from Fujian:** Ko-Lin Chin, *Smuggled Chinese: Clandestine Immigration to the United States* (Philadelphia: Temple University Press, 1999), 49–93.

45   **dollar vans and easy train access:** Guest, "Mott Street to East Broadway," 52.

46   **Flushing is no Chinatown at all:** Wei Li, *Ethnoburb: The New Ethnic Community in Urban America* (Honolulu: University of Hawai'i Press, 2009), 173–74.

46   **eating at Chinese-run restaurants:** "Chop Suey Resorts," *New York Times,* November 15, 1903.

53   **"There were many signs":** Yang Fan, "Chinese Protest Leader Seeks Asylum in US After Arrests," trans. Luisetta Mudie, *Radio Free Asia,* March 24, 2014, http://www.rfa.org/english/news/china/asylum-03242014165014.html.

54   **"The biggest fortune in life":** Echo Hui, "Chinese Authorities Just Won't Give Up, Says Wukan Protest Leader Who Fled to US," *South China Morning Post,* March 26, 2014.

Chapter 5: Work

58   **In 1890, Chinese men:** Peter Kwong, *The New Chinatown* (New York: Hill and Wang, 1987), 14.

58   **Their limited family lives:** Peter Kwong and Dušanka Miščevic, *Chinese America: The Untold Story of America's Oldest New Community* (New York: New Press, 2005), 135–52.

58   **wealthy Chinese investors:** Kwong, *New Chinatown,* 29–32.

60   **A statewide investigation:** Kim Barker and Russ Buettner, "Nail Salon Sweeps in New York Reveal Abuses and Regulatory Challenges," *New York Times,* February 29, 2016.

60   **multiple police raids:** Phillip Martin, "Human Trafficking: The Route Through Queens," WGBH News, January 10, 2013; Liz Robbins, "In a Queens Court, Women in Prostitution Cases Are Seen as Victims," *New York Times,* November 21, 2014.

61   **Some establishments served:** Chin, *Smuggled Chinese.*

64   **exposé on the working conditions:** Sarah Maslin Nir, "The Price of Nice Nails," *New York Times,* May 7, 2015.

Chapter 6: The Chairman

70   **warlords who ruled much:** Kwong and Miščevic, *Chinese America,* 2–38.

71   **found their way to Cuba:** Evelyn Hu-Dehart, "Latin America in Asian-Pacific Perspective," *Asian Diasporas: New Formations, New Conceptions,* ed. Rhacel S. Parreñas and Lok C. D. Siu (Palo Alto, Calif.: Stanford University Press, 2007).

71   **Drawn to San Francisco:** Kwong and Miščevic, *Chinese America,* 43–56.

71   **Deals were made:** Ibid., 75–89.

71   **"is a better addition":** Ibid., 49.

71   **built their own social support:** Ibid., 144–46.

72   **Chinese fishermen supplied:** Ibid., 10–17, 79–80.

72   **Chinatowns were, from the start:** Him Mark Lai, *Becoming Chinese American: A History of Communities and Institutions* (Walnut Creek, Calif.: AltaMira Press, 2004), 42.

72   **"pickaxe brigade":** Alexander Saxton, *The Indispensable Enemy: Labor and the Anti-Chinese Movement in California* (Berkeley: University of California Press, 1975), 113–15.

72   **In 1888 another measure:** Kwong, *Chinese America,* 106–18.

73   **They grilled new arrivals:** Ibid., 135–44.

74   **"gained the sky but lost":** Rowena Xiaoqing He, *Tiananmen Exiles: Voices of the Struggle for Democracy in China* (New York: Palgrave Macmillan, 2014), 15–36.

74   **Others moved to South Korea:** Jie Chen, "The Chinese Political Dissidents in Exile: Struggle for a Sustainable and Relevant Movement," *Open Journal of Political Science* 6, no. 1 (2016): 53–66.

Chapter 7: Sanctuary

84   **Chen had grown so famous:** Steven Jiang, "Batman Star Christian Bale Punched, Stopped from Visiting Blind Chinese Activist," CNN, December 16, 2011.

84   **New York City is estimated:** Pew Research Center Estimates based on the U.S. Census Bureau's augmented 2014 *American Community Survey.*

86 **"defensive" and "affirmative" asylees:** Nadwa Mossaad, "Refugees and Asylees: 2015," "Annual Flow Report," U.S. Department of Homeland Security, Office of Immigration Statistics, November 2016.

87 **Nationwide, more Chinese people apply:** Ibid.

88 **The persecution must have been:** Sec. 208 (13), U.S. Immigration and Nationality Act.

88 **an FBI raid on lawyers:** Kirk Semple, Joseph Goldstein, and Jeffrey E. Singer, "Asylum Fraud in Chinatown: An Industry of Lies," *New York Times*, February 22, 2014.

Chapter 8: Wukan! Wukan! A Death

101 **In a village just hours away:** Sui-Lee Wee, "Violent Protest Against Power Plant in Another South China Town," Reuters, December 21, 2011.

106 **"If you trust foreign media":** David Bandurski, "Guangdong Extends a Firm Hand to Wukan Villagers," China Media Project, December 21, 2011, http://cmp.hku.hk/2011/12/21/guangdong-leaders-move-to-end-wukan-incident/.

107 **"extreme actions" would be forgiven:** Ibid.

Chapter 9: Little Yan

114 **A vocational school graduate:** Yu Hong, *Labor, Class Formation, and China's Informationized Policy of Economic Development* (New York: Lexington Books, 2011), 143–45.

Chapter 11: Fortress Besieged

144 **they could, once again, pool their resources:** Kwong and Miščevic, *Chinese America* 328–29.

145 **Others spent months on boats:** Chin, *Smuggled Chinese* 3–5.

145 **The money her family collected:** "China People's Welfare Development Report 2013," China Family Panel Studies, University of Peking (2013) (Chinese).

146 **Visa officers were more suspicious:** These estimates, and remarks about the difficulty of obtaining a visa, were obtained from interviews conducted in Fujian Province, and among Fujianese immigrants in New York, in the spring and summer of 2015.

146 **a boat called the *Golden Venture*:** Chin, *Smuggled Chinese,* 193.

151 **founded on Long Island:** Long Island Business Institute website, http://www.libi.edu/about-libi/history.html.

Chapter 13: Wukan! Wukan! Land and Committee

168 **"Wukan offers democratic model":** Rahul Jacob and Jamil Anderlini, "Wukan Offers Democratic Model for China," *Financial Times,* January 30, 2012.

168 **"Rebel Chinese village prepares":** Malcolm Moore, "Wukan: Rebel Chinese Village Prepares to Hold Extraordinary Elections," *Telegraph,* January 31, 2012.

168 **"putting the public first":** Wu Gang, "Put Public First When Solving Land Disputes," *Global Times,* December 22, 2011.

168 **beginning of a sea change:** "Wukan a Model for Democracy," *South China Morning Post,* February 6, 2012.

168 **a political reform that had already failed:** Kevin J. O'Brien and Rongbin Han, "Path to Democracy? Assessing Village Elections in China," *Journal of Contemporary China* 18, no. 60 (2009): 359–78.

Chapter 15: Personal Shopping

198 **The system was so convenient:** "Mainland China's Luxury Spending Continued Its Decline in 2015, However, Emerging Signs Signal a Reversal in 2016," Bain & Company, January 20, 2016, http://www.bain.com/about/press/press-releases/China-Luxury -Report-2016-press-release.aspx.

Chapter 19: A Man of Wukan

240 **a bookseller who had been kidnapped:** Karen Cheung and Tom Grundy, "Detained Bookseller Lee Bo Says He Will 'Give Up' UK

Residency in Chinese TV 'Interview,'" *Hong Kong Free Press*, February 29, 2016.

240 **"Life is like a live broadcast":** Echo Huang and Isabella Steger, "Coming to You in an Eight-Part TV Series: Forced Confessions by Allegedly Corrupt Chinese Officials," *Quartz*, October 18, 2016.

240 **"I took kickbacks":** "Election 'Village Chief' Confesses to Taking 'Huge Bribes,'" China Global Television Network, June 21, 2016, https://www.youtube.com/watch?v=XXJ9Nj7jUzc.

Chapter 21: Politics

267 **progressives were banning:** Eileen Guo, "How WeChat Spreads Rumors, Reaffirms Bias, and Helped Elect Trump," *Wired*, April 20, 2017.

267 **less than half of the Asian Americans:** Karthick Ramakrishnan and Farah Z. Ahmad, *State of Asian Americans and Pacific Islander Series: A Multifaceted Report of a Growing Population* (Washington, D.C.: Center for American Progress, 2014), 64, https://cdn.american progress.org/wp-content/uploads/2014/09/AAPIReport-comp.pdf.

ABOUT THE AUTHOR

LAUREN HILGERS lived in Shanghai, China, for six years. Her articles have appeared in *Harper's, Wired, Businessweek, The New Yorker,* and *The New York Times Magazine.* She lives in New York with her husband and their daughter.